KU-263-454

Tolkien

Central Library
Y Llyfrgell Ganolog
02920 382116

ACC. No: 02699948

Also by Brian Rosebury and from the same publisher

ART AND DESIRE: A STUDY IN THE AESTHETICS OF FICTION

TOLKIEN

A Cultural Phenomenon

BRIAN ROSEBURY

Principal Lecturer
Department of Humanities
University of Central Lancashire

823.912
TOL

© Brian Rosebury, 2003

All rights reserved. No reproduction, copy or transmission of this
publication may be made without written permission.

No paragraph of this publication may be reproduced, copied or transmitted
save with written permission or in accordance with
the provisions of the Copyright, Designs and Patents Act 1988, or under the
terms of any licence permitting limited copying issued
by the Copyright Licensing Agency, 90 Tottenham Court Road, London W1T
4LP.

Any person who does any unauthorised act in relation to this publication may
be liable to criminal prosecution and civil
claims for damages.

The author has asserted his right to be identified as the author
of this work in accordance with the Copyright, Designs and
Patents Act 1988.

First published 2003 by
PALGRAVE MACMILLAN
Houndmills, Basingstoke, Hampshire RG21 6XS and
175 Fifth Avenue, New York, N.Y. 10010
Companies and representatives throughout the world

PALGRAVE MACMILLAN is the global academic imprint of the Palgrave
Macmillan division of St Martin's Press LLC and of
Palgrave Macmillan Ltd.
Macmillan® is a registered trademark in the United States,
United Kingdom
and other countries. Palgrave is a registered trademark in the European Union
and other countries.

ISBN 1—4039—1597—0 hardback
ISBN 1—4039—1263—7 paperback

This book is printed on paper suitable for recycling and
made from fully managed and sustained forest sources.

A catalogue record for this book is available from the British Library.

Library of Congress Cataloging-in-Publication Data
Rosebury, Brian.
    Tolkien : a cultural phenomenon / Brian Rosebury.— 2nd ed.
      p. cm.
    Includes bibliographical references (p.) and index.
    ISBN 1—4039—1597—0 — ISBN 1—4039—1263—7 (pbk.)
      1. Tolkien, J. R. R. (John Ronald Reuel), 1892–1973—Criticism and
interpretation. 2. Fantasy literature, English—History and criticism. 3. Middle
Earth (Imaginary place) I. Title.

PR6039.O32Z8183 2003
823'.91209—dc21

                                                                    2003053574

10   9   8   7   6   5   4   3   2   1
12   11   10   09   08   07   06   05   04   03

Printed and bound in Great Britain by
Antony Rowe Ltd, Chippenham and Eastbourne

For Janice, Tom and Will

Contents

Acknowledgements and Abbreviations

I am grateful to HarperCollins Publishers Ltd for permission to quote from their published works of J. R. R. Tolkien.

I acknowledge permission from Houghton Mifflin Company for quoting from the following: The Fellowship of the Ring, by J. R. R. Tolkien. Copyright © 1954, 1965 by J. R. R. Tolkien. Copyright © renewed 1982 by Christopher R. Tolkien, Michael H. R. Tolkien and Priscilla M. A. R. Tolkien. Reprinted by permission of Houghton Mifflin Company. All rights reserved. The Two Towers, by J. R. R. Tolkien. Copyright © 1954, 1965 by J. R. R. Tolkien. Copyright © renewed 1982 by Christopher R. Tolkien, Michael H. R. Tolkien and Priscilla M. A. R. Tolkien. Reprinted by permission of Houghton Mifflin Company. All rights reserved. The Return of the King, by J. R. R. Tolkien. Copyright © 1955, 1965 by J. R. R. Tolkien. Copyright © renewed 1983 by Christopher R. Tolkien, Michael H. R. Tolkien and Priscilla M. A. R. Tolkien. Reprinted by permission of Houghton Mifflin Company. All rights reserved.

In quoting from Tolkien's principal works I have used the following editions. Abbreviations used in the text and notes are shown here. Reprinted by permission of HarperCollins Publishers Ltd © J. R. R. Tolkien.

The Lord of the Rings, Second edition, 1966:
    The Fellowship of the Ring (FR)
    The Two Towers (TT)
    The Return of the King (RK)
The Hobbit, Fourth edition, 1946
Farmer Giles of Ham, paperback edition, 1983

Tree and Leaf, Second edition, 1988
The Adventures of Tom Bombadil, paperback edition, 1990.
Smith of Wootton Major, 1967
The Silmarillion, 1977 (S)
Unfinished Tales, 1980 (UT)
Mr Bliss, 1982
Roverandom, 1998

In the case of the series entitled *The History of Middle-earth*, I have used the sole available edition: hardback and paperback versions of these volumes have identical pagination. I have used the following abbreviations:

The Book of Lost Tales I: (LT1)
The Book of Lost Tales II: (LT2)
The Lays of Beleriand: Lays

I owe warm thanks to many colleagues, students and friends: not least to Ian Dennis, who introduced me to Tolkien's work at 'a formative age' many years ago, and to Christopher Garbowski, for persuading me to think further about Tolkien in the late 1990s, and for much recent encouragement. The final section of chapter 5 is based on material presented to the English Department at Marie Curie-Skłodowska University in Lublin, Poland: I am very grateful for their encouragement and hospitality. In expanding the book for this second edition, I have benefited particularly from consultation with Terry Hopton on parts of chapter 5, and Christopher Garbowski on both chapters 5 and 6. I have also learned much from the critical enthusiasm and cultural awareness of the students in my Tolkien class. Above all, I am deeply grateful to Janice Wardle, both for intellectual and for personal support, and to our sons Thomas and William, for their enthusiasm and assistance with parts of chapter 6. For all errors and misjudgements, I am alone responsible.

Introduction

When a shorter version of this book appeared in 1992, I began by saying that most people likely to read it would be familiar with *The Lord of the Rings* and *The Hobbit*, but that there would be two minorities: enthusiasts with an already wide knowledge of Tolkien's work, and newcomers in search of an introduction and a guide. The book, I explained, was intended to be of value to all of these types of reader: it would attempt to assess critically the whole of Tolkien's creative work, and to say at least some new things about it; to identify its most rewarding elements, and to explain what makes them effective. These are still among the main purposes of this new edition: its revised subtitle ('A Cultural Phenomenon') reflects the extension of its scope by the addition of two new, or mainly new, chapters.

I went on in 1992 to say that virtually all readers would know something of Tolkien's reputation, even if they had not actually read his work. It was essentially the reputation of a best-seller, not, as I believed it should be, that of a significant literary figure of the twentieth century, someone of comparable stature to, say, Poe or Peacock among nineteenth-century writers. A secondary purpose of my book, then, was (and is) to try to free Tolkien from the extremes of fan-club enthusiasm and critical disdain that often accompany best-seller status, and to locate him within literature and within the history of ideas.

We are now in the twenty-first century, and popular awareness of Tolkien has risen to unprecedented heights, thanks to the appearance of the remarkable film version of *The Lord of the Rings*, directed by Peter Jackson for New Line Cinema. In consequence, the number of casual newcomers to Tolkien's writing is likely to increase, while the dedicated admirers find themselves, with possibly mixed feelings, in a relatively smaller (though still absolutely large) minority. Jackson's creation is of great interest in itself, and its release brings to a head the cultural ferment that has been gathering around Tolkien's work for decades. At the same time, there have been significant advances in Tolkien scholarship since 1992. This revised and expanded edition of the present book is designed to take account of the most important of these developments.

Tolkien's reputation, meanwhile, has increasingly become a battlefield. A series of opinion polls in the late 1990s showed The Lord of the Rings to be the 'greatest' book of the twentieth century according to the votes – in the tens of thousands – of several categories of British readers, including Channel 4 viewers, shoppers at Waterstone's bookshops, and members of the upmarket book club, the Folio Society. The tale of these polls and the indignant reaction to them among metropolitan and academic critics has been too often told to bear repeating.[1] But one noteworthy feature of the reaction is the belief that the results had somehow been rigged by Tolkien's fans (supposedly a small and idiosyncratic group): that without their intervention the outcome would somehow have been quite different. As late as 2000, one reviewer was still asserting that 'almost no one' accepts Tolkien as one of the greatest writers of the last century, 'except the hard-core Tolkien addicts who've elevated his books to the status of a cult'.[2] The release of the first instalment of Jackson's adaptation in 2001 put the view that Tolkien is a minority obsession under further pressure, but triggered new – or rather, resurrected old – hostile responses. Germaine Greer, for example, claimed that the film, and by implication the book, sided with 'a leisured class' against those who 'actually do the work'; or again, that it expressed the hostility of people like ourselves in the West towards people who look different from us – which, she suggested, was a motive behind the military action which had recently overthrown the Taliban in Afghanistan.[3]

I will look at some of these criticisms later, but two points should be added right away. The first is that – if we set aside the efforts of Greer, John Carey, Valentine Cunningham and one or two others, which express themselves mainly in brief reviews and broadcasts rather than full-blown academic texts – the predominant response to Tolkien in the academic world has not been hostility. It has been bemused silence, or tacit dismissiveness. At best, there has been a willingness to accept Tolkien's membership of one or other marginalised genre. When I introduced an undergraduate module on Tolkien at my own university recently, one colleague complained that it was 'all Tolkien': which I took to mean that it would have been acceptable if I had smuggled Tolkien in as part of some wider field – 'children's literature', perhaps, or 'fantasy fiction' – into which any presupposition of his importance could safely be dissolved. Every academic who has worked on Tolkien will, I believe, have similar anecdotes of discouragement. In the discourse of literary critics, Tolkien's generally received significance remains that of a best-seller: oddly unlike other best-sellers, at least since Macpherson's pseudo-'Ossian' two centuries earlier, but, rather like 'Ossian', a matter for cultural historians interested in the transient phenomena of popular taste, not for critics pursuing questions of aesthetic quality.[4] 'I suspect that The Lord of the Rings is fated to become only an intricate Period Piece', remarks Harold Bloom, in his decidedly brief 'Introduction' to a recent collection of Critical Views.[5]

The second point that needs to be admitted is that aspects of the posthumous management, marketing and celebration of Tolkien's work since his death in 1973 have inevitably invited scepticism and irritation, much of it unfair but some of it at least understandable. The vast commercial value of the Tolkien account to the various publishers who have acquired it is well known, and the prominence in the bookshops of HarperCollins's seemingly inexhaustible output of reprints and spin-offs (audiotapes, calendars, diaries, art books, postcards and the like) would tempt many people to lob a rhetorical grenade or two in its direction. Moreover, much of the actual newly published work by Tolkien could not be expected to get, and did not get, favourable reviews – or before long, reviews at all, except from the most dedicated enthusiasts. The period 1983–96 saw the posthumous publication, under the devoted and persuasive editorship of Christopher Tolkien, of volume after volume of unfinished writings, including not only incomplete fragments but also justifiably discarded or revised drafts. These volumes (especially the series called The History of Middle-earth) are of value to scholars interested in Tolkien's creative development, to whom they represent, in effect, uniquely well-transcribed and well-presented manuscript sources; and they include works, or passages, of considerable interest and beauty. But in view of the high proportion of rudimentary, immature and mishandled material they also contain, it is difficult to feel sure that their commercial publication at such exhaustive length has been wise (I accept that there would have been practical and evaluative difficulties attached to selective publication), and I take leave to doubt the thoroughness with which they are usually read. No author's reputation could escape a certain risk from the publication of such materials on such a scale – certainly not that of Tolkien, who was, as I shall argue later, a slow developer who took many years to free himself from compositional misconceptions and unhelpful influences.

At the same time, there is a partly justified perception that Tolkien's admirers have mounted too uncritical, and too co-ordinated, a case on his behalf.[6] This perception goes back to Edmund Wilson's sceptical essay of 1956,[7] and often amounts to little more than incredulity at hearing Tolkien taken seriously at all, but there are some grains of truth in it. It seems churlish, for example, to criticise HarperCollins and Tolkien's earlier publishers – Houghton Mifflin, Allen & Unwin and the rest – for publishing critical works in praise of Tolkien, especially since these include most of the really good ones, but there is an appearance of industrial production about this steady output of favourably disposed commentaries. Similarly, the admirable Tolkien Society hosts a good deal of decent scholarship around Tolkien's works, but can hardly be in the business of probing his weaknesses. The very range and intensity of Tolkien's appeal to readers means that a high proportion of them will not, at least when initially challenged, be equipped to give a sophisticated explanation of the grounds of their pleasure, and it is easy to find naïve expressions of it and be irritated by them. Sometimes they surface even in published commentaries.

That Tolkien has attracted such an indifferent secondary literature (with some distinguished exceptions) might be taken by dismissive critics as a reflection on the quality of his own work – and perhaps it is, though not in the sense the dismissers intend. The truth is that it is difficult to write well about Tolkien because of the distinctive nature of his merits, not because he has no merits; yet if he is to be praised effectively, the praise must be justified in terms which bear an intelligible relation to the work of other writers. Many of his admirers have preferred to wrestling with this problem the easier option of isolating his work from the rest of literature. Analysis and evaluation are always comparative: it is no use declaring an anathema on modern literature and then worshipping Tolkien in a temple in which he is the solitary idol.

At all events, in this book I hope to write about the works of J. R. R. Tolkien without taking leave of a plausible general view of literary aesthetics and literary history. This book will not praise Tolkien by disparaging all, or even many of his contemporaries; it will not suggest that Tolkien is so extraordinary a writer as to be incommensurable with all other writers (though his works do have distinctive features which need to be acknowledged); it will not plead the superiority of 'the mythic mode' to 'the realist mode', or of traditional romance to 'modern' forms of literature; it will not substitute for literary analysis the classification of imaginary beings, places and sacred objects; it will not, I hope, rhapsodise, make coy puns on Tolkien's nomenclature, use metaphors borrowed from his works at every opportunity ('Tolkien's prose flows as boldly as the Great River Anduin', and so on), or play the game of pretending that Middle-earth really exists. And it will not detain the reader with excerpts from the autobiography of a devotee. What the book will aim to do is to understand and evaluate Tolkien's works as compositions, that is, as products of literary art which are for readers aesthetic experiences; to make sense of Tolkien's thought about art, religion, morality and politics; and to discuss the reception of his work and some of the cultural phenomena which have arisen in response to it.

In The Road to Middle-earth, the best of all critical studies of Tolkien, Tom Shippey observes the 'culture-gap' that yawns between this author and most of his critics, the sympathetic as well as the hostile. He attributes it in part to disparities – in age, in temperament, in intellectual training, in religious and moral values – between the author and his commentators (especially professors in American universities). But these types of disparity might occur between any writer and the majority of his critics. Something more specifically concerned with the relationship between Tolkien's work and the routine practices of literary criticism itself seems, as Shippey himself suggests, to be at issue in this case.

> Several writers have suggested recently that the toolkit of the professional critic at this time is too small: it does not work at all on whole *genres* of fiction (especially fantasy and science fiction, but including also the bulk of 'entertainment' fiction, i.e. what people most commonly read). Furthermore it has a strong tendency to falsify much of what it *does* attempt to explain by assimilating it, often unconsciously, to familiar models. Tolkien may be a peripheral writer for the theory of fiction. However it seems time to pay more attention to the peripheries, and less to the well-trodden centre.[8]

I agree with much of that. My own view is that weaknesses in the basic methods of literary criticism – weaknesses which the developments in literary theory of the last forty years have done nothing to remove – have harmed understanding of Tolkien's work. In particular, it has suffered from the projection upon it of meanings which it does not contain: sometimes reductive, tendentious, or historically impossible meanings. The main cause of this phenomenon (which has afflicted plenty of writers besides Tolkien) is the submergence, for much of the twentieth century, of the principle that a literary work, like any other product of complex human action, needs to be interpreted more or less correctly before it can be reasonably analysed, evaluated, applied or freely-associated about.[9]

Still, it is arguable that Shippey places the blame too unforgivingly on the critical practices: for there is something about Tolkien's art which eludes the conventional strategies of contemporary criticism, even when these are deployed with sympathy and patience. It is precisely this elusiveness, in fact, which proves the freshness of Tolkien's invention. His most important work, The Lord of the Rings, diverges in certain crucial respects from the various models against which it has seemed plausible to judge it: from medieval romance, notwithstanding Tolkien's professional interest in that genre; from the mainstream tradition of the English novel, though it owes more to this tradition than is often believed; from most fantasy and science fiction, especially the superficial imitations which its commercial success has encouraged; even from Tolkien's lesser works – which have, moreover, peculiarities of their own. The descriptive and analytical assumptions appropriate to most modern literature do, as Shippey suggests, need to be augmented if it is to be adequately explained. But this augmentation must be harmonised with a coherent overall view of literature, and of literary history, which holds good for Tolkien's contemporaries as well as himself. Tolkien belongs to the same century as Proust, Joyce and Eliot, and is read with pleasure by many of the same readers. Criticism needs to confront this fact and make sense of it.

Even Tolkien's ablest critics have had imperfect success in formulating a satisfactory critical language for discussing his work. *The Road to Middle-earth*, as its title suggests, [10] is preoccupied with the sources – that is, the exterior, discoverable sources – of Tolkien's invention. It displays with exceptional knowledge and penetration the relation of Tolkien's creativity to his learning, a relation which extended beyond a mere 'borrowing' from sources to an idiosyncratic rethinking of the nature of narrative art and of literary language: Shippey comes surprisingly close to vindicating his hyperbolic-sounding claim that Tolkien's mind (creative as well as scholarly) was one of 'unmatchable subtlety'. [11] He shows that Tolkien's reflections on language and on pre-modern literary modes yielded resources of expression, and of moral, political and psychological insight, which enabled him to speak powerfully to a twentieth-century readership: an emphasis he has greatly developed in his more recent, but in many ways similar, book, *J. R. R. Tolkien: Author of the Century*. [12] If there are limitations to Shippey's achievement they are the natural consequence of the brief he set himself. His defence of Tolkien is sometimes open to the objection that, while it demonstrates the ingenuity of Tolkien's creative workshop, that does not in itself demonstrate that the works produced are of high quality: certain preconceptions which might form obstacles to a sympathetic reading of Tolkien are superbly swept aside, but the strictly aesthetic defence is not always quite clinched. An impression is sometimes given, or might maliciously be taken, that instruction in Tolkien's (and Shippey's) philological interests is actually a *prerequisite* for a full recognition of Tolkien's literary merit – from which it is only a short step to that gibe about 'don's whimsy' which, with minor variations, has done such sterling service for three decades of literary opinion-formers and potted-historians.[13] Tolkien's 1938 Andrew Lang lecture 'On Fairy Stories', a complex essay in implicit self-analysis and self-exhortation from the most fruitful phase of his career, shows his awareness of the need for a strictly aesthetic vindication.

> It is precisely the colouring, the atmosphere, the unclassifiable individual details of a story, and above all the general purport that informs with life the undissected bones of the plot, that really count. Shakespeare's *King Lear* is not the same as Layamon's story in his *Brut*. ... In Dasent's words I would say, 'We must be satisfied with the soup that is set before us, and not desire to see the bones of the ox out of which it has been boiled'.... . By 'the soup' I mean the story as it is served up by its author or teller, and by 'the bones' its sources or material – even when (by rare luck) these can be with certainty discovered. But I do not, of course, forbid criticism of the soup as soup.[14]

Shippey's book does not, on the whole, deserve the application of these strictures, for its account of each of Tolkien's major works is attentive both to the unique force of individual details and its general purport. But it leaves a good deal, favourable and unfavourable, to be said about 'the soup as soup'. What I hope to do in this book is to arrive at a view of Tolkien which places him in the same frame as other twentieth-century writers, explores his originality and his modernity, and evaluates each of his individual works (except his strictly scholarly writings) without special pleading or hyperbole. I will say straight away that his reputation must, in my view, very largely rest on *The Lord of the Rings*, and the first two chapters will be devoted to analysing it at length. I hope through that analysis to establish, if not a definitive, at any rate a challengingly comprehensive, assessment of the work and explanation of its aesthetic basis. The third chapter will examine and evaluate Tolkien's other literary works, both for their individual qualities and for the light they shed on his creative development. The final three chapters are essays which aim to situate Tolkien's work and thought in various wider fields of knowledge. The fourth discusses the significance of his life and career within the literary and cultural history of the twentieth century, while the fifth suggests his distinctiveness as a thinker, and evaluates some attempts to construe and apply his vision from different ideological standpoints. The final chapter offers an analysis of the cultural 'after-life' of The Lord of the Rings, ending with a discussion of film versions of the work by Ralph Bakshi and Peter Jackson.

ONE

The Lord of the Rings: Imagining Middle-earth

I

In *The Lord of the Rings*, the work of his prime (it was begun in 1937, his forty-sixth year, and published in 1954–55), Tolkien realised for the first and only time the full potential of his creative imagination. The realisation was possible for two reasons: firstly because he constructed here a uniquely expansive form, which allowed the fullest embodiment to imaginative conceptions of (as it proved) great aesthetic and emotional potency; and secondly because he arrived in this work, after a twenty-year apprenticeship with many false starts, at a style, or range of styles, and an expertise in narrative, sufficient for those conceptions to be made transparent. Chapter 2 will be largely devoted to examining the execution of the narrative and its styles; the present one to the form, and to the nature and power of the imaginative conceptions. But the distinction is, of course, unsustainable at the highest level of aesthetic coherence, and this will, I hope, become apparent by the time the analysis is complete.

The *Lord of the Rings*, not a 'trilogy' but a unified work of some 600,000 words presented in three separately titled volumes, is set in a world called Middle-earth, of which the regions we encounter are broadly similar, in climate, geology and vegetation, as well as in scale, to Europe. It is, for the most part, a pre-industrial world, sparsely populated, and highly localised: trade is limited, and travellers are few. Men, gathered in communities of varying sizes, share Middle-earth with a variety of other 'speaking-peoples' (RK, 405), of whom Elves, Dwarves, Orcs and (half-Man-sized) Hobbits are the most common. Interaction among these peoples is rare (the very existence of Hobbits is unknown to distant communities) and often characterised by mutual suspicion. Nevertheless, Men, Elves, Dwarves and Hobbits are actual or potential allies, and primarily benign though variously corruptible. Orcs are the barbarous militia of the malign spirit or fallen angel Sauron, the Dark Lord, who has re-arisen in Middle-earth after a long age of oblivion. Sauron never appears in visible and speaking form, but his malevolent will, acting at a distance, is felt increasingly throughout the narrative, as he attempts to conquer or devastate the western regions of Middle-earth from his stronghold in the south-east, Mordor. He will succeed in doing so if he can recover the One Ring of Power, taken from him in an earlier epoch and invested with much of his own malevolent strength: its power cannot effectively be used against him, since it is intrinsically evil and its use corrupts the user. The Ring has come into the possession of the Hobbit, Frodo Baggins, and Sauron's servants are pursuing him. Salvation for Middle-earth depends on Frodo's destroying the Ring (resisting the corrupting temptation to claim and use it himself) by throwing it into the fire of Orodruin, Mount Doom in the heart of Mordor itself, where it was forged. Eventually this quest is accomplished and Middle-earth is duly saved.

Anyone who knows the work will recognise that this brief account omits innumerable complexities: it makes, for example, no reference to several major characters whose acts and attributes are of considerable importance to the overall sense of the work. Nevertheless, something of the appeal of *The Lord of the Rings* is, I hope, apparent from this bare synopsis. In part it is the appeal of an essentially simple, and exciting, plot; to that extent the work has affinities, as has often been noted, with a variety of story-telling traditions: with fairy-tales, quest narratives, and novels of adventure. But in part the appeal is attributable to the features described in the first half of the above account (without which, indeed, the narrative sketched in the second half would scarcely be intelligible). The circumstantial expansiveness of Middle-earth itself is central to the work's aesthetic power: once this is grasped, many other aspects of the work fall into place.

> They hastened up the last slope ... and looked out from the hill-top over lands under the morning. It was now as clear and far-seen as it had been veiled and misty when they stood upon the knoll in the Forest, which could now be seen rising pale and green out of the dark trees in the West. In that direction, the land rose in wooded ridges, green, yellow, russet under the sun, beyond which lay hidden the valley of the Brandywine. To the South, over the line of the Withywindle, there was a distant glint like pale glass where the Brandywine River made a great loop in the lowlands and flowed away out of the knowledge of the hobbits. Northward beyond the dwindling downs the land ran away in flats and swellings of grey and green and pale earth-colours, until it faded into a featureless and shadowy distance. Eastward the Barrow-downs rose, ridge behind ridge into the morning, and vanished out of eyesight into a guess: it was no more than a guess of blue and a remote white glimmer blending with the hem of the sky, but it spoke to them, out of memory and old tales, of the high and distant mountains. (FR, 146–7)

We shall return again and again to this quality of meticulously depicted expansiveness; and it will soon prove its relevance to a fundamental, and disputed, question, that of genre. The Lord of the Rings is a fictional prose narrative, and for a modern reader, or writer, the dominant category of such narratives is the novel. It has become conventional to insist – I have insisted myself in the Introduction – that The Lord of the Rings stands apart from the mainstream traditions of the novel, and this apartness has been taken by some as establishing the work's essential anachronism: in place of 'novel', terms such as 'epic' and 'romance', the names of pre-modern genres, have been proposed. Tom Shippey, more subtly, suggests that in The Lord of the Rings 'Tolkien set himself to write a romance for an audience brought up on novels',[1] which implies that the romance form and ethos are fundamental while the novelistic elements are a concessionary superstratum. Tolkien himself, in letters and in his Foreword to the work, avoids 'novel' and sometimes uses 'romance' – though he markedly prefers 'tale' and 'story', and, occasionally but revealingly, the more expansive 'history'. If, however, we try to identify the features of *The Lord of the Rings* that categorically exclude it from the canon of novels, as that canon has developed over three centuries or so, we meet with difficulties which reveal to us more about the nature of the work – and in passing about the nature of novels – than we would learn by summarily assigning it to a different genre.

The attempt may begin with a point which will have been obvious even from our brief summary. *The Lord of the Rings* deals not with imaginary events in the real world, but with imaginary events in an imaginary world. If novels, as the *Concise Oxford* supposes, portray 'characters and actions credibly representative of real life', and romances are tales with 'scene and incidents remote from everyday life', then on the face of it *The Lord of the Rings* is clearly a romance, at least if we assume that credible representation of 'real' life is impossible within an imaginary world. We might clarify the dictionary definition by glossing 'real' as 'historical': most novels are set in the historical world, while *The Lord of the Rings* offers an alternative 'history'. But the representation of an alternative world is widely assumed to involve a greater remoteness from actual human experience than the representation of a version of the historical world. Hostile readers tend to express the point by protesting that *The Lord of the Rings* 'fails to engage with the contemporary world' (or 'with social and political realities'); even a sympathetic critic like Derek Brewer, noting the conventional view that 'the novel shows life as it truly is, in all its concrete tragic elements', places *The Lord of the Rings*, as a 'romance', in schematic opposition to the novel, implicitly conceding that if we categorise the work as a novel we are bound to find it deficient on the essential novelistic criterion of realism.[2]

An immediate problem with this classificatory strategy is that a number of works which are non-realistic in this sense are in fact usually counted as novels: *The Castle*, *The Glass Bead Game*, *Vathek*, *The Time Machine*, *The Inheritors*. All of these, it is true, maintain at least a notional relation to the historical world; but so, as a matter of fact, does *The Lord of the Rings*, representing as it does not some distant planet but our geomorphically recognisable earth: its setting is 'the North-West of the Old World, east of the sea' (FR, 11). 'The theatre of my tale is this earth, the one in which we now live, but the historical period is imaginary', Tolkien affirmed.[3] The extra-chronological past of The Lord of the Rings is no more imaginatively remote from us than the pseudo-chronological future of Wells's Eloi and Morlocks (creatures who are themselves, as Tolkien noted,[4] imaginatively akin to the elves and goblins of fairy-tale, human beings reconceived, transformed by desire or terror). And, as we shall shortly see, in many cultural respects the society of the Hobbits, with its small towns, farms, inns, parties, letter-writing and clannishness, is closer to the experience of modern, even 'bourgeois' – Western man than that glimpsed by Wells's Time-Traveller. (Tolkien once remarked on the more-than-verbal affinity between the Hobbits and that archetypal bourgeois, Sinclair Lewis's Babbitt.)[5]

The significant feature of the imaginative displacement from reality in The Lord of the Rings is not so much its distance as its systematic realisation (to use a word which is tellingly paradoxical in this context). Novels, it might be said, diverge from historical reality for specific and local effect, while The Lord of the Rings systematically shuts it out in favour of the construction of an alternative universe. But the temporal and spatial order, the historico-geographical extension and density, of the alternative universe represented in The Lord of the Rings are attributes of the real universe too: indeed, in so far as these structural aspects of reality are concerned, The Lord of the Rings might actually be called unusually mimetic. The structural relation of imaginary universe to real one is not, moreover, the kind of symbolic or allegorical relation in which the invented world is texturally quite alien to the actual (as in, say, Voltaire's Micromégas): on the contrary, there is a degree of naturalism in the narrative of The Lord of the Rings which is much closer to the realistic novel than to the simplifying, or encapsulating, procedures of allegory. In the following passage, for example, Frodo Baggins and three companions, travelling eastward from their homeland, the Shire, arrive in the Bree-land, a cluster of large villages, with communities both of Hobbits and of Men.

The village of Bree had some hundred stone houses of the Big Folk, mostly above the Road, nestling on the hill-side with windows looking west. On that side, running in more than half a circle from the hill and back to it, there was a deep dike with a thick hedge on the inner side.

Over this the Road passed by a causeway; but where it pierced the hedge it was barred by a great gate. There was another gate in the southern corner where the Road ran out of the village. The gates were closed at nightfall; but just inside them were small lodges for gatekeepers.

Down on the Road, where it swept to the right to go round the foot of the hill, there was a large inn.

... The hobbits rode on up a gentle slope, passing a few detached houses, and drew up outside the inn. The houses looked dark and strange to them. Sam stared up at the inn with its three storeys and many windows, and felt his heart sink. He had imagined himself meeting giants taller than trees, and other creatures even more terrifying, some time or other in the course of his journey; but at the moment he was finding his first sight of Men and their tall houses quite enough, indeed too much at the end of a tiring day. He pictured black horses standing all saddled in the shadows of the inn-yard, and Black Riders peering out of dark upper windows.

'We surely aren't going to stay here for the night, are we, sir?' he exclaimed. 'If there are hobbit-folk in these parts, why don't we look for some that would be willing to take us in? It would be more homelike.'

'What's wrong with the inn?' said Frodo. 'Tom Bombadil recommended it. I expect it's homelike enough inside.'

Even from the outside the inn looked a pleasant house to familiar eyes. It had a front on the Road, and two wings running back on land partly cut out of the lower slopes of the hill, so that at the rear the second-floor windows were level with the ground. There was a wide arch leading to a courtyard between the two wings, and on the left under the arch, there was a lamp, and beneath it swung a large signboard: a fat white pony reared up on its hind legs. Over the door was painted in white letters: THE PRANCING PONY by BARLIMAN BUTTERBUR. Many of the lower windows showed lights behind thick curtains.

As they hesitated outside in the gloom, someone began singing a merry song inside, and many cheerful voices joined loudly in the chorus. They listened to this encouraging sound for a moment and then got off their ponies. The song ended and there was a burst of laughter and clapping.

They led their ponies under the arch, and leaving them standing in the yard they climbed up the steps. Frodo went forward and nearly bumped into a short fat man with a bald head and a red face. He had a white apron on, and was bustling out of one door and in through another, carrying a tray laden with mugs.

'Can we – ' began Frodo.

'Half a minute, if you please!' shouted the man over his shoulder, and vanished into a babel of voices and a cloud of smoke. In a moment he was out again, wiping his hands on his apron.

'Good evening, little master!' he said, bending down. 'What may you be wanting?'

'Beds for four, and stabling for five ponies, if that can be managed. Are you Mr Butterbur?'

'That's right! Barliman is my name.' (FR, 162, 164–5)

I have quoted at some length, though with a large excision, in order to bring out the leisurely pace, and the patient attention to sensory impressions, typical of the narrative. The Prancing Pony is no conceptual stopping-place on a Bunyanesque spiritual journey: there is far more detail here than could possibly be required for allegory. The reader's attention is drawn to spatial relationships (the lines of Road, dike and hedge, the topography of the inn and the sloping land, the turn to the left under the arch), to gestures (Butterbur's wiping his wet hands on his apron, at once a natural action and a courtesy), to ornament, furnishing and ambience (the fat white pony rearing on the inn-sign, the thickness of the curtains, the smoke and laughter emanating from the common-room). There is psychological realism too. The passage focuses on the emotional experience of arriving at an unfamiliar place: the little-travelled and socially deferential Sam (Frodo's servant) feels an anxiety from which the others are relatively free. The Prancing Pony is neither a symbol of comfort, nor the abode of giants which it half-appears to Sam: it is simply an inn which evokes different feelings in different people. It will, as it turns out, be the setting for both comforting and terrifying events, but it remains resolutely unallegorical, a place where certain things happen to happen.

Moreover, countless details of the episode at the Prancing Pony implicitly direct our attention to the rest of the huge world on which it is a tiny speck. If we are continually aware (as we are when visiting a real inn) of its geographical location, this is not simply a question of its appearing on a map in the end-papers. In the passage quoted, we note the size and lively activity of the inn, and the expectation of stabling for ponies and horses. We have already been told that the inn was built 'long ago when the traffic on the roads had been far greater', and that 'Strange as News from Bree was still a saying in the Eastfarthing [part of the Shire], descending from those days, when news from North, South and East could be heard in the inn, and when the Shire-hobbits used to go more often to hear it' (FR, 162). Note that the time-dimension is invoked, and that – characteristically of Tolkien – language, in this case a proverbial phrase, is used to give depth and authenticity to a historical statement. Later we meet the mixed company of the inn: hobbits (a range of family names are given, and their differences from those of the Shire mentioned); men both from the Bree-Land (whose four villages have been carefully located in relation to each other and to the landscape) and from the distant South; a few dwarves – we have learned a hundred pages earlier that dwarves use the 'ancient East–West Road ... on their way to their mines in the Blue Mountains' (FR, 52) – and 'a strange-looking weather-beaten man' with 'a travel-stained cloak of heavy dark-green cloth' and 'high boots of supple leather that fitted him well, but had seen much wear and were now caked with mud' (FR, 168).

> 'He is one of the wandering folk [Butterbur explains] – Rangers we call them. He seldom talks: not but what he can tell a rare tale when he has the mind. He disappears for a month, or a year, and then he pops up again. What his right name is I've never heard: but he's known round here as Strider. Goes about at a great pace on his long shanks; though he don't tell nobody what cause he has to hurry. But there's no accounting for East and West as we say in Bree, meaning the Rangers and the Shire-folk, begging your pardon.' (FR, 168–9)

This second authentic-sounding proverbial phrase serves as a comic rejoinder to the first, reinforcing it in fixing the geographical contact-but-distance between the two communities. Strider's muddy boots, obscure name and business, traveller's tales, and intermittent visits to the inn suggest the isolation of the Bree-landers, amid wide, uncertain regions of which they know little: '"Strider" I am to one fat man who lives within a day's march of foes who would freeze his blood', Aragorn son of Arathorn will declare some chapters later (FR, 261). Butterbur, the fat man in question, has been charged with sending a letter to Frodo in the Shire, but 'I put it by safe. Then I couldn't find nobody willing to go to the Shire next day, nor the day after, and none of my own folk were to spare; and then one thing after another drove it out of my mind' (FR, 179).

The rudimentary methods of communication this implies are in contrast to the efficient postal system which, we have earlier been told, operates in the Shire (FR, 19). The delay in Frodo's receipt of the letter – an entirely mundane event – has combined with a number of less mundane contingencies to bring the plot to its present juncture, and will contribute to its subsequent development.

All this should begin both to suggest Tolkien's skill in planning and executing 'novelistic' complexities of narrative, and to confirm at least one sense in which The Lord of the Rings is exceptionally realistic: its Middle-earth, like our world, is a complicated place, full of banal mischances, full of surprises which bring home the limits of our knowledge, full of space and multiplicity. ('The world being after all full of strange creatures beyond count', observes the Prologue (FR, 11) with delightful off-handedness, 'these little people [the Hobbits] seemed of very little importance'.) In comparison the world of, say, The Castle is confined and repetitive, with the obsessiveness and underdevelopment of an uneasy dream. (I mean the comparison to mark a difference in temper, not in quality, between the two works.) On the other hand the world of a Jane Austen novel seems less confined than Kafka's, but that is at least partly because (since it is set in a version of the real world, and unlike Kafka's work maintains an impression of social normality) we assume the presence of the historical universe beyond the boundaries of the explicit narrative. One would have to turn to the great Victorian novelists, or even to Tolstoy, to find a canonical novel which realises the amplitude of life in space and time as thoroughly as The Lord of the Rings.

The point of my argument here is not to suggest that The Lord of the Rings is a canonical novel after all, or to award it a paradoxical victory in a contest of realism. It is, in the first place, to identify as a distinguishing extra-novelistic feature of the work the representation of an imaginary world at a high level of interior authenticity, and to point out that the achievement of that authenticity has entailed a resourceful deployment of what can only be called realistic elements. It remains true, of course, that in some crucial senses novels of social realism are more realistic than *The Lord of the Rings*: they exclude the supernatural, they confine themselves to historical societies, they engage with human experience through human characters alone, instead of dividing it across a spectrum of imaginary races. But social realism too involves selectivity and structuring, and for that matter invention, in the representation of human experience: life is not the same as novels, not even the novels of Tolstoy or Arnold Bennett. Indeed an ethic of fictional realism based on factuality would be absurdly self-defeating if pressed to its logical conclusion. The relation of any work of fiction to reality is ultimately demonstrated, not by its literal correspondence to fact (which could only be achieved, if at all, by an abrogation of aesthetic order, that is, by the work's ceasing to be a work of fiction), but by its capacity to evoke a psychological response in readers – a response which could not be evoked by the imaginative conceptions of fiction unless at some level those conceptions were intelligible to readers on the basis of actual 'historical' correlatives. In social realism, some of the most complex conceptions (such as those of societies), as well as the simplest, have specific historical correlatives, while other complex conceptions (such as those of characters) are non-factual: the 'Dublin' of Ulysses correlates to the historical Dublin, the 'key' which Leopold Bloom leaves in the wrong pair of trousers correlates to a commonplace object in the historical universe, but 'Leopold Bloom' is non-factual, though constructed out of a multitude of details which have historical correlatives. In other kinds of fiction, the complex conceptions may all be non-factual, but are still built up from simpler conceptions which have historical correlatives, as the Prancing Pony and the hill-top view over the valley of the Brandywine river are built up from conceptions – slightly differently realised in each reader's mind, but necessarily always founded in experience – of architectural and landscape details. Certain passages in *Ulysses*, especially the phantasmagoria of the 'Circe' episode, are intelligible only in this way: the guarantee of their relation to reality, in spite of their grotesquely counter-factual scenes and incidents, is not their factuality but their aesthetic power, their effectiveness in promoting a response on the part of real persons.

On this view, when Brewer maintains that 'the claim for The Lord of the Rings is simply that ... it has symbolic power. And this power corresponds to human needs and desires',[6] he is propounding a formula which does not so much distinguish Tolkien's work from other types of fiction as identify the rationale for fiction in general: that it brings aesthetic order and intensity to 'human needs and desires', drawing on whatever imaginative conceptions, factual or non-factual, are required to achieve this end. Tolkien himself makes a suggestive remark along similar lines. In accounting for his own childhood enthusiasm for fairy-stories, he reports that

> fairy-stories were plainly not primarily concerned with possibility, but with desirability. If they awakened desire, satisfying it while often whetting it unbearably, they succeeded ... I desired dragons with a profound desire.[7]

The first sentence here can be adapted as a justification for all fictional departures from literal correspondence to fact, even those within social realism: especially if 'desirability' is taken to include its opposite. Since we can desire or undesire (to coin a term) both what we have encountered in fact and what we merely imagine, the degree of conformity to, or variance from, historical reality in a fictional work can be seen as determined by the nature of the desire the work is calculated to arouse.

I will pursue this general issue no further for the moment, but I will return to the question of desire towards the end of this first section of the chapter, and it will form the unifying theme of the second and final section. I wish now to turn to a second point of difference between The Lord of the Rings and the mainstream novel, a difference in the use of language. The supposed anachronism of The Lord of the Rings, its alleged remoteness from modern narrative practices, evidently has something to do with a particular perception of its style. According to Catharine Stimpson, 'like a director dressing an actor in doublet and hose to play Hamlet, [Tolkien] puts the English language into costume. ... Shunning ordinary diction, he also wrenches syntax. If we expect, "They got angry", he will write "Wrathful they grew".[8] The suggestion is of a clumsy pastiche, marked by lexical and syntactical outrages upon 'ordinary' language.

The passages already quoted from the work are enough, I think, to demonstrate the falsity of this claim, at least as a generalisation. They are written in a transparent, even plain, prose which avoids primness or formality: 'he had a white apron on', for example, is preferred to 'he was wearing a white apron', and 'they ... got off their ponies' to 'they ... dismounted from their ponies'. Far from sporting stylistic doublet and hose, the style is distinguished by an unobtrusive economy and precision in the use of 'ordinary diction', especially though not exclusively in verbs and verb phrases: 'the Brandywine River *made a great loop* in the lowlands'; 'the land *ran away in flats and swellings*'; where it *pierced* the hedge it was *barred* by a great gate'. Archaic inversions in the manner of 'Wrathful they grew' are absent. Not that Tolkien is casual or inflexible in the sequencing of phrases: he will often opt for the slightly less common alternative, either for grace and euphony or to maintain semantic fluency with preceding and following sentences. If the reader will glance back at the third sentence in each of the first two long quotations in this chapter (from FR, 146 and FR, 162 respectively), it should be clear that both these motives are at work. In the first case, the final clause is sequenced so as to leave the mind's eye on the Brandywine, which the following sentence further visualises. (It also leaves the mind's ear on the long melodious syllables of the name, instead of on 'lay hidden'.) In the second case, the sentence might have read, 'The Road passed over this by a causeway; but it was barred by a great gate where it pierced the hedge': the actual sequencing ensures that the opening and terminal phrases achieve maximum semantic continuity with the adjacent sentences.

The influence of the conviction that for 'romance' one must adopt a special stylistic costume (archaic, heroic, sublime, Ossianic), in contrast with the low-mimetic plainness of the novel, is detectable in some of Tolkien's earlier writing. But as the next chapter will show more fully, it can largely be discounted in an analysis of *The Lord of the Rings*. At points, it is true, a more dignified, even an archaic, style is employed, especially in dialogue. But the archaic is part of contemporary language: 'archaic' is not the same as 'obsolete'. There is no attempted stylistic reversion to the age in which the romance, rather than the novel, was the staple form of narrative. As Tolkien wrote at an early stage during the composition of *The Lord of the Rings*, the words chosen, however remote they may be from colloquial speech or ephemeral suggestions, must be words that remain in literary use ... among educated people ... . They must need no gloss. The fact that a word was still used by Chaucer, or Shakespeare, or even later, gives it no claim, if it has in our time perished from literary use ... . Antiquarian sentiment and philological knowingness are wholly out of place.[9]

Tolkien is here discussing the translation of a poem, *Beowulf*. But the logic of his argument is that a twentieth-century writer of fiction must adhere to 'words that ... need no gloss' for educated readers of literature – which, so far as fictional narrative is concerned, means readers of the novel. And the range of twentieth-century novel styles countenanced by readers is extremely wide, given that many modern novelists have 'shunned ordinary diction, and wrenched syntax', while others have reacted against this tendency by practising a studied plainness. Amid the stylistic diversity of the twentieth-century novel, from *Ulysses* to *Brighton Rock* to *Pale Fire* to *Trainspotting* – or simply within *Ulysses* – the stylistic scope of *The Lord of the Rings* is neither unusual nor intimidating.

Considerations of style, then, are hardly sufficient in themselves to exclude *The Lord of the Rings* from the category 'novel'. Yet there is something absolutely distinctive in the linguistic texture of *The Lord of the Rings*, quite apart from the personal stylistic resources evolved by Tolkien as by any other writer. It is the linguistic counterpart of the expansive conception of the invented world: a diversity and multiplicity of discourses, each of which has its place in a complex cultural-historical macrocosm. Its most obvious form is the use of a range of invented languages, mainly in proper names but also in occasional lines of verse or song, salutations or invocations. Once more I quote from an early stage of the narrative of the hobbits' journey: here, still within the Shire, they encounter a company of Elves.

> At length Gildor turned to the hobbits. ... 'We think you had best come now with us. It is not our custom, but for this time we will take you our road, and you shall lodge with us tonight, if you will.'
> 'O fair folk! This is good fortune beyond my hope', said Pippin. Sam was speechless. 'I thank you indeed, Gildor Inglorion', said Frodo

bowing. 'Elen síla lúmenn' omentielvo, a star shines on the hour of our meeting', he added in the high-elven speech.

'Be careful, friends!' cried Gildor laughing. 'Speak no secrets! Here is a scholar in the Ancient Tongue. Bilbo was a good master. Hail, Elf-friend!' he said, bowing to Frodo. 'Come now with your friends and join our company! You had best walk in the middle so that you may not stray. You may be weary before we halt.' (FR, 90)

Tolkien is not, of course, the first writer to invent names in pseudo-languages – Swift in Gulliver's Travels is probably the best-known example in English – but the scale and elaboration of his system is unprecedented: there are literally hundreds of personal and place-names in The Lord of the Rings, based on several distinct tongues, each of which is so elaborately individuated that, from proper names alone, the reader can recognise characteristic phonetic styles and begin to identify recurring features of word-formation. This effect of internal coherence and authenticity, coupled with the sheer profusion of names which rarely echo those of English, crucially negates the temptation to read into the nomenclature external allusions, and so preserves the integrity of the invented universe as well as enriching its complexity. Whereas Swift's 'Lilliput' functions essentially parasitically, through its suggestion of English 'little', only the most inexperienced of Tolkien's readers would be troubled by the resemblance of 'Inglorion' to 'inglorious': rather its melodious syllables harmonise with those of 'Gildor', and mark the contrast between the serene and exalted culture of the high-Elves and the homely, half-comic world which confers such names as Frodo, Sam and Pippin. The contrast is apparent too in the dialogue: Frodo, a rare instance of a hobbit who has dealings with Elves, manages a brief greeting in their tongue; Pippin, Frodo's social equal, echoes Gildor in adopting a courteous and stately style of English (which is to be conceived as a translation from the lingua franca of Middle-earth, the 'Westron' or 'Common Speech'); the servant is too overawed to speak. Differentiated styles of English speech are used in this fashion throughout the work to represent different peoples and different levels of formality in discourse. At the same time, the aesthetic qualities of the invented tongues reinforce our sense of the cultural and even moral character of their habitual users: the Elves literally stop their ears when the inscription on the Ring, in Sauron's Black Speech, is recited (FR, 267); the guttural and strenuous, but not unpleasing, Dwarvish seems appropriate to a 'tough, thrawn race ... secretive, laborious ... lovers of stone, of gems' (RK, 410); and the interminably agglomerated speech of the tree-like Ents corresponds to their enviably 'unhasty' existence.

> 'Real names tell you the story of the things they belong to in my language, in the Old Entish as you might say. It is a lovely language, but it takes a very long time to say anything in it, because we do not say anything in it, unless it is worth taking a long time to say, and to listen to.
>
> 'But now ... what is going on? What are you doing in it all? I can see and hear (and smell and feel) a great deal from this, from this *a-lalla-rumba-kamanda-lind-or-burúmë*. Excuse me: that is a part of my name for it; I do not know what the word is in the outside languages: you know, the thing we are on, where I stand and look out on fine mornings, and think about the Sun, and the grass beyond the wood, and the horses, and the clouds, and the unfolding of the world. What is going on? I like news. But not too quick now.' (TT, 68–9)

It is this deployment of linguistic variety as an integral part of the narrative content, a deployment in which the styles available within contemporary English assume the guise of an intermediate resource, to be exploited or even dispensed with entirely in the process of realising an imaginary linguistic universe, that sets The Lord of the Rings apart, at the level of verbal texture, from other fictions.

By this point it should be clear that a theme is emerging from the analysis. If The Lord of the Rings stands at a tangent to the novel as a genre, it is not because of a general abstention from realism or archaism of style – neither of which can really be attributed to it – but because of a highly specific feature for which precedents are hardly to be found in the novel tradition: the complex, and to an extent systematic, elaboration of an imaginary world. (The frequent, and otherwise odd-seeming, comparison of The Lord of the Rings to science-fiction derives its plausibility from this feature; but I know of no science-fiction text which displays it at a comparable level of amplitude and subtlety.) Let us keep this theme in mind, and proceed to a third and final attempt to justify the exclusion of The Lord of the Rings from the category of novels.

By comparison with almost any novel, The Lord of the Rings is episodic in structure, especially in the first volume. Gradually a complex plot evolves, as the strategies of Sauron, his adversaries and his allies, interact and produce unexpected results. But at first the plot is, arguably, relatively simple – in this respect it reproduces the perspective of the hobbits, who have no experience of the world outside their Shire, and initially grasp little more than that a malevolent power is searching for the Ring – and there are numerous adventures along the way, held together by the single thread of Frodo's flight from pursuit by Sauron's Black Riders. Frodo and his companions are tracked by the Riders through the Shire; they find refuge with the journeying Elves; they are tracked again; they find refuge with farmer Maggot; leaving the Shire, they lose their way in the Old Forest; they are rescued by the jovial and unaccountable Tom Bombadil; they stay in his house for some days; they proceed, and are captured by ghoulish Barrow-wights; Tom Bombadil again releases them; they arrive at the Prancing Pony; the inn is attacked by the Black Riders, but the hobbits escape with 'Strider'; they journey through the wilderness; they are attacked and Frodo is wounded; and so on. This string of episodes might be attributed to naïve construction, or to deliberate anachronism of genre: the structural features of The Lord of the Rings, it might be said, remind one of Pilgrim's Progress (except that the episodes lack allegorical significance); or of medieval romances; or of the Odyssey; but emphatically not of the modern novel, in which symphonic tightness of construction, the integral significance of each episode to plot and theme, the sustained development of material from exposition to closure, are of the essence.

But once again this separation of categories proves unsustainable. The model of the novel just propounded may hold for Tom Jones or Madame Bovary, but it scarcely holds for Robinson Crusoe or Tristram Shandy or Ulysses (again), let alone for the structurally pluralistic world of post-modern fiction. It is, in fact, an essentially nineteenth-century, or a Fielding-to-Flaubert, model. Conversely, the actual structural features of The Lord of the Rings have much in common with many novels, even nineteenth-century ones. Tom Shippey argues persuasively that 'the basic structural mode' of *The Lord of the Rings* is 'the ancient and pre-novelistic device of *entrelacement*'[10] in which a number of individual threads of plot, typically the adventures of various characters, are intertwined in a way which the characters themselves do not perceive, or only dimly intuit, but which becomes gradually apparent to the reader as the plot is clarified and fulfilled. This is perfectly true, even for the early episodes in Frodo's journey: certain details of these, it becomes clear from the subsequent narrative, reflect the actions of the wizards Gandalf and Saruman – particularly the former, Frodo's friend and advisor, whose worrying absence is a counter-theme during these chapters. Shippey's claim is abundantly true, as he demonstrates, of the later stages of the narrative. But as Shippey himself points out, the plot of *The Lord of the Rings* is integrated in a way which is not the case with its 'pre-novelistic' models: its 'separations and encounters and wanderings ... are controlled first by a map (something no Arthurian narrative possesses), and second by an extremely tight chronology of days and dates'.[11] These elements, and the attitude to plotting which they imply, put one in mind rather of the elaborate implicit chronology of *Wuthering Heights*, or of R. L. Stevenson's declaration that story-telling should always begin with a map,[12] than of the 'meaningless confusion' (Shippey's own description)[13] of some Arthurian romances. The technique of narrative interlacement may be pre-novelistic in origin, but the novel (perhaps especially the large, discursive Victorian novel of Dickens, Thackeray or Wilkie Collins) has appropriated it, or reinvented it. The interlacement of *The Lord of the Rings* differs essentially from that of, say, *Little Dorrit* only in the sense that, as we shall see, in the former the overall design which the individual characters cannot perceive has a mythical, in fact religious, dimension which is absent (unless at a very deeply implicit level) in Dickens's novel. But that is not a matter of structural mode.

The structural singularity of *The Lord of the Rings* is of a kind which cuts across any categoric distinction between novel and romance. Certainly the narrative permits, especially at first, an unusually leisurely succession of episodes. The whole of Book I (the first half of *The Fellowship of the Ring*) is required to bring Frodo, over some four hundred miles and twenty-seven days, to the Elvish sanctuary

of Rivendell, where various representative opponents of Sauron
resolve to attempt the destruction of the Ring. Shippey observes
that

> Frodo has to be dug out of no less than five 'Homely Houses' before his
> quest is properly launched: first Bag End, then the little house at
> Crickhollow with its redundant guardian Fredegar Bolger, then the house
> of Tom Bombadil, then the Prancing Pony, and finally Rivendell with its
> 'last Homely House east of the Sea'.[14]

Shippey's point is that The Lord of the Rings does not really get into
its stride – or get its interlacement working – until Book II. But
there is, I believe, a misconception here. It is true that Frodo's 'quest'
is not formalised until the Council of Elrond meets at Rivendell,
and that the journey which brings him to Elrond's House is at first
a walking holiday and then a flight from pursuit. If we are looking
for structural unity conferred by the declared quest, these chapters
must seem an anomalous, or at least over-protracted, preamble,
whether The Lord of the Rings is conceived as a novel or as a romance.
But it is doubtful whether this notion of the post-Rivendell quest
as the unifying concept is an apt one. As several critics have pointed
out, whereas the purpose of most quests is to acquire a sacred or
precious object, such as the Holy Grail, the purpose of this quest
is to get rid of something unholy, or, more particularly, to withhold
it, first temporarily and then permanently, from the malevolent
quester who is 'the Lord of the Rings'. Frodo and his friends do
not choose to pursue a quest, but have an unwelcome responsibility thrust upon them by ill-fate – not at the Council of Elrond, but
at the moment in Frodo's home, in chapter 2, when Gandalf reveals
to him that his golden ring, bequeathed by the departed Bilbo
Baggins, is Sauron's lost and coveted Ring of Power. In this sense the
opening chapters are fully coherent with the remainder of the
'quest': every furtive step Frodo takes is part of it. There is, however,
a deeper structural level at which the model of a quest narrative
seems in any case inapplicable, or at least inadequate. Though the
word 'quest' is used (mainly though not exclusively in dialogue, at
moments of formality or reflectiveness) it is scarcely emphasised:
in the 143 pages of Book IV, which is devoted to the journey of

Frodo and Sam to the mountain passes into Mordor, I can find only one, unobtrusive occurrence (TT, 285). The characters in non-formal discourse generally speak of 'our course', or 'our road'; and, as passages already quoted illustrate, we are above all aware of a journey in the most physical sense. Indeed it is the journey, rather than the quest, which serves as the unifying image.

> When their breakfast was over, and their packs all trussed up again, it was after ten o'clock, and the day was beginning to turn fine and hot. They went down the slope, and across the stream where it dived under the road, and up the next slope, and up and down another shoulder of the hills; and by that time their cloaks, blankets, water, food and other gear already seemed a heavy burden. The day's march promised to be warm and tiring work. After some miles, however, the road ceased to roll up and down: it climbed to the top of a steep bank in a weary zig-zagging sort of way, and then prepared to go down for the last time. In front of them they saw the lower lands dotted with small clumps of trees that melted away in the distance to a brown woodland haze. They were looking across the Woody End towards the Brandywine River. The road wound away before them like a piece of string.
>
> 'The road goes on for ever', said Pippin … . He sat down on the bank at the side of the road and looked away east into the haze, beyond which lay the River, and the end of the Shire in which he had spent all his life. … Frodo was silent. He too was gazing eastward along the road, as if he had never seen it before. Suddenly he spoke, aloud but as if to himself, saying slowly:
>
>> The Road goes ever on and on
>>> Down from the door where it began.
>> Now far ahead the Road has gone,
>>> And I must follow if I can,
>> Pursuing it with weary feet,
>>> Until it joins some larger way,
>> Where many paths and errands meet.
>>> And whither then? I cannot say.
>
> 'That sounds like a bit of old Bilbo's rhyming', said Pippin. 'Or is it one of your imitations? It does not sound altogether encouraging.'
>
> 'I don't know', said Frodo. 'It came to me then, as if I was making it up; but I may have heard it long ago. Certainly it reminds me very much

of Bilbo in the last years, before he went away. He used often to say there
was only one Road; that it was like a great river: its springs were at every
doorstep, and every path was its tributary. "It's a dangerous business,
Frodo, going out of your door", he used to say. "You step into the Road,
and if you don't keep your senses, there's no knowing where you might
be swept off to. Do you realise that this is the very path that goes through
Mirkwood, and that if you let it it might take you to the Lonely Mountain
or even further and to worse places?" ...' (FR, 82–3)

The homespun symbolism is transparent enough, and indeed
Bilbo's speech makes it virtually explicit: the Road stands for life,
or rather for its possibilities, indeed probabilities, of adventure,
commitment, and danger; for the fear of losing oneself, and the
hope of homecoming. At the same time it is markedly true of
Middle-earth, as a narrative locale, that it is a world of roads. Both
The Lord of the Rings and its predecessor, *The Hobbit* (which features
Bilbo, Frodo's elder cousin, as its hero), literally begin and end at
the door of Bag End after many hundreds of miles of journeying:
their heroes are travelling for much longer stretches of narrative
than they are resident anywhere. In fact only a few pages at each end
of *The Lord of the Rings* (FR, 51ff., RK, 301ff.) can be said to describe
sustained periods of residence by the principals, and in both cases
there are repeated references to journeying, actual or contemplated:
even before the revelation about the Ring, Frodo looks longingly at
maps, dreams about mountains he has never seen, and takes to
'wandering further and further afield by himself' (FR, 52). Gandalf,
the benevolent wizard, 'never made for himself any lasting abode',
we are told, but 'wandered' throughout the west of Middle-earth
(RK, 365); Aragorn is a 'Ranger', and 'the greatest traveller ... of
this age of the world' (FR, 67). The first episode in *The Lord of the
Rings* is Bilbo's farewell party, at the end of which he departs eastward
to an unknown destination; and the work closes with a final journey
for Frodo, a departure from the shores of Middle-earth, and Sam's
sad return to Bag End: the last words of the narrative are '"Well,
I'm back", he said' (RK, 311). Lest we should miss the point, the
'Road' song itself recurs in variants throughout *The Lord of the Rings*,
and returns, poignantly transformed, in the final chapter.

The 'journey', then, rather than the more narrowly defined 'quest', is the appropriate name for the image which unifies the heterogeneous narrative of The Lord of the Rings; the specific quest, Frodo's 'errand' as it is sometimes called, is merely the axis of the main action. The 'errand' pertains to the plot, the journey to the story, or 'history'. The difference is important. Whereas the quest as a unifying device is integrative, and relegates the locales to a subordinate status (every episode must represent a significant obstacle overcome, or a significant gain in enlightenment), the journey is expansive and exalts the locales: it permits diversions, loose ends, and celebrates the contingency and variety of the world. Certainly many – indeed, to varying extents, all – of the episodes of the hobbits' journeys are integrated into subsequent narrative developments; but these connections are contingent, and, as it were, life-like, not systematic or necessarily thematically significant. The short sword Meriadoc Brandybuck recovers from a haunted barrow in The Fellowship of the Ring he uses to wound the diabolic Witch-King in The Return of the King; but the previous episode, the encounter with Tom Bombadil, is only briefly touched upon thereafter, and Tom is not waiting to greet the travellers on their return journey. The Ents, encountered by the wandering Merry and Pippin in The Two Towers, are roused by them to join the war against the treacherous wizard Saruman; but the Ents' abandoned search for the Entwives, of which a good deal is said and sung in this episode, is destined never to be resumed. The maps of Middle-earth show countless lands, rivers, mountains, villages that do not feature in the narrative; and again and again the characters gaze in passing over landscapes that they will never, in fact, traverse. If, as I have suggested, the energetic elaboration of an imaginary world is the essence of the distinctiveness of The Lord of the Rings from the novel tradition, this structural use of the journey is a crucial part of that distinctiveness.

It might be protested at this point that expansiveness and contingency hardly make for coherence – that an emphasis on journeying looks like an excuse for rambling and superfluous invention, rather than a unifying device. On this view The Lord of the Rings offends not merely against widely accepted principles of novelistic unity, but against classical principles of proportion between the parts and the whole, of sufficiency of means to ends, which transcend distinctions of genre. The multiplication of places, peoples and personages, it might be said, goes far beyond what is necessary to secure the excitement of the climax and dénouement. Though the invention is enjoyable enough episode by episode, it overweights the structure: Tom Bombadil, for example, could safely be cut – as dramatic adaptations of the book, from the BBC radio version to Peter Jackson's film, have generally done.[15] A slimmed-down version of the work, retaining the essentials of the plot but without the leisurely proliferation of detail, would have been more fully effective.

But no one who knows the book well will feel that this makes sense. It is not merely that some episodes are too good to miss. The proposition that slimming-down would make the book as a whole more effective rings false. On the contrary, most readers are likely to agree with Tolkien himself (FR, 6) that the book is defective in being too short. The reason is that the amplitude of the world described in The Lord of the Rings is itself both structurally and thematically significant. What looks like excess from the point of view of a plot-based structure is wholly necessary for a different kind of structure: and the two types of structure are here ultimately integrated in a single aesthetic complex.

Here I would like to return to the point about desire, and to offer some generalisations which I hope will not be too contentious. The aesthetic dynamic of a plot-based structure is, in general and stating the point somewhat crudely, the creation in the reader's mind of certain hopes and fears, the resolution of which, in one way or another, forms the terminal objective of the plot. This is as true of, say, a Jane Austen novel (where the hopes and fears relate to the vicissitudes of courtship, or to the conflicts between good sense and folly) as of any melodrama. Whether the reader's engaged desires are, broadly speaking, gratified, as in Pride and Prejudice or The Winter's Tale, or, broadly speaking, denied, as in Tess of the D'Urbevilles or Othello, the structure of the narrative or drama is correlated to the process of their arousal, quickening, gratification or denial. Individual scenes or episodes serve not only to display events, engendering and resolving suspense, but to arouse those attractions and aversions towards particular conceptions (often, but not exclusively, characters) which motivate the reader to take an interest in the sequence of events. Not all literary works have plot-based structure. In the case of certain works of fiction, including some celebrated modern novels (Virginia Woolf's *The Waves*, for instance), the sequence of events may seem relatively unimportant; in other types of work, such as lyric poems, there may be effectively no events. In these cases, the aesthetic experience becomes an experience of response to plotless conceptions (which may at their simplest be no more than visual images), and different kinds of structure are employed to give coherence and clarity to this response.[16]

The Lord of the Rings has a plot-based structure, simple in outline but complex in detail. As Frodo, still bearing the Ring, draws nearer to Mordor, his scattered companions become involved in the war waged by Sauron, and his quasi-independent ally Saruman, against the two kingdoms of Men which lie to the west of Mordor – Gondor and Rohan. At length Saruman is overthrown and imprisoned in his own stronghold, Isengard; but the chief city of Gondor, Minas Tirith, is besieged, and it becomes clear, after various shifts of fortune, that military victory must sooner or later lie with Sauron. Books III and V narrate these developments; book IV and the early chapters of VI follow Frodo and Sam, pursued or accompanied by the degraded former Ring-bearer Gollum, to Mount Doom. The work's climax, when Frodo, finally yielding to the corrupting power of the Ring, refuses to destroy it in the volcanic fire, even as Sauron's hordes overrun the last defenders of the West, has an overpowering force, the culmination of several hundred pages of carefully accumulated tension, which no quotation can begin to suggest.

But the work also has an overarching, indeed all-inclusive, structure. As I have been aiming to suggest throughout this chapter, the work is unified by the imaginative authenticity of the invented world itself: by the internal coherence of its history, geography, philology. The complexities of the plot, the interlacing journeys, the multitudinous discourses, all conduce to this end. This expansiveness, which might be supposed to threaten incoherence, paradoxically has the opposite effect, since every additional detail, providing it is consistent with the rest, reinforces the impression of a world which has the interior consistency of the real world, as well as its capacity for newness, for surprise, its inexhaustibility.

The work's least novelistic sections of all – the six antiquarian Appendices, which supplement the main narrative with a hundred pages of lesser narratives, chronicles and essays, without ever producing the impression that the historical record has run dry – further authenticate this unifying expansiveness: one feels that they could go on for ever, and that an essential feature of the invented world (as of the real one) is this exhilarating illimitableness.

This comprehensive structure is effective aesthetically because the imaginary world and its contents are affectively highly charged. The point may be expressed aphoristically by saying that Middle-earth, rather than any of the characters, is the hero of The Lord of the Rings; and Middle-earth, as an imaginative conception, is coterminous with the entire work. Just as the emotional power of a novel may be derived primarily from our engagement with the personality of the protagonist, and only secondarily from the events in which the protagonist becomes involved, so the emotional power of The Lord of the Rings is at least as much a matter of the fascination and beauty of Middle-earth (including its peoples and their cultures) as of the excitement of the plot. But the crux of the plot is, precisely, the threatened destruction of Middle-earth: its conversion by Sauron, if he obtains the Ring, to the likeness of Mordor, a sterile, undifferentiated waste-land in which, we may presume, all cultures will have been obliterated and all peoples slaughtered or enslaved. ('He'll eat us all if He gets it, eat all the world', as Gollum warns Frodo (TT, 245).) In this way the two aesthetic structures – the dynamic structure of the plot, and the comprehensive structure of the invented world – are integrally related: our desire for Middle-earth is the keynote, so to speak, of our desire for the fulfilment of Frodo's errand. The Lord of the Rings is a consummate work of art because it co-ordinates these desires (each of which is itself a complex of many desires) into a compelling unity.[17]

II

In his Foreword to the second edition of The Lord of the Rings, Tolkien tells us that his 'prime motive was the desire of a tale-teller to try his hand at a really long story that would hold the attention of readers, amuse them, delight them, and at times maybe excite them or move them deeply' (FR, 6). Though expressed with calculated modesty, this account of his intentions is a more accurate pointer to his actual achievement in the work than many critical analyses. If *The Lord of the Rings* is to be esteemed, the reason which is prior to all others is that, like a great painting or piece of music, it promotes, and gives shape to, emotional responses which we value.

Tolkien notably does not say that his aim was to inculcate moral values, and I shall argue at the end of this chapter that an important appeal is made to desires which are not in themselves moral, though they are congruent or compatible with moral values. Nevertheless any analysis of the aesthetic power of *The Lord of the Rings* needs to take into account the fact that its values are organised around a moral conflict: Sauron's despotism is not only to be 'undesired', it is to be undesired in the specific sense of being perceived as categorically morally bad. Nothing could be more false, however, than the notion that *The Lord of the Rings* represents a deterministic, or Manichean, universe of struggle between the innately and unalterably good and the innately and unalterably evil. On the contrary, as several critics have noticed, the imagined world is underpinned by an optimistic, and occasionally explicit, theology of a quite different kind. 'Nothing is evil in the beginning', Elrond observes. 'Even Sauron was not so' (FR, 281). Though God is not referred to in *The Lord of the Rings* (except fleetingly in an Appendix, RK 317), and though its world is pre-Christian, there is no doubt that we are in an Augustinian universe, in which all Creation is good, and evil is conceived in terms of freely-chosen negation, of a wilful abdication from an original state of created perfection. Sauron, the Dark Lord, is not a countervailing deity, but a fallen angel who, for all his awesome power, cannot create new life, only strive to annihilate it or pervert it into abominable forms.[18] Whether the reader consciously recognises the theology is unimportant: the essential point is that the negativity of evil, and the intrinsic goodness of 'the effoliation and multiple enrichment of creation' (to quote Tolkien's words from a different context)[19] are consistently and palpably maintained.

CARDIFF

Whatever the clarity of the underlying moral ideas, however, any fictional narrative which attempts to embody a successful struggle of good against evil, not in allegorised abstractions, but in an elaborately 'realised' world, is exposed to a number of risks. There is the risk — which allegory is able to make into a virtue — of perceived over-simplification, such that the reader loses confidence in the moral significance of the action; the risk of making good seem dull and evil interesting; and the risk that the victory of good may seem either implausible, or all too plausible but in a way which undermines its claim to be good. W. H. Auden suggests that

> if ... Good and Evil are to be incarnated in individuals and societies, we must be convinced that the Evil side is what every sane man, irrespective of his nationality or culture, would acknowledge as evil. The triumph of Good over Evil ... must appear historically possible, not a daydream. Physical, and to a considerable extent, intellectual power must be shown as what we know them to be, morally neutral and effectively real: battles are won by the stronger side, be it good or evil.[20]

To take Auden's latter point first, the defeat of the forces of Evil should ideally appear, not as a lucky accident, or as a punishment inflicted from outside by a superior power (which deprives the actual process of defeat of any moral significance), but as the practical consequence of wickedness itself: Evil must appear as intrinsically self-defeating in the long run. Auden himself indicates several reasons why this is so in The Lord of the Rings. Sauron and his servants, despite their steadily growing superiority in crude strength and terror, are hindered by weaknesses which are themselves vices: their lack of imagination, the irrational cruelty which denies them the option of voluntary assistance (the victim must be made to act against his own will), and the selfishness which disables their alliances. The mutual deceptions between Sauron and Saruman, the murderous animosities among, and within, orc-tribes which aid the escape of Frodo and Sam from capture and pursuit in Mordor, the contrast between the sullen or terrified acquiescence of the enslaved and the energetic co-operativeness of free men (and, towards the end of the work, free hobbits revolting against Saruman's petty tyranny over the Shire) all contribute towards the 'historical possibility' of unforeseen victory over evil. In comparison, the few discreetly suggested providential interventions – the reincarnation of Gandalf after his fatal struggle with the demonic Balrog, the sea-wind from the South that speeds Aragorn's ships to the rescue of the beleaguered city of Minas Tirith – are at most correctives to blows struck by the forces of evil: they counteract the strength of the Dark Lord, but do not diminish it.

It is the intellectual myopia of Evil, however, on which greatest explicit emphasis is laid in the text. Just as the created world is intrinsically good, so disinterested curiosity about that world is an attribute of good; the negativity of evil entails a loss of insight and of the desire to understand others. 'Whereas the light perceives the very heart of the darkness, its own secret has not been discovered' (FR, 366). The inability of complete evil to understand self-renunciatory motives is consciously exploited by Sauron's antagonists in their decision to attempt the destruction of the Ring, even at the risk of sending it into Sauron's own territory.

> 'Let folly be our cloak, a veil before the eyes of the Enemy! For he is very wise, and weighs all things to a nicety in the scales of his malice. But the only measure that he knows is desire, desire for power; and so he judges all hearts. Into his heart the thought will not enter that any will refuse it, that having the Ring we may seek to destroy it. If we seek this, we shall put him out of reckoning.' (FR, 283)

The subsequent strategy of Gandalf and Aragorn is to mount a hopeless but diversionary military challenge to Sauron, drawing out his attention and his forces from Mordor to crush (as he will suppose) the embryonic power of a rival aggressor. Meanwhile Frodo and Sam proceed into Mordor on the errand that Sauron cannot imagine until, as Frodo claims the Ring for himself, Sauron recognises too late 'the magnitude of his own folly' (RK, 223).

At this moment, it is worth noting, Frodo himself is performing a wrongful, and indeed potentially calamitous, act: yielding at last in his exhaustion, when the moment to destroy the Ring is before him, to its fearsome, but in principle resistible, corruptive power. His failure of will takes him to the edge of the spiritual abyss into which Sauron has fallen ages earlier. In the event, Gollum, who has accompanied or tracked him to the end of his journey in his passion to regain the Ring, seizes it, biting off Frodo's finger, and falls – propelled by the Ring's own curse – into the physical abyss of the volcano. Frodo is saved by the practical consequence of earlier acts of mercy shown to Gollum, by Frodo himself, by Sam, by Bilbo, by Gandalf, by Aragorn, by Faramir the captain of Gondor, by the wood-elves of Mirkwood. Nevertheless, claiming the Ring is a culpable deed, and one which, it is made very clear, any of the characters (except the sublimely self-sufficient demigod Tom Bombadil) might have committed: indeed several of Sauron's opponents refuse to take or even handle the Ring, for fear of corruption by its inherent malignity and by the power to dominate others that it offers in proportion to the strength of the user. The well-intentioned Boromir, son of the ruling Steward of Gondor, covets it as a weapon for military exploits against Mordor, and finally assaults Frodo in an attempt to steal it; his father Denethor, more insidiously tempted, proposes to keep it in reserve in the vaults of his citadel (RK, 78). Frodo himself, possessive towards the Ring, and not without a streak of native priggishness, calls the devoted Sam a 'thief' when the latter offers to carry it for a while (RK, 188); and when the elderly Bilbo, the previous Ring-bearer, asks to see it once again, Frodo feels 'a desire to strike him' (FR, 244). These examples should make us cautious about accepting, so far as The Lord of the Rings is concerned, Auden's premise that 'Good and Evil are to be incarnated in individuals and societies.' Certainly the invented world presents us with intensified or encapsulated representations of good and evil, which in figures such as Gandalf and Sauron, or societies such as the Shire and Mordor, manifest themselves with a clarity of focus seldom if ever encountered in the historical world. But the implicit theology of free will is clear enough in The Lord of the Rings: no character is intrinsically (that is, by original and unalterable nature) evil or good in the way that, so far as we can gather from the stories, the wicked stepmother or good fairy of the traditional fairy-tale, or for that matter Uriah Heep and Agnes Wickfield in David Copperfield, are intrinsically evil and good respectively. The 'good', as we have seen, are morally fallible, and the evil have not been evil from the first. The crooked counsellor of Rohan, Grima 'Wormtongue', 'was not always as it now is. Once it was a man, and did ... service in its fashion' (TT, 125). Saruman 'was great once, of a noble kind that we should not dare to raise our hands against' (RK, 299). Nor are the guilty always irredeemable. Boromir, after his attack on Frodo, redeems himself by confessing to the deed and sacrificing himself to defend Merry and Pippin. King Théoden of Rohan, fallen into despair and inaction under the persuasions of Wormtongue, is revived by Gandalf, repudiates his false counsellor, and reprieves the loyal nephew he has victimised. Saruman and Gollum, both stained with repeated murder, come close, especially the latter, to repentance; one of the saddest moments in the narrative is the episode in which Gollum, painfully wavering over his scheme to betray Frodo and Sam to their deaths, resembling

> an old weary hobbit, shrunken by the years that had carried him far beyond his time, beyond friends and kin, and the fields and streams of his youth, an old starved pitiable thing ... (TT, 324)

tenderly touches the sleeping Frodo's knee, only to be accused by Sam of 'sneaking'. Sam's tetchy behaviour at this point, and his later reluctant compassion for Gollum after he has briefly shared the latter's experience of the burden of Ring-bearer, provide a further example of moral development among the principal characters, as does the striking contrast between Frodo's near-pacifism at the end of the narrative, when his only involvement in the Battle of Bywater is to prevent enraged hobbits from revenging themselves on Saruman's men (RK, 295–6), and his declaration near the beginning (FR, 68) that Bilbo ought to have killed Gollum when he had the chance.

As for the societies of Middle-earth, they too 'incarnate' good and evil only in the sense that they embody moral qualities recognisable from the historical world with an aesthetic clarity which is not to be found in history. Mordor is not a worse society – in the sense of quantity or intensity of accomplished evil – than, say, Hitler's Germany or Pol Pot's Cambodia or the Aztec Empire, but it is a uniformly – so to speak, harmoniously – evil society in a way that no real society can be. Mordor is the only morally unequivocal society in Middle-earth because it is the only society created wholly

in the image and according to the will of a single being: it is
necessarily evil because only an evil being would subordinate all
other wills to his own, and because the act of subordinating other
wills makes a being evil. (Contrast with Sauron's version of lordship
the following dialogue between Frodo and Goldberry, the wife of
Tom Bombadil.)

> 'Fair lady!' said Frodo … 'Tell me, if my asking does not seem foolish,
> who is Tom Bombadil?'
>   'He is', said Goldberry, staying her movements and smiling.
>   Frodo looked at her questioningly. 'He is, as you have seen him', she
> said in answer to his look. 'He is the Master of wood, water and hill.'
>   'Then all this strange land belongs to him?'
>   'No indeed!' she answered, and her smile faded. 'That would indeed
> be a heavy burden', she added in a low voice, as if to herself. 'The trees
> and grasses and all things growing or living in the land belong each to
> themselves. Tom Bombadil is the Master. No one has ever caught old Tom
> walking in the forest, wading in the water, leaping on the hill-tops under
> light and shadow. He has no fear. Tom Bombadil is master.' (FR, 135)

The relation of Bombadil to his little country is like that of an
unfallen Adam to the Garden of Eden. Bombadil's freedom from
fear is co-ordinate with his freedom from tyrannical intent: secure
in a gardener-like status which it does not occur to him to exceed,
his will cannot afflict or be afflicted by the wills of others. All
societies other than Mordor (unless one counts the miniature
tyranny of Saruman's Isengard) are predominantly good, though
with an admixture of actual or potential evil: even the unblemished
Elvish land of Lothlórien would, we must suppose, have degenerated
if its ruler, Galadriel, had yielded to the temptation to accept the
Ring from Frodo; and 'even in the Shire there are some as like
minding other folk's business and talking big' (RK, 281). The pre-
dominance of good is greater, no doubt, in these two communities
than in any real society: we are told, for example, that 'no hobbit
has ever killed another on purpose in the Shire' (RK, 285). But, as
this carefully qualified statement suggests, the exceptional peace-
fulness of the Shire, as of Lothlórien, is presented as the result of
specific and transitory historical circumstances, as well as of the
comparatively pacific nature of Hobbits and Elves. The Shire is

sheltered from conflict, both by the protective Rangers and by its geographical position, and enjoys a benign climate and fertile soil; in pre-Shire days Hobbits have in fact fought 'to maintain themselves in a hard world' (FR, 14). Lothlórien is an enclave defended by arrows as well as by the invisible power of Galadriel's own Ring, Nenya; when Galadriel, wearing Nenya, spreads out her hands 'towards the East in a gesture of rejection and denial' (FR, 380), it is not because the Elves are incapable of being seduced by Sauron, but on the contrary because they have been seduced in earlier times, and have learned their lesson – Nenya itself is a product of this period of collaboration.

If, then, in Auden's words, 'we are convinced that the Evil side is what every sane man ... would acknowledge as evil', it is at least partly because the represented conflict between good and evil is schematic only to an extent which is consistent with the internal authenticity of the invented world. Granted the initial 'mythical' premises, of which the most significant is the incarnation (in the literal sense) of formidable immortal spirits upon the surface of a great continent inhabited by mortal creatures, the manifestations of good and evil in The Lord of the Rings have a complexity more familiar from the realistic novel than from fairy-tale, and invisible only to the most determinedly cursory reading.

Mere complexity, however, is not enough to make the moral dimension of the work compelling. The interplay between good and evil in The Lord of the Rings forms part of the more comprehensive interplay between conceptions designed to arouse desire and conceptions designed to arouse 'undesire', or rejection: for the work to be effective, the reader must respond appropriately, at least to a sufficient extent for the affective structure which unites the plot to the invented world to hold firm. To put it more specifically and perhaps more clearly, the reader must be delighted by Middle-earth in order to care that Sauron should not lay it desolate, and must endorse with a lively emotional response the claims of the Shire, Rivendell, Lothlórien and Gondor, of Gandalf, Aragorn and Frodo, to constitute images of a life that is to be desired, of attitudes and motives that are to be desired in oneself and in others, and must correspondingly feel that Sauron and all his works are images of what is to be rejected and abhorred.

Vital to the achievement of this response is the contrast between the diversity of good and the sameness of evil. The benign societies of Middle-earth have few uniform features, except those incident upon the imagined pre-industrial stage of economic development. (Mostly, for example, they are hereditary monarchies – but this is not true of the Shire, which has an elected Mayor, nor, apparently, of the Bree-land.) As the hobbits journey among them, it is their dissimilarities which are most often underlined. There is a wide tolerance, even a relish in diversity, both in trivial and in comparatively serious matters.

Now more torches were being lit. A cask of wine was broached. Storage barrels were being opened. Men were fetching water from the fall. Some were laving their hands in basins. A wide copper bowl and a white cloth were brought to Faramir and he washed.

'Wake our guests,' he said, 'and take them water. It is time to eat.'

Frodo sat up and yawned and stretched. Sam, not used to being waited on, looked with some surprise at the tall man who bowed, holding a basin of water before him.

'Put it on the ground, master, if you please!' he said. 'Easier for me and you.' Then to the astonishment and amusement of the Men he plunged his head into the cold water and splashed his neck and ears.

'Is it the custom in your land to wash the head before supper?' said the man who waited on the hobbits.

'No, before breakfast', said Sam. 'But if you're short of sleep cold water on the neck's like rain on a wilted lettuce. There! Now I can keep awake long enough to eat a bit …'

Before they ate, Faramir and all his men turned and faced west in a moment of silence. Faramir signed to Frodo and Sam that they should do likewise.

'So we always do,' he said, as they sat down: 'we look towards Númenor that was, and beyond to Elvenhome that is, and to that which is beyond Elvenhome and will ever be. Have you no such custom at meat?'

'No', said Frodo, feeling strangely rustic and untutored. 'But if we are guests, we bow to our host and after we have eaten we rise and thank him.'

'That we do also', said Faramir. (TT, 284–5)

Both parties to the clash of washing-rituals are attractive, the Men because of their attentive hospitality, Sam because of his democratic spirit ('Easier for me and you') and his comically informative reply ('No, before breakfast') which misses the emphasis of the question. The exchange sets the tone for what immediately follows. Frodo *feels* strangely rustic and untutored, but it is only a feeling, an effect of cultural perspective; and to feel rustic and untutored is not to feel guilty: there is no implied reproach to the hobbits for irreligion. Middle-earth is, in fact, a world without churches or organised piety, though not without celebration and reverence: the Elves, for example (to whose poetry and song any distinction of 'sacred' from 'secular' seems inapplicable), sing in spontaneous praise of Elbereth, under the stars she has kindled. Dogma and sectarianism are absent. The hobbits, as we see here, lack even the minimal religious ritual of the Men of Gondor: their ethical culture, learned in ancient times from Elves or Men, has become almost wholly tacit, and in the Shire, we gather, they now fear Elves and know nothing of the realms of Men. But this unwritten yet entrenched ethic, its origins only glimpsed in a few proverbial phrases – 'there had been no king for a thousand years … yet the Hobbits still said of wild folk and wicked things (such as trolls) that they had not heard of the king' (FR, 18) – has its own charm, correlated to the hobbits' easy-going way of life and lack of ambition.

The universal value of courtesy, to be sure, is upheld here, and elsewhere. 'You have courteous speech', declares the venerable Denethor to a nervous Pippin, 'strange though the sound of it may be to us in the South. And we shall have need of all folk of courtesy, be they great or small, in the days to come' (RK, 28). That special degree of courtesy which enables individuals actually to transcend differences of culture and race, to understand and respect the customs of others, marks out characters of especial wisdom, like Galadriel who receives and conciliates the Dwarf, Gimli, in Lothlórien. But it is not universal even among the benign. Galadriel's own people are suspicious of Gimli (and he of them), while to the people of Rohan, 'Elvish wights' are sinister figures associated with sorcery (TT, 34–5; RK, 59). The hobbits of the Shire are for the most part incorrigibly parochial. When Frodo returns to the Shire, wounded and subdued, he receives little honour from the people he has saved from enslavement or death – indeed they remain largely unaware of, or indifferent to, the events beyond their own borders. Sam's father, 'Gaffer' Gamgee, greets Frodo not with gratitude but with uncomprehending reproof.

> 'Good evening, Mr Baggins!' he said. 'Glad indeed I am to see you safe back. But I've a bone to pick with you, in a manner o' speaking, if I may make so bold. You didn't never ought to have a' sold Bag End, as I always said. That's what started all the mischief. And while you've been trapessing in foreign parts, chasing Black Men up mountains from what my Sam says, though for what he don't make clear, they've been and dug up Bagshot Row and ruined my taters!' (RK, 293)

But the comic tone is important. While this circumscribed vision is not exactly commended – we will soon feel, with Sam, the poignancy of the ailing Frodo's retirement – it is accepted with good humour. The Shire has its own values and mores, appropriate, in normal circumstances, to a peaceful land, untouched for centuries by momentous events. The Gaffer's protest against Sam's wearing armour ('What's come of his weskit? I don't hold with wearing ironmongery, whether it wears well or no' (RK, 294)) is as sane and humane in these terms as his concern for his taters. Conversely, the military values of Gondor, of which Faramir speaks somewhat apologetically to Frodo (TT, 287) and Beregond to Pippin (RK, 39), reflect its position as historical antagonist and neighbour to Mordor. The geopolitical complexity of Middle-earth requires, in fact, if it is to be plausible, a certain variation in the expression and emphasis given to moral imperatives.

As for life-styles, modes of social organisation, and other cultural features, the principal societies are again extremely various, granted certain basic moral principles. (Polygamy, for example, is conspicuous by its absence.) Dwarves and Elves, 'the Mountain and the Wood' (FR, 392), have antithetical preferences, reconcilable only by exceptional friendship: Gimli consents to visit the alarmingly alive Forest of Fangorn, 'though with no great delight, it seemed' (RK, 259) only because the Elf, Legolas, has accompanied him into the caves of Aglarond. With these two races Tolkien greatly elaborates and dignifies traditional images: Dwarvish culture is based on crafts-manship, especially in metal, and on trade; Elven culture is sylvan, or maritime. The reclusive Wild Men of Drúadan Forest, with their poisoned arrows, gurgling speech and primitive mathematics ('I am great headman, Ghân-buri- Ghân. I count many things: stars in sky, leaves on trees, men in the dark. You have a score of scores counted five times and five' (RK, 106)) seem scarcely human to the neighbouring Rohirrim, who themselves, 'writing no books but singing many songs' (TT, 33) have a rudimentary culture by the sophisticated standards of Gondor. But these differences are not essentially evaluative. The 'return of the King' at the end of the work does not usher in a rule of the saints or a uniform polity: though Aragorn's formal sovereignty extends over both Drúadan and the Shire, he consigns both to the exclusive government of their existing populations (RK, 254, 377). This endorsement of diversity, apart from its contribution to the internal realism of Middle-earth, protects The Lord of the Rings from any accusation of invoking a narrow and prescriptive version of the good life.

Conversely, evil tends to homogeneity. Its keynote is aggrandisement of self and negation of not-self, whether through the literal consumption of others, as with the giant blood-drinking spider Shelob, or through the enslavement and torture of other persons and the destruction of growing things. There is only one form of political order, a military despotism which terrorises its own soldiery as well as its enemies; sexuality is loveless, either diverted into sadism or confined to the organised breeding of warriors; economic life is based on slavery, and is devoted not to the cultivation, but to the exploitation, and ultimately the destruction, of resources. Industrial processes are developed solely for the purposes of warfare and deliberate pollution. In all these respects Saruman's despotism is just the same as Sauron's: his Isengard is 'only a little copy, a child's model or a slave's flattery' of Sauron's 'vast fortress, armoury, prison, furnace of great power, Barad-dûr' (TT,161). (There is narrative discretion here: Tolkien avoids the risk of duplication, and at the same time reinforces our sense of the literally indescribable terror of Sauron's Dark Tower, by depicting Isengard at close quarters and at length while suggesting Barad-dûr only through distant and momentary glimpses.) When Saruman escapes to the Shire, all he can do is initiate the same process once again at a petty level. Sauron's own vassals and slaves are robbed of distinct identity: the Lieutenant of the Tower of Barad-dûr has no recorded name, 'for he himself had forgotten it, and he said: "I am the Mouth of Sauron"' (RK, 164). When Sauron is overthrown, his orcs and trolls run 'hither and thither mindless; and some slew themselves, or cast themselves in pits, or fled wailing back to hide in holes and dark lightless places far from hope' (RK, 227). His service is a negation of personal autonomy. The Ring, likewise, assimilates individuals to one another. Gollum incessantly calls the Ring his 'precious'; Bilbo uses the same word (though only once), when reluctant to relinquish it (FR, 42); so does Aragorn's ancestor Isildur: 'it is precious to me, though I buy it with great pain' (FR, 266). The Ring gradually negates the particular identities of its owners, extending their lives (unless they die violent deaths) but causing them to fade – in the end, literally – into a depersonalised wraithdom, like the Men, ensnared with Rings by Sauron in an earlier age, who appear as the ghostly, menacing and indistinguishable Nazgûl, the Nine Riders. The hobbits, though physically resilient, suffer psychological attenuation. Bilbo, cheerfully unaware of the Ring's nature, feels himself 'stretched ... like butter that has been spread over too much bread' (FR, 41). Frodo, in the last stages of his journey, confides to Sam that he 'could not give it up, and if you tried to take it I would go mad' (RK, 214), and loses the ability to visualise anything but the hallucination of the fiery Ring.

> 'No taste of food, no feel of water, no sound of wind, no memory of tree or grass or flower, no image of moon or star are left to me. I am naked in the dark, Sam, and there is no veil between me and the wheel of fire. I begin to see it even with my waking eyes, and all else fades.' (RK, 215)

Gollum, obsessed by the desire to repossess the Ring, talks to it continually, speaks of himself in the third person or in the plural except at moments of intermittent rationality, and is effectively driven insane by the final crisis on Mount Doom, when he must either seize the Ring from Frodo or see it cast into the Fire and destroyed: he pursues Frodo to the Cracks of Doom 'with a wild light of madness glaring in his eyes', and in the few moments of possession dances 'like a mad thing' on the brink of the chasm (RK, 222, 224). Sympathetic though most readers will be towards Gollum, the state into which he degenerates, and by which Frodo and others are threatened, is genuinely frightening. One can imagine a person wishing to be like Wilkie Collins's Count Fosco, or Goethe's Mephistopheles, or even conceivably Milton's Satan (though not Dante's); it is one of the triumphs of Tolkien's literary judgement in The Lord of the Rings that fully accomplished evil is represented by states of personality (or unpersonality) which no sane reader could envy.

In many respects the polarities of value within The Lord of the Rings are based on an appeal to the centre of the moral consensus. Truthfulness is opposed to falsehood, loyalty to treachery, kindness to cruelty, and so on. This might become merely pious and facile, and end by alienating, rather than engaging, the reader's attention and sympathies. But the characters and their actions avoid copybook banality for two reasons. The first is that none of the core virtues is pressed as a dogma beyond the point of common sense. Faramir says that he 'would not snare even an orc with a falsehood' (TT, 272), but then Faramir is a powerful and well-armed warrior, fully capable of killing orcs by the dozen: the hobbits, when captured and otherwise helpless, do in fact resort to understandable deception at times, as when Merry and Pippin imply to the orc-captain Grishnâkh that they have the Ring (TT, 58–9). In the extremity of Denethor's madness, when he commands his guards to help him to commit suicide, and proposes to burn his wounded son on the same pyre, Beregond breaks his oath of fealty in order to save Faramir, and kills three loyal guards. 'And the others cursed him, calling him outlaw and traitor to his master' (RK, 128). It is important that Beregond should grieve at these actions, and should subsequently be brought to (a merciful) judgement for them, but the common-sensical principle is clear: obligations of loyalty, even when reinforced by solemn oaths, may be overridden by other moral imperatives. Even Frodo's kindness to Gollum is modified by the need to take precautions against a sudden murderous attack, or an attempt to seize the Ring.

'You revealed yourself to me just now, foolishly. *Give it back to Sméagol* you said. Do not say that again! Do not let that thought grow in you! You will never get it back. But the desire of it may betray you to a bitter end. You will never get it back. In the last need, Sméagol, I should put on the

Precious; and the Precious mastered you long ago. If I, wearing it, were to command you, you would obey, even if it were to leap from a precipice or cast yourself into the fire. And such would be my command. So have a care, Sméagol!' (TT, 248)

It is an instance of the psychological and moral complexity of the work that Frodo is speaking here both out of prudence and altruism (since catastrophe for everyone, including Gollum himself, is probable if the latter regains the Ring or hinders Frodo's errand), and – as the nervously repeated sentence suggests – out of his own steadily hardening possessiveness towards the Ring.

The second reason is that the attractiveness of the benign characters and societies lies not only in their practice of certain consensus virtues, but in their manifestation of what one might call peri-ethical qualities: qualities such as humour, learning, curiosity, creativity, and delight in life, which are ultimately related to more centrally moral qualities (such as freedom from self-absorption, and love for other creatures) but which often fall into the wrong hands, so to speak, in works of fiction.[21]

Humour, in particular, is almost exclusively associated with goodness in The Lord of the Rings. Tolkien is perfectly capable of creating comic villains in stories of less ethical seriousness – Chrysophylax in Farmer Giles of Ham, and to some extent Smaug in The Hobbit, are examples. In The Lord of the Rings, Gollum perpetrates one or two bleak jokes, while Saruman, Grishnákh and the Lieutenant of Barad-dûr engage in sarcastic sneering, but none of these is remotely funny: it is the menace and hatred, or in Gollum's case the extraordinary mixture of the sinister and the pathetic, on which the emphasis rests. Gollum cackles with laughter when the hobbits, stumbling at night through the Dead Marshes, see the faces of slaughtered soldiers, eerily illuminated, below the surface of the pools.

'The Dead can't be really there! Is it some devilry hatched in the Dark Land?'

'Who knows? Sméagol doesn't know', answered Gollum. 'You cannot reach them, you cannot touch them. We tried once, yes, precious. I tried once; but you cannot reach them. Only shapes to see, perhaps, not to touch. No precious! All dead.'

Sam looked darkly at him and shuddered again, thinking that he guessed why Sméagol had tried to touch them. 'Well, I don't want to see them', he said. 'Never again! Can't we get on and get away?'

'Yes, yes', said Gollum. 'But slowly, very slowly. Very carefully! Or hobbits go down to join the Dead ones and light little candles. Follow Sméagol! Don't look at lights!' (TT, 235–6)

Gollum is on his best behaviour here, and his black joke about the little candles is just sufficiently similar to the lugubrious humour in adversity in which Sam specialises ('Three precious little Gollums in a row we shall be, if this goes on much longer', he reflects a moment later (TT, 236)) to remind us that Gollum himself is a hobbit, though severed from his people by centuries of loneliness. The Shire hobbits are both intentionally and, as we have seen already, unintentionally humorous. Bilbo's farewell party is a gluttonous revelry, ending with his heckled, would-be-witty speech and the practical joke of his disappearance. ('Why worry? He hasn't taken the vittles with him', comments Rory Brandybuck (FR, 39).) Merry and Pippin banter freely with other characters, irrespective of rank, and Pippin engages in rather irritating horseplay at bathtime. Sam and Frodo both sing comic songs. The Elves of Lothlórien mock Sam for breathing so loudly that they could shoot him in the dark (FR, 356). Above all, the wizard Gandalf, despite – or appropriately to – the seriousness of his role as the Enemy of Sauron, is a partially comic figure, in the tradition of the genial yet peppery hero-sage of which Sherlock Holmes is the earliest example (oddly enough) that comes to mind;[22] his knowledge and authority are counterbalanced by self-mockery (evoked by his failure to make sense of the simple inscription on the west door of the mines of Moria (FR, 318–21)), and by a playfulness which expresses itself not only in his firework display at Bilbo's party but in his cat-and-mouse game with Aragorn, Gimli and Legolas when he returns, hooded and newly attired, from the dead. They suppose him at first to be Saruman, and apprehensively interpret his comments and inquiries as sarcastic challenges; the joke is that they are nothing of the kind, but conversational sheep in wolves' clothing. It is the quality of Gandalf's laughter, 'like the sudden bite of a keen air, or the slap of a cold rain that wakes an uneasy sleeper' (TT, 97) that gives Aragorn the first hint of his identity.

The contrast between Gandalf and Saruman also exemplifies the moral significance of certain qualities associated with the intellect: learning, disinterested curiosity, informativeness. Gandalf has knowledge of 'every language that had ever been spoken in the West of Middle-earth' (FR, 321); he travels for centuries, forming acquaintances among all the benign peoples; he 'goes in for hobbit-lore: an obscure branch of knowledge but full of surprises' (FR, 58) – a speciality which has originally no pragmatic motive, but which serves him well when the Ring falls into the hands of hobbits. Within the bounds of prudence he shares his knowledge readily: it is he who warns the White Council, of wizards and leaders of the Elves, of Sauron's return to Dol Guldur in Mirkwood (FR, 264). His narratives, at Bag End (FR, 56ff.), Rivendell (FR, 263ff.), and in the Forest of Fangorn (TT, 105–7) are among the longest and most eloquent in the text. Indeed the capacity to *narrate* – as distinct from making speeches, or issuing commands or threats – is a hallmark of the benign. Saruman too has great intelligence and eloquence, but of a different kind.

> 'A new Power is rising. Against it the old allies and policies will not avail us. There is no hope left in Elves or dying Númenor. This then is one choice before you, before us. We may join with that Power. It would be wise, Gandalf. There is hope that way. Its victory is at hand; and there will be rich reward for those that aided it. As the Power grows, its proved friends will also grow; and the Wise, such as you and I, may with patience come at last to direct its courses, to control it. We can bide our time, we can keep our thoughts in our hearts, deploring maybe evils done by the way, but approving the high and ultimate purpose: Knowledge, Rule, Order; all the things that we have so far striven in vain to accomplish, hindered rather than helped by our weak or idle friends. There need not be, there would not be, any real change in our designs, only in our means.' (FR, 272–3)

Saruman's argument is, of course, immoral, especially in terms of the deontological morality of *The Lord of the Rings*; but, equally importantly, it is foolish, since Sauron will quite certainly not reward – indeed does not have – 'friends', and, as Gandalf says, 'only one hand at a time can wield the One' (FR, 273). By opening hostilities against his benign neighbours, Saruman simply guarantees his own destruction by one side or the other sooner or later. The foolishness is rooted in Saruman's incapacity for unselfish curiosity and communicativeness: pursuing knowledge only for the sake of personal power, he withholds information about the Ring from the White Council, and hubristically uses the *palantir*, or Seeing Stone, housed at Isengard despite the risk of ensnarement by Sauron who possesses an answering Stone. Unlike Gandalf, who befriends the Ents, Saruman is indifferent to them and simply milks Treebeard for information. ('I told him many things that he would never have found out for himself; but he never repaid me in like kind ... . He does not care for growing things, except as far as they serve him for the moment' (TT, 76).) He consequently underestimates the Ents, takes liberties with their trees, and is quite unprepared for their onslaught on Isengard. Similarly, his incuriosity about hobbits defeats his assiduous quest for the Ring: even Sauron, from a much greater distance, gets his servants to the Shire more quickly.

The attractiveness of the hobbits is reinforced by their capacity for disinterested curiosity. Frodo and Bilbo are, in their unassuming way, 'learned' and curious about the wider world, and communicate this enthusiasm to their familiars, such as Sam. ('Crazy about stories of the old days he is, and he listens to all Mr Bilbo's tales [says the Gaffer]. Mr Bilbo has learned him his letters – meaning no harm, mark you, and I hope no harm will come of it' (FR, 32).) Most hobbits are emphatically not outward-looking in this way, but are, by way of compensation, thoroughly curious and communicative about their own world: 'they drew long and elaborate family trees with innumerable branches. ... By no means all Hobbits were lettered, but those who were wrote constantly to all their friends (and a selection of their relations) who lived further off than an afternoon's walk' (FR, 16, 19). Meriadoc Brandybuck writes a history of 'pipe-weed', and a study of 'Old Words and Names in the Shire' (FR, 24). In contrast, Gollum's curiosity, facilitated by the invisibility conferred by the Ring, is from the first directed to the gaining of advantage over others: 'he used [the Ring] to find out secrets, and he put his knowledge to crooked and malicious uses ... he took to thieving ...' (FR, 63). He shuns sunlight and moonlight, literally turns his eyes towards the ground, and goes hunting in mountain caves for 'great secrets' which prove to be 'just empty night' (FR, 63–4). Only the lure of the Ring is able to draw him out from his seclusion in darkness. His partial recovery during his journey with Frodo and Sam is reflected in an evanescent ability to think beyond his own despair. He remembers, weeping, 'tales from the South, when Sméagol was young, long ago ... wonderful tales' (TT, 249); but when, in a rare moment of relaxation, Sam recites a poem about an 'oliphaunt', Gollum is unable to respond.

> 'That,' said Sam, when he had finished reciting, 'that's a rhyme we have in the Shire ... I've heard tales of the big folk down away in the Sunlands. Swertings we call' em in our tales; and they ride on oliphaunts, 'tis said, when they fight. They put houses and towers on the oliphauntses backs and all, and the oliphaunts throw rocks and trees at one another ... . But now I don't suppose I'll ever see an oliphaunt. Maybe there ain't no such beast.' He sighed.
>   'No, no oliphaunts', said Gollum again. 'Sméagol has not heard of them. He does not want to see them. He does not want them to be.' (TT, 255)

As Gollum's aversions include not only the Sun and Moon, and oliphaunts, but scented plants – he coughs and retches amid the 'sweet-smelling herbs and shrubs' of Ithilien (TT, 258–9) – one is tempted to say that his corruption by the Ring has alienated him from 'nature'; but this would only be a half-truth. What he is alienated from is, more precisely, the humane, creative and expressive delight in life, including the natural beauty and resources of Middle-earth, variously enjoyed by the benign peoples. He cannot, or refuses to, eat *lembas*, the ambrosial 'waybread' of the Elves which sustains the hobbits: he complains at the very smell of the leaves in which the cakes are wrapped. He refuses cooked rabbit and fried fish, as well as herbs and vegetables. (In contrast, Sam clings to his cooking gear until the very last phase of the journey – when he casts his pans into a fissure in the desert plain of Mordor their clatter is 'like a death-knell to his heart' (RK, 215).) What Gollum will eat is the diet of the uncivilised, even bestial, carnivore, that is, everything which to cultivated human taste (at least in

Europe) is repellent: raw meat, raw fish, raw fowl, 'worms or beetles or something slimy out of holes' (TT, 232), and (if Sam's conjectures and the rumours of the Woodmen (FR, 67) are well-founded) hobbits, the flesh and blood of children, and even long-dead bodies. In this respect Gollum's degradation harmonises with that of the orcs of Sauron and Saruman, and with the Augustinian theology. It is not that these malign figures are contrary to, or outside, (benign) nature – they are themselves created beings, and therefore part of nature – but that they are perverted to hate the rest of nature, including not only living and growing things but the arts, artefacts and accomplishments (including the cuisines) of other created beings: like Shelob, perhaps like Wormtongue who, Saruman hints, eats the murdered Lotho Sackville-Baggins (RK, 299), they devour cannibalistically if they can because this mode of eating represents in ideal form the negation of others.

Conversely, the positive values to which the work appeals are those of a life which is civilised (in the widest sense) as well as altruistic. It celebrates not only the arts (especially poetry and song, and architecture) but friendship, love and marriage, work (especially craftsmanship), domesticity, the pleasures of food and drink, and the exploratory enjoyment of landscape and of the multitudinous kinds of nature – of plants and flowers for their fragrance and beauty, birds for their song, horses for their grace and swiftness, 'oliphaunts' for their terror and splendour. The proportion of the text devoted in *The Lord of the Rings* to conceiving these aspects of Middle-earth – a high proportion, as may already be apparent – provides a crucial index of a reader's understanding: anyone who regards these elements as 'padding', or as essentially subordinate in importance to the development of the plot, has simply not grasped the nature of the work. Many examples could be given, but one which will serve as a test case is the early episode in which Frodo, Sam, Merry and Pippin awaken in the house of Tom Bombadil, the morning after their rescue from the Old Forest.

They leapt up refreshed. Frodo ran to the eastern window, and found himself looking into a kitchen-garden grey with dew … . His view was screened by a tall line of beans on poles; but above and far beyond them the grey top of the hill loomed up against the sunrise. It was a pale morning: in the East, behind long clouds like lines of soiled wool stained red at the edges, lay glimmering deeps of yellow. The sky spoke of rain to come; but the light was broadening quickly, and the red flowers on the beans began to glow against the wet green leaves.

Pippin looked out of the western window, down into a pool of mist. The Forest was hidden under a fog. It was like looking down on to a sloping cloud-roof from above. There was a fold or channel where the mist was broken into many plumes and billows; the valley of the Withywindle. The stream ran down the hill on the left and vanished into the white shadows. Near at hand was a flower-garden with a clipped hedge silver-netted, and beyond that grey shaven grass pale with dew-drops …

'Good morning, merry friends!' cried Tom, opening the eastern window wide. A cool air flowed in; it had a rainy smell. 'Sun won't show her face much today, I'm thinking. I have been walking wide, leaping on the hill-tops, since the grey dawn began, nosing wind and weather, wet grass underfoot, wet sky above me. I wakened Goldberry singing under window; but nought wakes hobbit-folk in the early morning. In the night little folk wake up in the darkness, and sleep after light has come! Ring a ding dillo! wake now, my merry friends! Forget the nightly noises! Ring a ding dillo del! derry del, my hearties! If you come soon you'll find breakfast on the table. If you come late you'll get grass and rain-water!'

Needless to say – not that Tom's threat sounded very serious – the hobbits came soon, and left the table late and only when it was beginning to look rather empty … . The room looked westward over the mist-clouded valley, and the window was open. Water dripped down from the thatched eaves above. Before they had finished breakfast the clouds had joined into an unbroken roof, and a straight grey rain came softly and steadily down. Behind its curtain the Forest was completely veiled.

As they looked out of the window there came, falling gently as if it was flowing down the rain out of the sky, the clear voice of Goldberry singing up above them. They could hear few words but it seemed plain to them that the song was a rain-song, as sweet as showers on dry hills, that told the tale of a river from the spring in the highlands to the Sea far below. The hobbits listened with delight; and Frodo was glad in his heart, and blessed the kindly weather, because it delayed them from departing. The thought of going had been heavy upon him from the moment he awoke; but he guessed now that they would not go further that day.

The upper wind settled in the West and deeper and wetter clouds rolled up to spill their laden rain on the bare heads of the Downs. Nothing could be seen all round the house but falling water. Frodo stood near the open door and watched the white chalky path turn into a little river of milk and go bubbling away down into the valley. (FR, 139–40)

By any conventional criterion of narrative urgency, this section (a small part of the leisurely Bombadil episode) is uncalled for. Its importance lies in the finely observed skyscape and landscape, with their sharp effects of light and colour (the flowers glowing red against the pervasive grey, the yellow of sunrise beyond the soiled-wool clouds), and in the quietly blissful evocation of the cycle of mist, cloud, rain, river, Sea. Goldberry's rain-song has credibility because the evocativeness attributed to it has already been achieved by the prose, through images – their sensuous tonality announced by the word 'refreshed' at the beginning of the passage – which involve not only vision but all the senses, sometimes by the lightest implication: touch (wet grass underfoot, the open window, rain 'on the bare heads' of the Downs), hearing (water dripping from the eaves), smell (Tom 'nosing' the weather), and even taste (grass and rain-water for breakfast). Underlying this quickening of the senses is the impression of a calm domestic sanctuary, made actual by the beans, the clipped hedge, the chalk path, and the 'curtain' – actually of falling rain, but serving as a kind of extension of the sheltering homely house – which screens off the dangers of the Forest. That Frodo's eastward journey is delayed is no blunder in narrative construction, for it is just the kind of happiness encapsulated in this episode, the happiness of grateful contemplation of beauty, and of unforced, unhurried activity, practical and creative, which the work opposes to the nihilistic spirit of Mordor. We need to feel its allure, not only in order to sustain our interest in the fulfilment of Frodo's mission, but also because the imagining of such happiness (which like any object of desire is most compelling when transient or imperilled) is central to the purposes of The Lord of the Rings.

A near-contemporary of Tolkien, who produced a rather different best-seller in the same decade, wrote that for me a work of fiction exists only insofar as it affords me what I shall bluntly call aesthetic bliss, that is a sense of being somehow, somewhere, connected with other states of being where art (curiosity, tenderness, kindness, ecstasy) is the norm.[23]

Tolkien might not have relished being coupled with Nabokov, and would certainly not have chosen 'art' as the comprehensive term for those states of being that are to be desired, but the modest aspirations expressed in his Foreword are not too far from this patrician pronouncement of Nabokov's. Tolkien would certainly have echoed Nabokov's remark that 'I am neither a reader nor a writer of didactic fiction.'[24] As I have tried to show, there is moral force and subtlety in The Lord of the Rings, but the moral significance of the work – since it is a work of fiction, not of ethics or devotion – is dependent on the reader's delight and amusement, excitement and emotion, being aroused in an appropriately structured way. As our analysis of the work moves outwards from its moral core – or inwards from its moral periphery – we reach a point at which we can only speak of aesthetic bliss, or of the quickening of the heart's desire, however co-ordinated with moral values that bliss or quickening may be.

The expansive conception of Middle-earth is, as this chapter has consistently sought to show, the key to the work's appeal to the heart's desire. Expansiveness in time is as important as expansiveness in space – indeed the two are closely associated, since the yearning to explore an extensive terrain implies the desire for extensive quantities of time in which to explore it. The hobbits' longevity is just sufficiently greater than that of human beings to be enviable – the long-lived Bilbo is sprightly at 111, and still alive, if sleepy and forgetful, twenty years later. Dwarves, and some Men, also appear to have long life-spans by our standards, while Elves are immortal (in the sense that only grief, injury or the end of the world can terminate their physical being). Others enjoy still wider perspectives.

'Mark my words, my friends: Tom was here before the river and the trees; Tom remembers the first raindrop and the first acorn. He made paths before the Big People, and saw the little People arriving. He was here before the Kings and the graves and the Barrow-wights. When the Elves passed westward, Tom was here already, before the seas were bent. He knew the dark under the stars when it was fearless – before the Dark Lord came from Outside.' (FR, 142)

Though Tolkien himself spoke of the wish to escape from death as 'the oldest and deepest desire',[25] something more complex is at work here than a simple appeal to the longing for deathlessness, powerful though that primal longing may be. For one thing, the work also represents the burden of continuous existence, especially when it is purposeless or joyless. Bilbo's exceptional age is in part a sinister gift from the Ring – only his relinquishing it saves him from the centuries-long withering of Gollum. The Elves' immortality is charged with melancholy and regret. 'For the Elves the world moves,' says Legolas, 'and it moves both very swift and very slow. Swift, because they themselves change little, and all else fleets by: it is a grief to them. Slow, because they do not count the running years, not for themselves. The passing seasons are but ripples ever repeated in the long long stream. Yet beneath the Sun all things must wear to an end at last' (FR, 405). The Elves regard death as 'the gift of the One to Men' (RK, 344). But when Elrond's daughter, Arwen, assumes mortality in order to marry Aragorn, she finds it (at Aragorn's deathbed) 'bitter to receive' (RK, 344). Much of the power of the work, in this respect, seems to me to lie in its realising the exhilarating perspective of childhood and early youth, in which the time stretching before one seems virtually limitless, and the world, at first a tiny region intensely perceived and seemingly eternal, opens out in multiple horizons, as one's knowledge and imagination and physical strength develop. As Treebeard puts it, recalling the remote age before the 'Great Darkness' (the dominion of Sauron's master Morgoth),

'Those were the broad days! Time was when I could walk and sing all day and hear no more than the echo of my own voice in the hollow hills. The woods were like the woods of Lothlórien, only thicker, stronger, younger. And the smell of the air! I used to spend a week just breathing!' (TT, 72)

The nostalgia for this Eden-like state is familiar as a literary theme from Traherne, Vaughan, Wordsworth and many other writers. 'I was a stranger, which at my entrance into the world was saluted and surrounded with innumerable joys ... I knew not that they were born or should die, but all things abided eternally.'[26] Tolkien in *The Lord of the Rings* represents a universe which embodies this perspective, but also embodies the later aspirations of life, in which we seek happiness in spite of a fuller sense of our mortality, and at the same time attempt to preserve our original joy in the world, or at least to maintain an integrity between the freshness of the early experiences and the ripeness of the later. If (to impose an over-literal symbolism for the momentary sake of clarity) the Shire equals childhood, then the hobbits' venturing beyond it represents facing up to adult responsibilities; their returning to it, though sadder and wiser, expresses the desire to maintain lifelong psychological contact with one's childhood, until one has to renounce it, along with everything else, in death. The purposeful and enriching journey 'there and back again' (to quote the subtitle of *The Hobbit*) stands as an image for spiritual wholeness preserved through the vicissitudes of life. When Frodo and Sam pause to rest in a mountain pass above Mordor, Sam reflects on

> 'the brave things in the old tales and songs ... adventures, as I used to call them ... . Folk seem to have been just landed in them, usually ... . But I expect that they had lots of chances, like us, of turning back, only they didn't ... . We hear about those as just went on – and not all to a good end, mind you; at least not to what folk inside a story and not outside it call a good end. You know, coming home, and finding things all right, though not quite the same ... . But those aren't always the best tales to hear, though they may be the best tales to get landed in!' (TT, 321)

Life as a human being brings adventure (or negatively, disturbance) varied with peace (or negatively, boredom); it also involves the possibility of disaster, the likelihood of a price to be paid for one's own or others' happiness, and the certainty of transience. *The Lord of the Rings* presents a narrative in which adventure and peace are combined in such a way as to sharpen the edge of both, and in which disaster is averted, the price for happiness paid, and transience accepted. If disaster had not been averted, if the work had been not a comedy but a tragedy (as are many of the earlier tales of Middle-earth revealed in Tolkien's posthumously published writings), the 'aesthetic bliss' afforded by the expansive conception of Middle-earth would in principle have been still present, though differently flavoured by the outcome of the plot. In practice, it is difficult to imagine such a work, for the energy and delight with which the invented world is realised seems incompatible with any but an essentially affirmative conclusion. And only an essentially affirmative conclusion could sustain, by contrast, the ineffable poignancy of the close – impossible to evoke adequately by quoting anything less than the entire three volumes of the preceding narrative – in which Frodo departs for ever, leaving Sam, as the evening deepens to darkness at the Haven, standing in silence, 'hearing only the sigh and murmur of the waves on the shores of Middle-earth' (RK, 311).

Two

The Lord of the Rings:
Achieving the Narrative

I

The imaginative conception explored in chapter 1 poses formidable difficulties of narrative construction and of style. A design of exceptional amplitude, multiplicity and expansiveness needs somehow to be reconciled with narrative energy and cohesion; and the resources of twentieth-century English language have to be deployed, without being wrenched into obscurity or disfigurement, in the representation of an invented world remote from that of contemporary experience.

The Lord of the Rings is therefore an extremely ambitious work from a technical point of view; and the success with which the design is executed across its huge canvas is variable. At its weakest, the texture of the writing is no more than serviceable to the overall design, and occasionally there are moments of embarrassing banality or mannerism. At its best, the momentum of the narrative and the transparency of the imagined world are achieved with effortless resource and subtlety.

As I implied at the end of chapter 1, analysis, even supported by extensive quotation, can only hint at the effect of the finest passages, since they derive their quality, when the work is actually read and re-read, from their relation to the whole conception which is sustained in the reader's memory. It is true of any work, of course, that its parts are interdependent for their full meaning, but with The Lord of the Rings this consideration assumes an exceptional force. It is partly that the significance of numerous details, the most obvious cases being the names of persons and places, is wholly distinctive to the invented world, so that a paragraph out of context can leave the casual browser without even the limited cultural reference-points available to the browser of a realist novel. But the complexity of realisation is such that even a passage of comparatively straightforward narrative is, for the involved reader, a nexus of implied images and suggestions. The following passage, for example, describes a moment of repose during the journey of Frodo and Sam through Mordor.

> The land seemed full of creaking and cracking and sly noises, but there was no sound of voice or foot. Far above the Ephel Dúath in the West the night-sky was still dim and pale. There, peeping among the cloud-wrack above a dark tor high up in the mountains, Sam saw a white star twinkle for a while. The beauty of it smote his heart, as he looked up out of the forsaken land, and hope returned to him. For like a shaft, clear and cold, the thought pierced him that in the end the Shadow was only a small and passing thing: there was light and high beauty for ever beyond its reach .... Now, for a moment, his own fate, and even his master's, ceased to trouble him. He crawled back into the brambles and laid himself by Frodo's side, and putting away all fear he cast himself into a deep untroubled sleep. (RK, 199)

The point is not simply that we need to have picked up place-names as we go along in order to know that the Ephel Dúath is a mountain range, and not, say, a tower or a great wall. It is that the reader's experience of this passage in Book VI is profoundly determined by knowledge derived from numerous other passages, adjacent and distant in the text; and that this knowledge is co-ordinated around a sense of extremely precise physical location and orientation. Sam is sitting with his back to his destination, Mount Doom, still several days' march away across a pitted desert, and to the tower of Barad-dûr beyond, whence Sauron's supernatural Eye gazes, looking for the Ring which now hangs on a chain round the sleeping Frodo's neck. A ridge at their backs screens Frodo and

Sam from both the Mountain and the Dark Tower. The land, on the western margins of Mordor, is almost but not quite barren (as the concealing brambles remind us). For some time Frodo and Sam have been forced by the nature of the terrain to head north, rather than east towards the Mountain; orcs are hunting for them, and Gollum is lurking somewhere in the vicinity. (Sam's 'putting away all fear', despite the sly noises around, is a brief recession from the caution of weeks during which he and Frodo have rarely dared to sleep simultaneously; it is at once a necessary reaction to accumulated stress and an act of quasi-religious faith.) The Ephel Dúath Frodo and Sam have recently traversed, by a series of stairs, passes and tunnels: the 'dark tor high up in the mountains' will recall to the reader this hauntingly described nocturnal ascent, with its last vertiginous glimpse of the ravine from which it began. Beyond the mountains, in the lands that are not yet 'forsaken', are the other members of the party that set out from Rivendell with Frodo and Sam. (Their adventures have already been narrated, in Books III and V. We know, but Frodo and Sam do not, that Gandalf has returned from death.) That a star is visible in the sky above the mountains is significant: Sauron has for several days been pouring black cloud westward out of Mordor to accompany the advance of his armies, but a wind off the Sea has begun to disperse it. A passage three pages earlier shows Frodo and Sam observing this, and adds 'Théoden lay dying on the Pelennor fields' (RK, 196), thus fixing the point in the other narrative which we have reached. The solitary star, in addition to its natural beauty as an image, has associations with the Elves, not only because they worship the star-kindler Elbereth but also because Frodo carries an Elvish 'star-glass' in which the light of the morning star is captured. All this orientation in place, time and action is part of the experience of a reader who encounters the passage in its normal sequence: and only such a reader, after 170 pages of Frodo and Sam's watchful and laborious journey, will fully appreciate the exceptional nature of this moment of grace, release and self-abandonment.

The combination, noted here, of a precisely localised character-perspective (that of Sam) with an implicit or explicit 'objective' perspective upon the world within which the character is localised, is fundamental to The Lord of the Rings. It is adumbrated from the very start, for the work has two openings, not to mention two endings. The Prologue presents a brief 'documentary' account of the nature and history of Hobbits, relaxed and discursive as much as scholarly, and incorporating a reprise of the relevant events of *The Hobbit*, notably Bilbo's acquisition of the Ring. Chapter 1 maintains continuity to the extent that it retains the cheerful tone. But the work begins, like innumerable realist novels, in *medias res*, with a character-perspective: not so much that of Bilbo himself (or of Frodo, who is introduced on the first page) as that of the parochial community of Hobbiton.

> When Mr Bilbo Baggins announced that he would shortly be celebrating his eleventy-first birthday with a party of special magnificence, there was much talk and excitement in Hobbiton. Bilbo was very rich and very peculiar, and had been the wonder of the Shire for sixty years, ever since his remarkable disappearance and unexpected return. The riches he had brought back from his travels had now become a local legend, and it was popularly believed, whatever the old folk might say, that the Hill at Bag End was full of tunnels stuffed with treasure. (FR, 29)

The party and associated events are described at leisurely length, while hints about the nature of the Ring, and rumours about trouble beyond the borders of the Shire, are quietly insinuated through dialogue. For hundreds of pages the perspective of the hobbits, and particularly of Frodo, is preserved with unbroken temporal continuity, with careful linking passages accounting for the time-lapses between major incidents – Bilbo's party and sudden departure, Gandalf's return to Hobbiton to warn Frodo about the Ring, Frodo's flight, and so on. A gradually broadening sense of what is going on in Middle-earth is achieved, as under the pressure of events Frodo and his companions gain a measure of enlighten-ment. The *Prologue*, meanwhile, acts as a marker: our recollection of it maintains the awareness that Frodo's perspective is an incomplete one, and more generally that the hobbits' customs and values are not absolute or universal.

This double awareness is part of the work's paradoxical realism. In the real world we have individual perspectives, and we have collective knowledge, consolidated in documents: the sense of a gap between these, between the world we see before our eyes and the wider world of which we acquire fragmentary knowledge, is part of the structure of our experience. What we do not have in reality is access to omniscience; and Tolkien's 'donnish' device – favoured by non-donnish novelists from Defoe to Nabokov – of representing the fictional narrative as a document (or a collection of documents if we include the Prologue and Appendices), is a realistic reflection of this fact. Tolkien's own professional scholarliness served, one suspects, both to reinforce his awareness of human non-omniscience, and to afford him a certain playful pleasure in the act of 'documentary' composition.

In another respect, too, The Lord of the Rings adheres more closely than many imaginative works to the configuration of normal human experience. Many 'realist' novels and plays adopt a structure in which the action switches abruptly, or with minimal linkage, from one protagonist, locale or sub-plot to another, before (usually) integrating all the elements for the dénouement. This kind of structure (which might be called 'symphonic' by analogy with the separate exposition, and eventual integration, of themes in a sonata movement, or compared to the brisk switches of scene achieved by editing in film or television drama) can make for great force of contrast and complexity of development, but its sudden and frequent transitions tend to make the contrivances of the authorial hand very visible. Novelists like Thackeray, George Eliot or Trollope turn this visibility into a virtue by adopting an openly manipulative, often ironic, narrative persona ('let the gentle-hearted reader be under no apprehension .... It is not destined that Mrs Bold shall marry Mr Slope');[1] and its logical conclusion is reached in Proust's novel, a million-word essay which just happens, as the essayist reflects and remembers, to unfold a plot of Tolstoyan dimensions along the way. But there are advantages in occluding the hand of the designer if the imaginary world is to be as transparently 'realised' as possible. The Lord of the Rings does, it is true, achieve formidable complexity of action in its second and third volumes, but by then the invented world has been authenticated in great detail by the great continuous narrative of The Fellowship of the Ring. Moreover, when at the end of that volume the travellers who set out from Rivendell are scattered, and it becomes unavoidable to divide the narrative between the perspectives of different groups of characters, this is done with the maximum emphasis on narrative continuity. There is no cinematic cross-cutting; instead, the journey of Frodo and Sam is narrated in two long unbroken sections (Book IV, 143 pages, and 52 pages of Book VI) and the adventures of the other members of the Fellowship in extended chapters within continuous sections (Books III and V).

So far as possible, the intertwining of strands of action to create suspense is accomplished by plausible developments within the plot itself rather than by unmotivated manipulation of narrative sequence. The episodes in which Frodo meets Faramir in the battle-zone (TT, 265ff.), and in which Faramir, back in Minas Tirith, reports the meeting to Denethor and the newly arrived Gandalf (RK, 84ff.), are enough to provide the wizard with the information about Frodo's progress necessary to guide his later strategy. His fear that Frodo may have perished or been captured in the valley of Minas Morgul, and Sauron regained the Ring, is not less moving because we already know that (as is the way of half-informed dreads) it is both well-founded and ill-founded: Frodo has indeed been captured, but the Ring is in the possession of Sam, still at liberty. When later (RK, 165) the Lieutenant of Barad-dûr taunts Gandalf with the cloak and mail-coat taken from Frodo, Gandalf's anguish strikes home less because we are as yet unaware of Frodo's escape than because the Gandalf-perspective has been developed so fully over the preceding chapters that we can see the force of this apparent blow to his strategy and his carefully nurtured hopes.

Where, on the other hand, there is unmotivated narrative movement, the effect can be faintly meretricious. The clearest case is the inversion of chronological order which allows the 'surprise' of Aragorn's arrival during the Battle of the Pelennor Fields, before the besieged walls of Minas Tirith (RK, 123). The black sails of Sauron's allies, the Corsairs, appear up the river – but the ships contain Aragorn and his host, who have overthrown the Corsairs and liberated their galley-slaves. Despite a surge of triumphant rhetoric ('the mirth of the Rohirrim was a torrent of laughter and a flashing of swords, and the joy and wonder of the city was a music of trumpets and a ringing of bells') the episode fails to be the emotional climax of the battle, just because it comes out of the blue and not out of a developed situation. (The true climax is formed by the connected deaths of Théoden and the Witch-King, which both have complex resonances from far back in the narrative.) The subsequent retrospective account of the capture of the ships – narrated by Legolas and Gimli to Pippin – has an inevitably dutiful and 'staged' quality, as Tolkien was aware.[2] On the other hand, when Denethor, secluded within the Citadel while the battle rages, concludes his outburst of defeatism by saying to Gandalf, 'even now the wind of thy hope cheats thee and wafts up Anduin a fleet with black sails' (RK, 129), the dramatic irony is highly effective, because the grounds of Denethor's error have been so carefully prepared that the text does not even need to spell them out. (Denethor has used a *palantir* to scrutinise Sauron's strategy and view his armies from afar: Sauron's more powerful will has ensured that he sees those images most likely to drive him to despair. It is consistent with Denethor's intellectual pride that he should seize the opportunity to trump Gandalf's optimism with this misleading card.)

The danger that a narrative of such length may lose cohesion amid a profusion of highly localised points of view is avoided not only by the sustained presentation of characters' perspectives, and the interweaving of plot lines, but by a number of key passages in which an approach is made to a more nearly objective perspective. These passages can be divided into two kinds: passages of intellectual reflection, associated mainly with Gandalf, and passages of imaginative vision, associated mainly with Frodo. In the former category are the Council of Elrond, and the 'Last Debate' of the surviving Captains, at which the diversionary assault on Mordor is conceived. These episodes, in which the situation and the issues at stake are reviewed and summarised with Gandalf's exceptional authority, come at approximately one-fifth, and four-fifths, of the way through the main narrative; the latter may be said to reaffirm the dominance of Gandalf's moral and strategic perception, taken for granted when he makes his initial disclosures to Frodo, endorsed at the Council, but contested subsequently by Saruman, Théoden, Denethor and others, and of course removed entirely for ten chapters by his fall into the abyss. The Council completes the exposition of the strategic themes; the Debate prepares for their dénouement. Gandalf's wisdom, not infallible but validated repeatedly in action, signals the existence of a coherent reality beyond the circumscribed perspectives of individual characters; and (given the structural role of Middle-earth itself) this is both an aesthetic and an ethical matter: the work is cohesive because the history of Middle-earth is rationally and morally intelligible, not a chaos of perspectives.

Frodo's glimpses of cohesion are products of revelation rather than reason. Three times, once at Crickhollow (FR, 118–19) and twice in the house of Tom Bombadil (FR, 138, 146) his dreams disclose the unknown past or future – though in images whose significance is only apparent much later, and then only in part, for the evocation of the quality of dreams is throughout naturalistic and not allegorical. (Trapped by drifting snow in a mountain pass, Frodo has a brief wish-fulfilment dream of returning to Rivendell, ostensibly to report developments to Bilbo, who replies *'I don't think much of your diary ... . Snowstorms on January the twelfth: there was no need to come back to report that!'* (FR, 303).) In particular, certain images suggest Frodo's ultimate departure from Middle-earth by ship into the West. The dreams give momentary access to a world in which time future is contained in – though not determined by – time past: but the inhabitants of Middle-earth can achieve only hints and guesses about that world. The *palantiri* likewise guarantee the existence of a superindividual reality transcending time and space, while leaving even the most gifted individuals who use them at risk of error. The Mirror of Galadriel, likewise, 'shows things that were, and things that are, and things that may yet be. But which it is that he sees, even the wisest cannot always tell' (FR, 377).

'I will look', said Frodo, and he climbed on the pedestal and bent over the dark water. At once the mirror cleared and he saw a twilit land. Mountains loomed dark in the distance against a pale sky. A long grey road wound back out of sight. Far away a figure came slowly down the road, faint and small at first, but growing larger and clearer as it approached. Suddenly Frodo realized that it reminded him of Gandalf. He almost called aloud the wizard's name, and then he saw that the figure was clothed not in grey but in white, in a white that shone faintly in the dusk; and in its hand there was a white staff. The head was so bowed that he could see no face, and presently the figure turned aside round a bend in the road and disappeared out of the Mirror's view. Doubt came into Frodo's mind: was this a vision of Gandalf on one of his many lonely journeys long ago, or was it Saruman?

The vision now changed. Brief and small but very vivid he caught a glimpse of Bilbo walking restlessly about his room. The table was littered with disordered papers; rain was beating on the windows.

Then there was a pause, and after it many swift scenes followed that Frodo knew to be parts of a great history in which he had become involved. The mist cleared and he saw a sight which he had never seen before but knew at once: the Sea. Darkness fell. The sea rose and raged in a great storm. Then he saw against the Sun, sinking blood-red into a wrack of clouds, the black outline of a tall ship with torn sails riding up out of the West. Then a white fortress with seven towers. And then again a ship with black sails, but now it was morning again, and the water rippled with light, and a banner bearing the emblem of a white tree shone in the sun. A smoke as of fire and battle arose, and again the sun went down in a burning red that faded into a grey mist; and into the mist a small ship passed away, twinkling with lights. It vanished, and Frodo sighed and prepared to draw away. (FR, 378–9)

Most of the images in the last-quoted paragraph take on a fuller significance later. The ship with black sails suggests the Corsairs, and the white tree is Aragorn's emblem; the white fortress with seven towers is presumably Minas Tirith, and the populous city is perhaps Gondor's chief city Osgiliath (at an earlier time, since by the period of the main action it has long been deserted). But the images already have emotional force: they proceed in a sequence from calm to calm, with two episodes of turbulence of which the second is clearly more positively conceived than the first (contrast the emotional tone of 'sinking' with 'went down', 'blood-red' with 'burning red', 'wrack of clouds' with 'grey mist'). In between come the exhilarating images of wide river, white fortress, shining banner. The second turbulent episode resolves itself into the melancholy and blissful image of the receding ship: 'twinkling', visually apt given the mist and dusk, responds in a different key to the 'rippling' morning light on the water. Frodo's sigh is appropriately ambiguous – is it yearning or relief, sadness or enchantment? On a first reading we may just possibly remember Frodo's dream, at Crickhollow, of longing to climb a white tower and look out over the Sea (FR, 119);

on a second, the disappearing ship is recognisable as a prevision of his departure from the Grey Havens in the last chapter.

Lest this sense of a cohesion of past, present and future seem deterministic, and the serene close of the paragraph unduly comfortable, we are instantly reminded that the Mirror shows not what 'will be', merely what 'may yet be'.

> ... It vanished, and Frodo sighed and prepared to draw away.
>
> But suddenly the Mirror went altogether dark, as dark as if a hole had opened in the world of sight, and Frodo looked into emptiness. In the black abyss there appeared a single Eye that slowly grew, until it filled nearly all the Mirror. So terrible was it that Frodo stood rooted, unable to cry out or withdraw his gaze. The Eye was rimmed with fire, but was itself glazed, yellow as a cat's, watchful and intent, and the black slit of its pupil opened on a pit, a window into nothing. (FR, 379)

A serene and positive conclusion is not inevitable: Sauron is still to be reckoned with. The vision of the Eye not only marks a sharp and sudden emotional shift in this passage, but introduces the principal image through which Sauron's threat-at-a-distance will be expressed: his soldiers wear the Eye as a symbol on their livery, and Frodo comes to intuit the direction of Sauron's 'Eye', or hostile, questing will, 'as certainly as a man can tell the direction of the sun with his eyes shut' (TT, 238). At a crucial moment of decision, underlining the dependence of future events on the free choices of persons, Frodo, alone on a mountaintop and recklessly wearing the Ring, takes it off just as Sauron's commanding Eye, alerted by it, sweeps past like a kind of searchlight (FR, 117).

If the weaving into these paragraphs of important threads from elsewhere in the work is easily discerned, what of the brief previous paragraph, describing Bilbo in his room? The paragraph might seem superfluous: Bilbo has effectively dropped out of the plot, and whatever he may be doing at Rivendell is of no significance to the progress of events. Actually, however, this is part of its value: the glimpse of Bilbo prevents the revelations of the Mirror from seeming too calculatedly 'significant'. The discontinuity of what Frodo sees underlines the contingency and mystery within the historical unfolding of Middle-earth, even when it is apprehended with the special vision available to Galadriel. At the same time its resemblance to the discontinuities of dreaming makes the passage imaginatively accessible to us; and the clairvoyant status of the Mirror lends authority to the dreams of Frodo which resemble it. But the paragraph also has emotional force, recalling the secluded happiness of Rivendell (and the rain on the windows takes us back further, to the shelter of Bombadil's house). The disordered papers are a reminder that the story is incomplete, the quest still unaccomplished.

These passages which associate an approach to objectivity of perspective with practical wisdom (Gandalf's purpose and strategy) and with joyful imagination (Frodo's poignant intuitions of past and future) underline a point made in chapter 1: the essentially comedic (in contradistinction to tragic) nature of The Lord of the Rings. The experiences of its characters do not float in a void, but have significance within a larger metaphysical pattern – the pattern of an expansive narrative, rather than a rigid and enclosed system – and that pattern is joyful, in the eyes of the humane as well as the divine, and in part amenable to humane intelligence; though the world is mysterious and contingent, it is not the veil of Maya, illusory or incomprehensible, and happiness does not depend on renouncing it. Even Sam in the darkness of Mordor sees eternal beauty in the stars, and this experience is described in terms which validate it objectively: 'the beauty of it smote his heart ... hope returned to him ... the thought pierced him' (RK, 199). The character-perspective and the objective perspective are differentiated in The Lord of the Rings, and the former greatly predominates, but their moments of convergence are affirmative. It is this underlying harmony between the thoughts and intuitions of the humane and the tran-scendently significant order, a harmony which is woven into the detail of the narrative, which gives authenticity to the most obviously comedic feature of The Lord of the Rings, its happy ending – or 'eucatastrophe', to borrow Tolkien's own term for the joyful resolution, the 'sudden and miraculous grace, never to be counted on to recur',[3] which he held to be distinctive of the fairy-tale as a genre. Of course the eucatastrophe, the destruction of the Ring, is made plausible at the level of sequential cause-and-effect by the errors of Sauron, the strategies of his opponents, the merciful treatment of Gollum by Frodo and others, the Ring's curse on

Gollum, and so on: sufficiently plausible, in a contingent world, for us to reflect that it might have been different. The eucatastrophe is aesthetically compelling not because it is predetermined – on the contrary, it is essential to its emotional impact that we should regard the outcome as resting on a knife-edge – but because its optimism is emotionally consonant with the work's pervasive sense of a universe hospitable to the humane. And the dual, but converging, perspective of the narrative is the structural expression of this sense. The fundamentally optimistic tonality is as apparent in the two endings of the work as in the two openings discussed above. Just as the Prologue and chapter 1, though 'objective' and character-based respectively, share a light and cheerful tone, so the close of the final chapter and the close of the last Appendix share a modulation from nostalgic resignation to homely cheerfulness. Sam, Merry and Pippin, journeying home from their farewell to Frodo at the Grey Havens, ride in silence for many miles, but at last Merry and Pippin break into song, and Sam comes home at evening to 'yellow light, and fire within', and takes his small daughter on his knee (RK, 311). And the scholarly Appendix F, after closing its main text with a lyrical, elegiac passage on the fading of the Elves ('they dwell now beyond the circles of the world, and do not return'), actually concludes with a jocular note, in smaller type, on the meaning of a hobbit place-name (RK, 416).

II

If the handling of narrative perspectives is, in general, effectively integrated with the larger aesthetic purposes of the work, the handling of style, or rather styles, sometimes stretches Tolkien's resourcefulness to its limits. He had confronted himself with the daunting task of presenting a wide range of scenes, incidents and cultures in a pre-modern world, of giving voices to a variety of 'speaking-peoples', human and otherwise, in the medium of an English which must seem to twentieth-century readers both intelligible and appropriate to its subject-matter. I have suggested already – and numerous quotations from the work should by now have borne this out – that what one might call the bread-and-butter style of *The Lord of the Rings*, the basic style of narration and description which accounts for perhaps 90 per cent of the text, is transparent, and largely free from archaic, let alone obsolete, forms. That is not to say that it lacks distinctive features. Catharine Stimpson's exasperated claim that 'shunning ordinary diction, he wrenches syntax ... . If we expect, "He came to an island in the middle of a river", he will write, "To an eyot he came"'[4] is demonstrably false (quite apart from its question-begging notions of 'ordinary' diction and normative, unwrenched syntax), for Tolkien employs the style 'we expect', as Stimpson has it, far more often than the inversions and rarer syntactical forms which trouble her. But her overstatement conceals two truths: firstly, that Tolkien's phrase-order in sentences, though rarely archaic, is carefully considered for expressive effect – he does not simply employ the sequence most likely to occur in colloquial speech; and secondly that his diction draws on the full range of 'words that remain in literary use ... among educated people'.[5] 'Eyot' is certainly among these: indeed it is still (just) in non-literary use, for the good reason that it is much the briefest way of referring to 'a small isle in the middle of a river' (though in fairness to Catherine Stimpson it should be said that it is little used in US English).[6] A glance at three actual appearances of 'eyot' in *The Lord of the Rings* is illuminating, and will also serve to suggest the prevalence of 'unwrenched' syntax in the text.[7]

> That night they camped on a small eyot close to the western bank. (FR, 398)

> A long whitish hand could be dimly seen as it shot out and grabbed the gunwale: two pale lamplike eyes shone coldly as they peered inside, and then they lifted and gazed up at Frodo on the eyot. (FR, 400)

> ' ... Still there are dangerous places even before we come there: rocks and stony eyots in the stream ...' (FR, 401)

We might ask ourselves how, without a loss of meaning or economy, 'eyot' could be replaced in any of these cases. In the first case, 'a small eyot' is decisively smaller than 'a small island': this helps to establish that Gollum has no cover on land, and must approach Frodo out of the water, as indeed he does in the second sentence. In the third, 'island' perhaps might be substituted, but 'eyot' more firmly suggests something small enough to be overlooked until one runs aground. All three sentences are syntactically unexceptional by any twentieth-century standards: Ernest Hemingway could have written them. My next example shows a more idiosyncratic phrase-order; in order to highlight Tolkien's compositional choices, I have preceded it with a notional 'primitive version' in a more commonplace syntactical mode, making minor changes of diction when the altered syntax seemed to require this.

> A grey mist gathered about Saruman's body, to the dismay of those standing by. It rose slowly to a great height, like smoke from a fire, and loomed over the hill as a pale shrouded figure. Then it wavered for a moment, looking to the West; but a cold wind came from that direction. The figure bent away, and dissolved into nothing with a sigh. ['Primitive version']

> To the dismay of those that stood by, about the body of Saruman a grey mist gathered, and rising slowly to a great height like smoke from a fire, as a pale shrouded figure it loomed over the Hill. For a moment it wavered, looking to the West; but out of the West came a cold wind, and it bent away, and with a sigh dissolved into nothing. (RK, 300)

The rules of the 'primitive version' are, firstly, that subject and main verb initiate each sentence, and the remaining clauses then fall into line behind them; and secondly, that each sentence is rationed to a single conjunction. In other words, there is an inhibition, in the name of stylistic modernity, on inversion (in the sense of the delayed appearance of the subject) and on the potentially dignifying, or 'biblical', cadences ('and … and … and …') latent in multiple conjunctions. The consequence is four sufficiently competent sentences. Tolkien's version, by abandoning these inhibitions while avoiding archaism, achieves greater clarity and fluency as well as an appropriately grave tone. By making flexible use of phrase-order, and converting the first and second, and the third and fourth, sentences in each case into a single sentence, it brings into proximity the crucial verbs describing the continuous motion of the mist ('gathered, and rising slowly' ... 'it loomed over the Hill. For a moment it wavered') which are widely separated in the primitive version. It also juxtaposes the cold wind and the bending away which is its consequence. The repetition of 'West' becomes stylistically acceptable if the subject of the second clause ('wind') is delayed to produce the compact and rhythmically symmetrical formula 'looking to the West; but out of the West ...' whereas a moment's reflection will show that the repetition becomes awkward if the subject–verb–predicate sequence is maintained. The immediate verbal echo is important, for the West is more than a geographical 'direction': it represents the other-world from which the Wizards have been sent, incarnate, to the aid of Middle-earth, and the shade of Saruman should be felt here to be engaging in a brief, fatal dialogue, signalling an appeal which meets with rejection. Both sentences are sequenced for expressive effect. The first begins with an indication of emotional tone ('dismay'), invites us to share the attentiveness of the bystanders, and then closes in on the body and follows the movement of the mist that rises from it. The second displays the 'dialogue' across the brief pause of the semi-colon, and comments on its pathos by the winding-down effect of the two 'and ...' clauses and the strategic placing of 'nothing'.

The narrative style of *The Lord of the Rings* is by no means uniform: as in this example, episodes of grandeur or solemnity or violence bring out expressive nuances of syntax and diction. Books III and V, which are dominated by warfare, generally display the most highly wrought narrative passages, with occasional definite shifts into heroic diction.

> But lo! suddenly in the midst of the glory of the king his golden shield was dimmed ...
>
> The great shadow descended like a falling cloud. And behold! it was a winged creature; if bird, then greater than all other birds, and it was naked, and neither quill nor feather did it bear, and its vast pinions were as webs of hide between horned fingers; and it stank. (RK,115)

One might well wish away the 'lo!' and the 'behold!'. Tolkien is generally not at his best with instances of *sudden* action: in less exalted crises, he tends, at least in the first volume, towards an over-reliance on the formula 'at that moment … (x happened)'.[8] If these intensifying exclamations are defensible, it is because they are used sparingly, serving in this case to signal the approach of a supremely terrible moment in a battle which has already raged with great ferocity; and because the last quoted phrase is equally typical of the narrative: 'and it stank'. The exalted, as it were scriptural, style invites us to perceive the intervention of the Witch-king on his pterodactyl-like steed as an epiphany of the diabolic, the next worst thing to an encounter with the fallen angel Sauron himself; but at the same time we are asked to imagine the creature with great sensory vividness – its stench, its physical structure, and a little later its croaking cry, and its weight as it settles on Théoden's dying horse and digs in its claws. This concreteness, the issues that depend on the encounter, and the elaborately developed 'history' we already possess for each of the two antagonists, authenticate the stylistic fortissimo of which 'lo!' is (an admittedly crude) note. How else, Tolkien might ask, could such an episode be appropriately narrated? If it is to be effectively narrated in the twentieth century, it must be treated in language not obsolete (lest it be unintelligible) but rare to the same degree that, in an ironic literary age, heroic episodes are themselves rare.

Even in such passages, moreover, the risky heroic mannerisms are the exception rather than the rule. The presence of Merry as an observing consciousness generates numerous examples of plain syntax: 'Merry crawled on all fours … . He dared not open his eyes or look up … . He opened his eyes and the blackness was lifted from them. There some paces from him sat the great beast … . The face of their enemy was not turned towards him, but still he hardly dared to move' (115–16). This stylistic variation could make for an unsightly patchwork, but in fact the amplitude of the narrative is such as to allow gradual modulations between the exalted style and the plain. The point may be illustrated by a passage towards the end of the episode, when the Witch-king and Théoden are both dead, the battle has moved to another part of the field, and Merry stands wounded, having used his short sword, retrieved from the Barrow many chapters earlier, to pierce the sinew behind the Witch-king's knee.

And still Meriadoc stood there blinking through his tears, and no one spoke to him, indeed none seemed to heed him. He brushed away the tears ... . Then he looked for his sword that he had let fall; for even as he struck his blow his arm was numbed, and now he could only use his left hand. And behold! there lay his weapon, but the blade was smoking like a dry branch that has been thrust in a fire; and as he watched it, it writhed and withered and was consumed.

So passed the sword of the Barrow-Downs, work of Westernesse. But glad would he have been to know its fate who wrought it slowly long ago in the North-Kingdom when the Dúnedain were young, and chief among their foes was the dread realm of Angmar and its sorcerer king. No other blade, not though mightier hands had wielded it, would have dealt that foe a wound so bitter, cleaving the undead flesh, breaking the spell that knit his unseen sinews to his will. (RK, 119–20)

The first paragraph opens with essentially plain syntax, with phrases that might be modelled on Merry's speech-patterns ('no one spoke to him ... now he could only use his left hand'). Yet woven into the clauses are nuances of diction – 'heed'; 'let fall' rather than 'dropped'; 'for', in the sense of 'because'; 'even as', in the sense of 'at the very moment that', and not least the full version of Merry's name, which keeps in touch with the heroic tonality, so that when attention shifts from Merry to the sword, and its historic relation to the Witch-king, the accompanying stylistic shift is not too abrupt. The 'behold!' signals Merry's shock of surprise (and alarm, when he makes the connection with his numbed arm) at the dissolution of the sword-blade, so eloquently conveyed through the sustained image of the burning branch; and by placing the sword in the same stylistic frame as the Witch-king, it prepares us for the revelation in the next paragraph: the Witch-king's unholy perpetuation of 'undead' existence has been ended by the indirect agency of his long-dead victim, the sword's maker. (And yet there is no facile determinism: the blow might not have been struck had Merry's courage failed him, as it almost does; and in any case it is Éowyn's stroke, not Merry's, which actually kills the Witch-king.)

The dignified prose of the second paragraph effectively sustains the heroic tone, though the archaic adjective 'dread' is a superfluous note, except rhythmically. The quasi-conclusiveness of its first sentence prepares us for a sudden shift of focus and mood, confirmed by the opening phrase of the second (another emotional marker). The sentence employs inversion as much for economy and elegance as for expressive effect. (Compare the awkward uninverted version, 'But he who wrought it long ago, etc., etc., etc. ... would have been glad to know its fate'.) The final sentence triumphs over its elements of cliché through its musicality – the widely-spaced assonances ('blade ... wield ... dealt ... cleaving ... flesh ... spell ... will'), the alliterative group 'wield ... wound ... will', and the sinuously memorable 'unseen sinews' – and the ruthless simultaneity of its present participles, 'cleaving ... breaking': the suppression of 'and' here is as important as its elegiac repetition in the passage describing Saruman's death.

Certainly there are stylistic failures in The Lord of the Rings. The early chapters of The Fellowship of the Ring, initially drafted as a sequel to the children's book The Hobbit, before Tolkien himself realised the scale and seriousness the new work would assume, show occasional signs of imperfect revision.[9] The Prologue and first chapter, with their circumstantial accounts of hobbit society in the Shire, their elements of satire, and the undertow of melancholy associated with Bilbo's decision to leave Bag End for ever, have nothing to do with the conventionalities of the children's story: the half-bourgeois, half-rustic inhabitants of Hobbiton and Bywater are nearer to the world of Silas Marner (or, except for their general cheerfulness, of Hardy's Wessex) than to that of Swallows and Amazons, let alone The Marvellous Land of Snergs[10] (an apparent influence on The Hobbit). But there are a few incongruous lapses into a style better suited to the children's story originally conceived.

> There was a terrific splash, and a shout of Whoa! from Frodo. It appeared that a lot of Pippin's bath had imitated a fountain and leaped on high ...
>
> Hobbits have a passion for mushrooms, surpassing even the greediest likings of Big People. (FR, 112)

A rare incongruity of a different kind is the express-train metaphor in the first chapter (FR, 36). And there are one or two attempts, in the early chapters, to force the dramatic and emotional pace with assertive rhetoric instead of allowing the tension to build naturally. 'Fear seemed to stretch out a vast hand, like a dark cloud rising in the East and looming up to engulf [Frodo]', we are told at quite an early stage in Gandalf's first narration at Bag End (FR, 60).[11] But with Mordor still a thousand miles distant, this is psychologically incredible as well as aesthetically premature, and the imagery of the dark cloud looks merely trite because nothing has happened yet to substantiate it concretely: it will be precisely the achievement of much later chapters to give renewed life to this, and other, metaphors for fear and evil which are in themselves apt but have become staled by casual, imaginatively undeveloped use.

While the first half of the first volume, though written with great freshness, is sometimes unsure in tone, the occasional weakness of the later sections lies in a certain dutifulness and stiltedness in executing passages which may be necessitated by plot or theme but are not central to the work's imaginative vision – passages which might, so to speak, appear in any 'romance'. The courtship of Faramir and Éowyn is one such episode (RK, 237–41); another is Aragorn's healing of Faramir, Éowyn and Merry after the battle of the Pelennor Fields (RK, 139–46), with its energetic but somehow unconvincing attempt to suggest the paradisal scent of the healing herb athelas. (Tolkien, so skilled at evoking sensory experience, sometimes founders in attempting to praise the indescribable: of the stream Nimrodel in Lothlórien, he writes that 'it seemed to [Frodo] that he would never again hear a running water so beautiful, for ever blending its innumerable notes in an endless changeful music' (FR, 360) – which has a fair claim to be the most tired sentence in the whole work.)

It is perhaps no accident that these two episodes feature a high proportion of dialogue, for it is in dialogue, given the nature of the work, that the danger of stiltedness and artificiality is at its greatest. The underlying rationale for dialogue styles in The Lord of the Rings is that the peoples of Middle-earth share a 'Common Speech', the variations of which must be represented by variants of English. But variants on a single modern tongue will inevitably – as Appendix F, 411 concedes – fall somewhat short of evoking the cultural and ethical diversity to which they are supposed to correspond; and highly characterised English dialogue styles will always risk seeming derivative from literary or historical models. (This no doubt explains the tendency of cursory disparagers like

John Carey to cite bits of dialogue, quoted out of context, to exemplify 'the feebleness of Tolkien's stylistic grasp'.)[12]

Not all styles are problematical. The conversation of the hobbits, and the Bree-landers, among themselves is essentially contemporary English, socially modulated to a certain extent (Frodo speaks differently from Sam, and Barliman Butterbur differently from Aragorn), and denuded of incongruously modern references; their adjustments, according to their varying expertise, to more stately discourse with Elves, or Men of Gondor and Rohan, are plausibly handled. Gandalf's speech has comparable range and, as one should expect, much greater rhetorical power: he deploys irony and benevolent humour, and can argue and expound as well as narrate; his utterance, in fact, as befits his nomadic life, linguistic skill and far-reaching intelligence, displays variations of style comparable to that of the main narrative, from relaxed conversation with the hobbits ('I am glad to find you visible ... I wanted to catch you and have a few final words' (FR, 40)) to exalted narration ('A great smoke rose about us, vapour and steam. Ice fell like rain. I threw down my enemy, and he fell from the high place and broke the mountain-side where he smote it in his ruin' (TT, 106)). His fellow-wizard Saruman, too, is convincingly shown to have a range of styles: colloquial, diplomatic, intimidatory, vituperative. Gandalf's comprehensive scope leaves little stylistic elbow-room for the other senior figure in the original fellowship, Aragorn, who labours under the further disadvantage of having to transform himself from the taciturn, weather-beaten Ranger 'Strider' into King Elessar. As Strider, he shows a gleam of Gandalf-like asperity in his description of the unfortunate Butterbur as 'a fat innkeeper who only remembers his own name because people shout it at him all day' (FR, 180), but is otherwise stylistically distinguishable from the wizard mainly negatively, by a lack of expansiveness and humour: he tends to reprimand the hobbits for imprudent jokes. The later Aragorn talks with a somewhat generalised dignity: few of his speeches could, I think (except by their content) be confidently assigned to him rather than, say, Gandalf or Faramir.

Elizabeth Kirk suggests, in a fine essay on Tolkien's styles, that 'each style [is] used not primarily to define the individuality of the given speaker or situation, but to enact the kind of consciousness he shares with others who have a comparable stance before experience'.[13] As an aesthetic defence this principle works for the hobbits, whose stance before experience is unheroic yet adaptable and irrepressible, and for the wizards, whose stance is intellectual, ethical, inquisitive and self-consciously superior; but these are precisely the groups whose utterance is characterised by flexibility. I am not so sure that the principle is sufficient to explain a certain stylistic sameness among a range of, broadly admirable and dignified, characters. For example, the Elf Legolas and the Dwarf Gimli share the retrospective narration of the journey on the 'Paths of the Dead' (RK, 150–4), but it is difficult to discern any stylistic difference between them. Similarly, Rohan and Gondor are culturally differentiated in terms of politics, arts, and customs, but less markedly in speech-styles. It is true that Denethor would not liken himself, as Théoden does, to an 'old badger in a trap' (TT, 144); and Théoden would not construct Denethor's 'I will have naught: neither life diminished, nor love halved, nor honour abated' (RK, 130): it tells us something about the two societies that homely metaphors come naturally to the ruler of one, and symmetrical abstractions to the ruler of the other. But most of the discourse among Men, and indeed Elves and Dwarves, is indeed a 'Common Speech', dignified and slightly archaic.

Perhaps this stylistic homogeneity can be defended, in Kirk's terms, as reflecting the deliberate approximation of language when mutually sympathetic cultures communicate. Certainly, in a very broad sense, all these peoples might be said to have 'a comparable stance before experience': all of them would esteem a person like Aragorn, for example, and all are enemies of Sauron. But in other respects it is their diversity that is emphasised. The most marked stylistic differences among them are, in fact, not in speech, but in poetry, and in nomenclature: if we come to imagine Gimli's speech to be of a different texture from that of Legolas, it is mainly because we recall his invocation of dwarvish place-names ('Dark is the water of Kheled-zâram, and cold are the springs of Kibil-nâla' (FR, 296)), his guttural battle-cry, and the brooding melancholy of the verses he chants in Moria. Likewise, our impression of the collective 'voice' of the Rohirrim comes much more clearly from their sung alliterative verse than from their spoken prose: the distinctiveness of the former does much to induce us to forget the merely serviceable nature of the latter. As Kirk says, an important function of the verse is 'to provide an intensification of the qualities of a given style which could not be so pronounced in the main narrative'.[14] It must be an open question whether Tolkien, or anyone using the resources of English, could have differentiated the dialogue styles of the principal cultures more sharply than he has done.

With the more grotesque, comic or eccentric speakers, Tolkien certainly achieves differentiation. Tom Bombadil's 'prose' almost entirely observes the metre of his song. Treebeard's 'unhasty' Entish thought and speech are signalled not only by his bassoon noises ('Hrum, Hoom') but by a non-heroic syntactical informality, and a colloquialism not unlike the hobbits': his speech ambles along, without troubling much to put itself into dignified order.

> 'Hm! Not bad, not bad', said Treebeard. 'That would do. So you live in holes, eh? It sounds very right and proper. Who calls you hobbits, though? That does not sound elvish to me. Elves made all the old words: they began it.' (TT, 68)

The most memorable success – and here, contrary to Kirk's thesis, it clearly is a case of defining the individuality of the speaker – is Gollum's extraordinary idiolect, with its infantile cringing and pleading, its obsessive repetition of words and phrases that, like the Ring itself, have become for him talismans of desire or resentment, its undeveloped syntax and unstable sense of grammatical person (suggesting mental dissociation), its sibilance and gurgling. If it has a partial model, it is perhaps the playful, wheedling, sentimental argot of the nursery: Gollum promises 'to be very very good' (TT, 225), uses 'nice' and 'nasty' habitually, talks about 'little hobbitses' and 'poor mices' (TT, 221), and whimpers to the distant Eye of Sauron, 'Don't look at us! Go away! Go to sleep!' (TT, 223). Gollum's moral deformity is like that of an unregenerate child grown old, in whom the unattractive infant qualities of selfishness, cruelty and self-pitying dependency are monstrously preserved and isolated. (And yet this infantilism may partly account for the sympathy it is difficult to withhold from Gollum.) Other characterising styles, such as that of the Wild Men of Druadan Forest, are distinctive but less original.

> 'No, father of Horsemen … we fight not. Hunt only. Kill *gorgûn* in woods, hate orc-folk … . Wild Men have long ears and long eyes; know all paths.' (RK,106)

Francis Hope's comment – 'Heap good writing'[15] – is apt and not unfair: rudimentary syntax and diction, designed to suggest a tribal people striving to converse in the few known fragments of an unfamiliar tongue, inevitably take a limited number of forms. With the Orcs, whose speech is intended to suggest a closed militaristic culture of hatred and cruelty, Tolkien draws on a number of models. Indeed there are at least three different dialogue-types for Orcs, corresponding to differences of rank and of tribe. (None of them, incidentally, is 'working-class', except in the minds of critics who – themselves, it seems, unconsciously equating 'degraded language' with 'working-class language' – have convinced themselves that the Orcs' malign utterances betray Tolkien's disdain for 'mere working people'.)[16] The comparatively cerebral Grishnâkh, for example, talks like a melodrama villain, or a public-school bully.

> 'My dear tender little fools … everything you have, and everything you know, will be got out of you in due time: everything! You'll wish there was more that you could tell to satisfy the Questioner, indeed you will: quite soon. We shan't hurry the enquiry. Oh dear no! What do you think you've been kept alive for? My dear little fellows, please believe me when I say that it was not out of kindness: that's not even one of Uglúk's faults.' (TT, 59)

The Uruk-hai, Grishnâkh's rivals, are an arrogant warrior horde, not without a certain *esprit de corps*, and are given to yelling war-cries. ('Bring out your king! We are the fighting Uruk-hai! We will fetch him from his hole, if he does not come. Bring out your skulking king!' (TT, 145).) Lastly, the dialogue between individual orcs at moments of animosity (which is most of the time) is brutal and squalid in a rather underpowered way.

'The Black Pits take that filthy rebel Gorbag!' Shagrat's voice tailed off into a string of foul names and curses. 'I gave him better than I got, but he knifed me, the dung, before I throttled him … '

'I'm not going down those stairs again', growled Snaga, 'be you captain or no. Nar! Keep your hands off your knife, or I'll put an arrow in your guts.' (RK, 182)

If Tolkien is reduced here to stylised snarls, and bowdlerised suggestions of excremental vituperation, one recognises his difficulty: more overt obscenity and violence would not so much have offended twentieth-century sensibilities as have evoked, incongruously, the world of the twentieth-century crime novel. Most readers, engrossed in the narrative, will absorb this functional, and sufficiently expressive, dialogue without being unduly detained by its artificiality or derivativeness.

A final example may serve to represent the style of *The Lord of the Rings* at its distinctive best – not in moments of instantaneous action, or in dialogue, but in narrative that is at once dynamic and sensuously alert.

Light was fading fast when they came to the forest-end. There they sat under an old gnarled oak that sent its roots twisting like snakes down a steep crumbling bank. A deep dim valley lay before them. On its further side the woods gathered again, blue and grey under the sullen evening, and marched on southwards. To the right the Mountains of Gondor glowed, remote in the West, under a fire-flecked sky. To the left lay darkness: the towering walls of Mordor; and out of that darkness the long valley came, falling steeply in an ever-widening trough towards the Anduin. At its bottom ran a hurrying stream: Frodo could hear its stony voice coming up through the silence; and beside it on the hither side a road went winding down like a pale ribbon, down into chill grey mists that no gleam of sunset touched. There it seemed to Frodo that he descried far off, floating as it were on a shadowy sea, the high dim tops and broken pinnacles of old towers forlorn and dark. (TT, 306)

The visual imagination is at its sharpest here. Characteristically, the passage takes up a vantage-point and constructs a panorama around it. The scene is appropriately gloomy: Frodo and Sam are soon to attempt to enter Mordor; and it is no surprise when the following morning reveals only a 'dead brown twilight' (TT, 308), as Sauron's pall of black cloud rolls westward. But there is no anthropomorphism in the prose: even the 'stony voice' is, first and foremost, literally the sound of water flowing over rocks. It is instructive to compare the passage with part of Hardy's famous description of Egdon Heath in *The Return of the Native*.

> It was at present a place perfectly accordant with man's nature – neither ghastly, hateful, nor ugly; neither commonplace, unmeaning, nor tame; but, like man, slighted and enduring; and withal singularly colossal and mysterious in its swarthy monotony. As with some persons who have long lived apart, solitude seemed to look out of its countenance. It had a lonely face, suggesting tragical possibilities.[17]

Where Hardy, one is tempted to say, describes like a poet or a philosopher, Tolkien describes like a painter: his descriptions appeal to the emotions through the senses, not the other way round. Hardy projects human significances at the landscape; Tolkien evokes the human experience of perceiving a landscape. (For some readers this difference will suggest the greater seriousness of Hardy's concerns: I have tried to show, in chapter 1, that Tolkien's interest in 'Middle-earth' itself is part of an entirely serious system of values.) But the analogy of a painter is imperfect, not merely because sound and silence are heard but because the visual scene is not experienced statically. Frodo arrives at this vantage point, after long journeying, at the beginning of the paragraph; and his (and our) perception of the land ahead is suffused with an awareness of the continuing journey. The long valley comes out of the darkness, but Frodo must go into it. And the description is full of verbs suggesting movement, though most refer to static features of the landscape: 'sent', 'gathered', 'marched', 'came', 'ran', 'went winding down', and the participles 'falling', 'ever-widening', 'hurrying', 'coming up', and (arguably) 'floating'. The paradox of movement in stillness reinforces that of an audible silence: we sense the nervously attentive eyes and ears of the travellers. Already the absence of living creatures, and the heavy, stifling atmosphere, have been stressed. Frodo now looks at the road and imagines invisible things moving up and down on it. The landscape becomes suffused with a tension which will be intensified in the following pages (with moments of relief – a brief dream, a glimpse of sunlight at dusk), and will culminate in the nightmarishly slow transit, as if 'between the raising of a foot and the setting of it down minutes of loathing passed' of the valley of Minas Morgul, with its tower lit with a light 'paler ... than the moon ailing in some slow eclipse', its 'topmost course' revolving 'slowly, first one way and then another, a huge ghostly head leering into the night' (TT 312–13).

Syntactically the passage is entirely 'unwrenched', though it has certain structures typical of Tolkien: the three-part sentence with at its centre a somewhat lyrical adjectival phrase ('blue and grey under the sullen evening', 'remote in the West', 'floating as it were on a shadowy sea') qualifying a noun in the preceding or following phrase; and the use of both colon and semi-colon to punctuate a single complex sentence. The diction too is in Tolkien's most representative, resourceful but non-archaic, style, with a few unexpected words: 'descried' (chosen probably for rhythm, and for precision of meaning in preference to the rhythmically similar 'perceived', which less clearly implies conscious effort); 'hither' perhaps for euphony (the distant alliteration with 'hurrying' and 'hear'?); 'chill' for its secondary suggestion of 'chilling' (to the view; productive of fear) in preference to 'cold' which has a less apt metaphorical force in this case and could not sensibly be construed literally. The exact (and in context euphonious) 'top' in the final sentence shows that Tolkien does not always opt for the dignified or learned alternative. The coinages 'forest-end' and 'fire-flecked' are descriptive economies. Only 'like snakes' strikes a jarring note: as a visual simile it is felicitous enough, and its removal leaves a rhythmical awkwardness, but snakes large enough to serve the metaphorical purpose are too 'tropical' to harmonise with this scene, and no overtones of reptilian menace are needed in a passage which evokes a much subtler and more diffused sense of danger.

The inversion 'old towers forlorn and dark' is for euphony, and to vary the adjective–noun sequence, already used three times in the sentence. Out of context, it might be dismissed as a Gothic cliché; actually it is an instance of one of the work's greatest strengths, though a strength difficult to illustrate by quotation. The point is that the towers are literally forlorn: they belong to Osgiliath, the 'populous city' glimpsed in the Mirror of Galadriel, but long ago abandoned in Gondor's retreat before the expansion of Mordor. Not only do we recall this historical detail when we read the phrase, but the visual scene brings home the distinctive kind of forlornness to which Osgiliath is condemned: it stands in no man's land between the two opposed powers, East and West; and the haunted impression it makes under the gathering dark reminds us that it is Mordor, rather than Gondor, the spirit of decay rather than the spirit of growth, that dominates in this disputed territory. Roger Sale observes, in a rather backhanded compliment to Tolkien, that he 'can make the world live just by taking all the dead metaphors he knows and writing them as if they were not dead'.[18] For Sale, the success of this enterprise depends on the wide-eyed receptiveness of the hobbits, for whom the dead metaphors 'come to life'. But it is more than that. Tolkien here restores power to a jaded image by constructing around it a new historical and geographical context, which displays afresh its original aptness: the very simplicity which made it a cliché becomes again its virtue. (Conversely, when Tolkien concludes a passage describing the fragrant beauty of Ithilien with the sentence, 'Ithilien, the garden of Gondor now desolate kept still a dishevelled dryad loveliness' (TT, 258), the very ingenuity of the phrasing tends to discredit it. With its nymph's-hair conceit, its incongruous classicism and abstraction, and its obtrusive and contrived-looking alliteration, it is too obviously drawn from a specialised stylistic jewel-box (of a kind which Tolkien usually keeps firmly closed) to have the inevitability and transparency, the quality of seeming to draw upon the most natural and unaffected expression, 'the word neither diffident nor ostentatious', which his descriptions generally achieve.)

To some critics the sense of inevitability is precisely the cause of their disapproval. Catharine Stimpson again represents the hostile consensus forcefully when she asks 'why Tolkien so blandly, so complacently, so consistently, uses the symbol of light and of white to signify good and the symbol of dark and black to signify evil'.[19] One answer is that Tolkien does not do anything so crude, and does not much employ symbolism anyway (though some of his characters do: Saruman, for example, uses the device of a White Hand on his soldiers' livery; and Aragorn's standard is predominantly black). Names can be misleading: the Black Riders, for example, are not black – if anything they are white (see, for example, FR, 208); it is only their outer garments that are black, and their inner robes are 'white and grey' (FR, 226). The Black Stone of Erech is associated with the essentially positive figure of Isildur, and his war against Sauron. If Tolkien were a Manichean he might employ the symbolic system Stimpson suggests, but he is not, as I have pointed out: the corruption of 'Saruman the White' is sufficient to show this.

Nevertheless it is true that Tolkien draws upon the emotional potency of images of light and dark. These are by no means invariably correlated respectively with good and evil, joy and fear: among the most eerie images in the work are the candles that glow in the Dead Marshes, and the 'corpse-light', the 'light that illuminated nothing' of the tower of Minas Morgul (TT, 312). Still, Tolkien's use of imagery assumes that certain associations of image with emotion can be depended upon among his readers. Many modern writers have worked on that assumption: it is integral to the symbolist movement in poetry, and to Eliot's notion of the objective correlative. But there is also a tradition of radical scepticism which would question it. As Elizabeth Kirk says, some disparaging judgements of Tolkien's style 'reflect a comparatively modern assumption that the function of language in any work of art is to force the reader out of the reactions, awarenesses, associations of ideas and value judgements which he shares with others and to substitute for them sharper, more distinctive, individual and original modes of awareness ... . This is a function of post-Romantic views of the artist as a privileged sensibility.'[20] Tolkien, she suggests, stands outside this tradition: for him the artist speaks to our common nature, and his aim is the 'recovery' (to use his own term),[21] the recreation in new materials, of a clear and lively and generally accessible vision of beauty and value. Kirk's cites in support Eliot's lines from *East Coker*.

> There is only the fight
> To recover what has been lost, and found and lost
> Again and again; and now under conditions
> That seem unpropitious.

To align Tolkien with a modernist (whom he did not particularly admire) against a tradition derived from Romanticism is challenging; but of course many Romantics supposed themselves to be 'men speaking to men', to be engaged in revealing 'the primary laws of our nature'.[22] The rejection of the very notion, however qualified, of human nature, is intrinsic neither to Modernism nor to Romanticism. But this question takes us beyond the scope of the present chapter.

THREE

Fiction and Poetry, 1914–73

Early Writings: Imagining Arda

Tolkien's literary career spans almost sixty years, from shortly after the outbreak of the Great War in 1914, when he was twenty-two, until shortly before his death in 1973. Roughly the middle third of his creative life (1937–55) is dominated by the composition of *The Lord of the Rings*. But the first third was a period of apprenticeship, of scholarly eminence and literary obscurity. Tolkien's most influential contributions to scholarship and criticism – notably the edition (with E. V. Gordon) of *Sir Gawain and the Green Knight*, and the essay on *Beowulf* – date from this period, and the essays 'On Fairy Stories' and 'On Translating *Beowulf*' followed only a little later. The only literary compositions to achieve publication before 1937 were a handful of poems, printed in obscure magazines: one, 'Goblin Feet', which Tolkien came to dislike intensely for its prettified and diminutive 'fairy' imagery,[1] appeared in a couple of anthologies in the early twenties.

But Tolkien was writing prolifically during this period, as is abundantly demonstrated by the first five volumes of the posthumous series 'The History of Middle-earth', edited by Christopher Tolkien: *The Book of Lost Tales* (two volumes), *The Lays of Beleriand*, *The Shaping of Middle-earth*, and *The Lost Road*. Even during and after the composition of *The Lord of the Rings*, Tolkien continued to work on this great narrative cycle, which achieved its nearest approach to a definitive form in the posthumously published Silmarillion and Unfinished Tales of 1977 and 1980 respectively. The last four volumes of 'The History of Middle-earth' document the other phases of Tolkien's continued work on the cycle, ending with short texts from his last few years. The series would actually be better called 'the History of Arda', since its narratives extend beyond the land-mass of Middle-earth proper and encompass a myth of the creation and early history of Arda, the world (an imagined version of our own world) of which Middle-earth is merely a part.

In these writings, which often take the form of multiple versions of an evolving tale, Tolkien strove to construct a unified corpus of myth and legend – a process he continued until the end of his life. This mythical 'history', which never assumed a completely fixed form, stands in the position of a remote background to the events of The Lord of The Rings, which are dated several thousand years later. The numerous allusions to the earlier history in that work are internally consistent, and indeed contribute greatly to its exhilarating sense of wide expanses of time; but there is not complete consistency – even on matters of detail, let alone in overall aesthetic character – between The Lord of the Rings and any other version of the history. Tolkien hoped during the late 1940s to publish the entire historical sequence as a unified narrative, but for reasons which will be discussed later I am confident that this would not have worked. A reader who wishes to enjoy Tolkien's work to the fullest is best advised to treat the various tales and poems of the (fictionally) earlier epochs essentially as discrete inventions, and not as 'extensions' to The Lord of the Rings.

These writings are difficult, often fragmentary and contradictory, and, it must be said, only intermittently rewarding. The earliest works of all are lyrical poems, written around the time of Tolkien's graduation from Oxford and enlistment in the Lancashire Fusiliers; in the more effective of these, the impact on the emerging 'history' of the peculiar poignancy of youthful experience is touchingly visible, in spite of a highly derivative style. These poems of Tolkien show beyond doubt that Humphrey Carpenter's assertion that 'for him English literature ended with Chaucer' is an overstatement.[2] Among a number of post-medieval, mainly nineteenth-century, influences, the shadows of Keats and early Tennyson, and of Milton's 'Lycidas', fall particularly heavily across them.

> Now are thy trees, old, old Kortirion,
> Seen rising up through pallid mists and wan,
> Like vessels floating vague and long afar
> Down opal seas beyond the shadowy bar
> Of cloudy ports forlorn …
> Bare are thy trees become, Kortirion,
> And all their summer glory swiftly gone.
> The seven lampads of the Silver Bear
> Are waxen to a wondrous flare
> That flames above the fallen year.
>> ('Kortirion among the Trees', 1915, ll.
>> 108–112, 119–23: LT1, 33–6)

Winter (personified) comes in with 'icy shears' and 'blue-tipped spears', and the melodious phrasing ranges from Tennysonian sonorousness ('sunlight dripping on long lawns') to Keatsian airiness ('whirl ye with the sapphire-winged winds'). If we strip away the surface of conventional romantic style, we find above all the aching intensity of a young man's response to place. 'Kortirion' is a town of the Elves in Alalminorë, the Land of Elms; but it is also Warwick in its wooded shire, for at this early stage Tolkien proposed to relate his mythology to the history of England. Elvish Kortirion would be Warwick at an earlier epoch, or as perceived by a visionary, nostalgic imagination: it embodies a lost ideal beauty, which at exceptional moments – especially, it seems, in autumn and after sunset – the poet glimpses in 'the little faded town' of the present.

> O! gentle time
> When the late mornings are bejewelled with rime,
>> And the blue shadows gather on the distant woods.
> The fairies know thy early crystal dusk …
> They know the season of the brilliant night,
>> When naked elms entwine in cloudy lace
> The Pleiades, and long-armed poplars bar the light
>> Of golden-rondured moons with glorious face.
>> (ll. 90–3, 97–100)

Tolkien's gift for admitting the reader to a transparent view of landscape is already at work here: only the dutifully complicated 'lace' metaphor clutters the visual field. The sound-patterning, too, is gracefully handled, especially the liquid and labial assonances, and discreet alliteration, of the last two quoted lines. In a slightly later poem, 'The City of Present Sorrow' (1916: LT2, 297), the speaker recollects the beauty and ancientry of Oxford, and laments the departure of its men to war. The city, though easily identified, is not actually named, as if to heighten, by 'defamiliarising', the elegiac vision. Once again, the best lines in a thoroughly conventional poem are the most limpidly and particularly observed, or recalled:

> I see thy clustered windows each one burn
> With lamps and candles of departed men ...
> To thee my spirit dances oft in sleep
> Along thy great grey streets, or down
> A little lamplit alley-way at night,
> Thinking no more of other cities it has known.
>   (ll. 14–15, 22–5)

An even more personal poem, 'You & Me; and the Cottage of Lost Play' (LT1, 28–30) uses the image of a cottage inhabited by playful fairies (and discovered in sleep) to express the intimacy and shared imaginings of two children, 'a dark child and a fair'. This poem is in a simpler style, with hints of Christina Rossetti, Allingham's 'The Fairies' and (as Christopher Tolkien suggests)[3] Francis Thompson's 'Daisy', but also a deeper resemblance in mood to the nostalgic nineteenth-century ballads of which Hood's 'I remember, I remember' and Peacock's 'Love and Age' ('I played with you 'mid cowslips blowing / When I was six and you were four')[4] are examples. Evidently it is a homage, deliberately projected backwards in time and transformed into fairy-tale mode, to an aspect of Tolkien's adolescent romance with his fellow-orphan Edith Bratt. Its opening focuses realistically if sentimentally on the reveries of childhood ('the blue-spun twilit hours / of little early tucked-up beds'), and it ends in a mood of shared regret for the unreclaimable permanence of an imagined land 'where all things are, that ever were'.

These poems, rooted in immediate personal experience, yearning towards elusive intimations of eternity discerned in the transitory joys of the present and of memory, seem to me more successful than those of the same period, such as the 'Eärendel' group (LT2, 267–74), which initiate the actual narrative content of the mythology in wholly imaginary settings. The derivativeness even of the better poems, and their proneness to romantic cliché ('to thee my spirit dances oft in sleep') means that they can only be regarded as immature works, by a writer whose genuine but limited talent for verse was destined never to be reconciled with twentieth-century taste. That the twenty-three-year-old Tolkien should write in this style is not so extraordinary, for the effects of his romantic temperament would have been reinforced by the poetic values still prevalent in the Edwardian England of his formative years: in his teens Housman's *Shropshire Lad*, and Yeats's early volumes with their mythical and 'faery' themes, were freshly minted; Swinburne and Francis Thompson were still alive, and Robert Bridges was beginning his long term as Poet Laureate. But English poetry was about to take a decisive turn away from the romantic tradition: Eliot's 'Love-Song of J. Alfred Prufrock' appeared in *Poetry* in June 1915, and Yeats had renounced his early manner a few years earlier. Nevertheless, it is in the mimetic particularity of these poems, as well as in their commendable fearlessness in expressing ecstatic, nostalgic, and even sentimental emotions, that the promise o. Aolkien's later achievements can be seen.

The 'Cottage of Lost Play', reconceived, and relocated in Kortirion, served as a linking device for the first version of the mythological history: the tales comprising the history were to be narrated there to a traveller, Eriol, through whom a connection with pre-Saxon England would subsequently be established. This cumbersome and aesthetically redundant narrative framework was eventually dismantled, and the legends allowed to stand independent of any association to English history. At the same time the element of diminutiveness associated with the Cottage and its numerous inhabitants, fairies and mortal children, was mercifully abandoned: for while the laughing children and 'very little folk' (LT1, 14) of the Cottage conception work well enough as a poetic objective correlative for private tenderness, they are quite incompatible with the immense, and often violent and tragic, history which was now evolving.

Most of the myths and legends concerning the 'First Age' (as it came to be identified – The Lord of the Rings is set at the end of the Third) have now been published in several conflicting versions; even the names of principal characters change from one version to the next. However, the overall scheme remained fairly stable, and can be set out, with drastic simplification and many omissions, as follows. Eru Ilúvatar (God) creates the Ainur (who may be conceived as angels, though they have the distinctive personalities and functions of classical gods). The Ainur make music before Ilúvatar, at his bidding and around themes propounded by him, and he translates their music into the form of the World, 'globed amid the Void' (LT1, 56; 5, 17). Some of them descend into it to participate in its history; among these is the powerful but wilful Melkor, whose discords introduced into the Music are now to be expressed in destructiveness and cruelty on Earth.

Despite the depredations of Melkor, the Valar (Ainur within the World) establish a paradisal realm, Valinor, illuminated by golden and silver light from two great Trees. Now the Elves (the elder 'Children of Ilúvatar', not conceived by the Ainur in their Music) appear in Middle-earth, far from Valinor; at length many of them journey to Valinor by starlight. There Fëanor, a gifted Elf, creates the Silmarils, jewels which imprison light from the Two Trees. Melkor steals the Silmarils and destroys the Trees, fleeing to Middle-earth. Fëanor and his clan disobey the Valar by pursuing Melkor. They establish various settlements of Elves in Middle-earth, and wage futile war on Melkor's northern stronghold, Angband. Meanwhile the Valar create the Sun and Moon to re-illuminate the Earth.

The war between the Elves and Melkor (during which the younger Children of Ilúvatar, Men, appear on the scene, as do the Dwarves), provides the historical background to the three most developed tales of the cycle, all tragic in character: 'Beren and Lúthien', 'The Children of Húrin' and 'The Fall of Gondolin'. From the protagonists (Men and Elves) of the first and third of these is descended Eärendil, who finds Valinor and successfully pleads for the Valar to intervene. Melkor is overthrown in an apocalyptic battle, and thrust out of the world into the Void.

The reader who intends to explore these legends should certainly begin with *The Silmarillion*, in which a complete version of the cycle, based largely on the latest forms the individual tales assumed in Tolkien's manuscripts, is presented. Most of the earlier texts will, I suspect, only begin to be digestible by a reader who already has an acquaintance with the main lines of the narrative; and so far as the quality of the prose and the clarity of the action is concerned, the later versions can generally be regarded as supplanting the earlier, incorporating almost everything of aesthetic value in them, and so rendering them superfluous except to the scholar. Some of the ancillary texts are explicitly mere sketches, or dated 'annals' designed to clarify the sequence of events: though couched in sufficiently dignified prose, they make no pretence to narrative fluency. Others are fully developed narratives, but marked, especially in the early versions, by derivative conceptions out of keeping with the tragic seriousness which elsewhere had been achieved: the figure which would ultimately evolve into Sauron, for example, appears in an early form of the Beren and Lúthien tale ('The Tale of Tinúviel', LT2, 15ff.) as a giant cat which sets Beren to catch three mice of 'a very wild, evil and magic kind' (LT2, 16). Certain aspects of the nomenclature, such as the punning use of 'Gnomes' to denote the most learned and enlightened branch of the Elves,[5] strike one as inadvisable, though I suppose it is just conceivable that had he persisted with the term Tolkien might have reclaimed a dignified meaning for 'Gnome' as he has done for 'Elf'. Morally, too, there is in the early Tales often only a rudimentary glimpse of the profundity to come: the divine Valar quarrel among themselves, and heroes such as Beren engage in vulgar trickery. (Here the influence of the classical pantheon is evident – but the moral universe of Tolkien's mature work, with its devout sense of an immanent benevolence in the world, is very different from Homer's, and this feature alone would make the 'Lost Tales' conceptually irreconcilable with the published *Silmarillion*, let alone *The Lord of the Rings*.)

Above all, the prose in the pre-1937 legends is far removed from the transparency, and flexible use of elevated style, achieved in *The Lord of the Rings*. Instead there is a sustained archaism, strongly reminiscent of the prose romances of William Morris a generation and more earlier.

> The most of that folk were gone a-hunting with the Gods, but many there were gathered about the beaches before their dwellings and dismay was abroad among them, yet still were no few busy about the places of their ships, and the chief of these was one that they named Kópas, or more fully Kópas Alqaluntë, the Haven of the swanships. Now Swanhaven was like a bason of quiet waters, save that towards the eastward and the seas the ring of rocks that enclosed it sank somewhat, and there did the sea pierce through, so that there was a mighty arch of living stone. So great was this that save of the mightiest ships two might pass therethrough, one going out maybe and another seeking inward to the quiet blue waters of the haven, nor would the mast-tops come nigh to grazing on the rock. ('The Flight of the Noldoli', LT1, 164)

Though the passage contains no words which are archaic in the sense of requiring a glossary, there is a persistent preference for forms which have no rationale except to push the language back into a generalised pre-twentieth-century idiom. The obsolete 'bason' for 'basin' is characteristic. 'Save', still common in The Lord of the Rings, is almost always rhythmically more fluent than 'except', but there is no such defence for 'nigh'. The unnecessary negatives ('no few'; 'nor would the mast tops …'), with their irritating air of disputing what no one has asserted, the superfluous articles and particles ('the most'; 'a-hunting'), the mannered tentativeness (Kópas, or more fully Kópas Alqaluntë; 'one going out maybe and another seeking inward'), and the mishandled inversions which create ambiguities (as with 'there' in the first sentence, and less seriously in the second), all obscure a potentially beautiful description. Tolkien might have reflected that, since the legends belong to no specific period in the history of the English language, and therefore have no 'fitting' historical style, uniform archaism could only convey the impression of a lack of confidence in the communicability of his vision to a contemporary readership. 'High style' for especially exalted moments might be justified, but this is by no means an especially exalted moment and too much sublimity becomes self-defeating. (In fact I suspect Tolkien was still too bewitched by Morris's prose mannerisms to make this kind of independent compositional judgement.)

The reader prepared to brave the archaic prose style, but not perhaps to persevere through the two densely annotated volumes of The Book of Lost Tales, should at any rate look at 'The Fall of Gondolin' (LT2, 149–97), in which the vividly imagined betrayal and destruction of the last Elvish city is narrated with ruthless energy, and an impressive capacity for evoking panic and disorder while maintaining narrative coherence. However, the major exception to the rule that The Silmarillion supersedes in quality the earlier versions of the legends is the tale of Beren and Lúthien. Certainly the earliest prose version of this story ('The Tale of Tinúviel', LT2), is weak. But in the 1920s Tolkien embarked upon two narrative poems, a treatment in alliterative verse of 'The Children of Húrin' and a version of 'Beren and Lúthien' in octosyllabic rhyming couplets. These now appear in The Lays of Beleriand (Beleriand being a region of Middle-earth). 'The Lay of the Children of Húrin', though it has an impressive narrative urgency, suffers in the end from the unadaptableness of modern English to the metrical and assonantal idiom of Beowulf: diction and syntax are too often, and too obviously, constrained by the demands of the medium:

> Not Morgoth's might nor meed nor torment
> them vowed, availed to reveal that lore;
> yet lights and lamps of living radiance,
> many and magical, they made for him.
> No dark could dim them the deeps wandering;
> whose lode they lit was lost seldom
> in groundless grot, or gulfs far under.
>
> (ll. 793–9, Lays, 35)

The effect is of a resourceful pastiche. The Lay is also somewhat unvaried in its grimness of mood. But 'The Lay of Leithian, or Release from Bondage', begun in 1925 after the abandonment of 'The Lay of the Children of Húrin' is a different matter. One of the best-known moments in the publication history of Tolkien's works is the scathing reaction to the poem by Allen & Unwin's reader in 1937, and his preference for the 'stinging pace' of an accompanying prose version.[6] Almost certainly these comments were salutary in reinforcing Tolkien's move towards a more 'novelistic' kind of fiction, for twentieth-century taste, so responsive to a plurality of prose fictions, has shown no tolerance at all for narrative poetry. Nevertheless, 'The Lay of Leithian', though unfinished and seriously flawed, seems to me to contain the most rewarding work Tolkien produced before the 1930s, and to be much the best account of the Beren and Lúthien story.

In its essence the story is a classically simple fairy-tale with a tragic ending. The hero (Beren, a mortal man) falls in love with a heroine of superior 'status' (Lúthien, an immortal Elf). Her father (Thingol, King of the Elvish realm of Doriath) opposes their union, and sets the hero a seemingly impossible task as the price of her hand (to bring him a Silmaril from the iron crown of Morgoth, alias Melkor). The hero succeeds in the task, but dies as a result.

The basic story is enriched by a number of complexities which only enhance its emotional power. The tragic colouring is established from the start. Morgoth's dark power extends over wide lands in which Thingol's Doriath is an enclave. Beren is the only survivor of a band of outlaws, betrayed to Morgoth's servants by one of their number, Gorlim, after he is deceived into believing that Morgoth will reunite him with his lost wife. After Gorlim is killed by Morgoth, his ghost (preceded by apparitions of carrion-birds with bloody beaks) visits Beren in a dream and urges him to warn his fellow-outlaws, who include Beren's father; but Beren arrives too late to do more than bury them. After further fighting, and then flight, the exhausted Beren, 'grey in his hair, his youth turned old' ('The Lay of Leithian', l. 552, Lays, 175), glimpses Lúthien, dancing in a lonely woodland clearing to the music of the piper, Daeron, who is hidden in the branches of an oak. (The jealous Daeron will be an enemy of Beren.) He searches for her through the seasons from summer to spring before finding her and winning her love. Later, when Beren, against all hope and with the help of Lúthien, prises the Silmaril from Morgoth's crown and grasps it in his hand, the hand is bitten off by Morgoth's giant Wolf, Carcharoth. Beren escapes, presents himself before Thingol, and declares that 'even now a Silmaril is in my hand' (S, 184). Thingol relents and the lovers are betrothed. The Wolf, maddened by the Silmaril blazing in his belly (for it burns unholy flesh), invades Doriath: Beren completes the quest by hunting it to death, but he himself is killed.

Lúthien relinquishes her immortality in order to follow Beren 'beyond the confines of the world' (S, 187).

This story has a powerful three-part structure, with intense but transient joy at its centre and grief, of different kinds, at either end; and there are episodes, or scenes, of great dramatic potential. One can imagine it as a Wagnerian music-drama: Act One – Beren and the outlaws, with the apparition and narration of Gorlim at its centre; Act Two – Beren's pursuit of Lóthien, with the changing seasons, the intrusions of Daeron, and a final love scene; Act Three – the quest for the Silmaril, punctuated by the two contrasting confrontations of Beren with Thingol and his court, and closing with Beren's death and Lúthien's *Liebestod*. There are, however, some weaker features in the tale as actually presented. The mechanics of Beren's theft of the Silmaril involve complicated and implausible disguises, and too facile an appeal to benevolent 'magic'. Morgoth improbably allows himself to be sung to sleep by Lúthien. (There is an undeveloped suggestion that he is sexually attracted by her, but this somehow diminishes and humanises him in an incongruous way.) Another problem arises from what is, in the long term, a welcome development in the legendary conception – indeed a development which will terminate in the expansive world of *The Lord of the Rings*. The tale of Beren and Lúthien becomes involved in the 'political' complexities of Middle-earth, the shifting alliances and hostilities among the enemies of Morgoth (the sons of Fëanor, the other Elves, the various Houses of Men, the Dwarves). As a result the journey to Morgoth's fortress is duplicated by an exciting, but structurally intrusive, episode in the dungeons of his vassal Thû (later, Sauron), and Lúthien becomes irrelevantly embroiled with Fëanor's corrupt sons Celegorm and Cerufim. Even after death there are complications: Beren and Lúthien are permitted to return to Middle-earth for a while, and Beren becomes involved in a war between Thingol and a Dwarf-Lord.

In *The Silmarillion*, the tale of Beren and Lúthien, mostly reduced to a bare prose narrative of events, becomes so enmeshed in the wider history that its integrity and simplicity, and certainly its intensity, are lost. The 'Lay', however, focuses intensively upon the story, combining steady narrative impetus with, as A. N. Wilson says, 'passages of quite stunning beauty'.[7] The effect of the lyrical passages describing Lúthien and her enchanted surroundings, and Beren's yearning pursuit of her, is cumulative: the individual line that might seem trite or clichéd in isolation ('By dawn and dusk he seeks her still') is carried off by sheer profusion of verbal melody and precision of imagery.

> An autumn waned, a winter laid
> the withered leaves in grove and glade;
> the beeches bare were gaunt and grey,
> and red their leaves beneath them lay.
> From cavern pale the moist moon eyes
> the white mists that from earth arise
> to hide the morrow's sun and drip
> all the grey day from each twig's tip.
> By dawn and dusk he seeks her still;
> by noon and night in valleys chill,
> nor hears a sound but the slow beat
> on sodden leaves of his own feet.
>
> (ll. 673–84)

The middle four lines here, especially, represent the poem at its best, with their subtly-spaced assonances, their shiveringly exact meteorology, and the onomatopoeic dripping of three successive stresses on 'each twig's tip'. The aerial 'cavern' of moonlit darkness, bounded by cloud or risen mist, as well as being visually well-observed, brings the moon down into the scene as a quasi-observer, heightening Beren's loneliness (so far as human, or Elvish, company is concerned) and, by compressing the scene somewhat, reinforcing our sense of his imprisonment within it – that is, within the enchanted woods of Doriath – by the bewitching memory of Lúthien. C. S. Lewis objected to 'beat' in line 683, calling it 'utterly inappropriate to the sound described',[8] but he was wrong: 'beat' clearly denotes not the timbre of a drum, but musical 'beat' or rhythm, the 'measured sequence of strokes or sounds' as the OED has it, with an added suggestion of Beren's crushing weight: the two long syllables that conclude the line (and the effect is repeated in the next) reinforce the sense of weary trudging. Not all the poem is on this level, but enough of it is to make one regret that Tolkien abandoned it at the moment when Carcharoth bites off Beren's hand, leaving the final scenes, including Beren's death, to be narrated only in prose versions. It has a distinctive place in his *oeuvre*, representing in some ways not so much a precursor of the later accomplished fictions as a final expression (at least until *Smith of Wootton Major* forty years later) of the deeply personal romantic vision glimpsed in the earliest poems.

The Silmarillion, Unfinished Tales, and Later Narratives of Arda

During the same period, the late twenties, in which he worked on 'The Lay of Leithian', Tolkien was preparing the brief first version of 'The Silmarillion'. The volume eventually published under that title in 1977 resembles a huge canvas, worked on over forty years, of which some parts have been painted over repeatedly while others have been little modified, except where minor details have been touched up to avoid serious inconsistency. The subsequently published volumes of drafts show (to simplify a little) three early versions, which can be roughly associated with the dates 1926, 1930 and 1937; a further major revision took place at the beginning of the 1950s, and revision continued intermittently for another two decades. Comparison of the early versions with the published *Silmarillion* is revealing, and leads to the conclusion that, while the post-1950 revisions and additions marked a considerable advance in stylistic maturity, the essential content of the 'history', and – equally important – its chronicle-like narrative perspective, were firmly fixed before *The Lord of the Rings* was begun at the end of 1937. As the work evolves there is, to be sure, a modest but discernible move in the direction of the more expansive and novelistic conception fulfilled in *The Lord of the Rings*. An example of this is the narration of the Elves' first journey, from their place of awakening in starlit Middle-earth, by the lake of Cuiviénen, to the divine realm of Valinor. In 'The Book of Lost Tales' the land journey through Middle-earth is passed over in a few lines, but the narrative is progressively expanded until in the 1977 published *Silmarillion* we have a protracted migration of peoples, proceeding by fits and starts through wide territories which are at any rate sketched geographically.

> And it came to pass after many years of journeying in this manner that
> the Eldar took their course through a forest, and they came to a great
> river, wider than any they had yet seen; and beyond it were mountains
> whose sharp horns seemed to pierce the realm of the stars. This river, it
> is said, was even the river which was after called Anduin the Great, and
> was ever the frontier of the west-lands of Middle-earth ... Now the
> Teleri abode long on the east bank of that river and wished to remain
> there, but the Vanyar and Noldor passed over it, and Oromë led them into
> the passes of the mountains. And when Oromë was gone forward the
> Teleri looked upon the shadowy heights and were afraid. (S, 53–4)

On the other hand, as this passage illustrates, The Silmarillion
remains locked into a certain stylistic 'distance'. Rarely is the visual
realisation any more detailed than here; the love of the particular,
unrepeatable landscape, of changing light and weather, that we find
in The Lord of the Rings is absent (or rather it is attributed to the Elves
without, on the whole, being evoked for the reader). The narrative
speeds through tumultuous events, chronicled briefly and
externally: the close perspective of individuals, of the kind that in
The Lord of the Rings is provided mainly by the hobbits, seldom appears.
Characters succeed one another in sometimes bewildering
profusion: with a few exceptions (Fëanor, Húrin, Túrin, Eöl,
Maeglin) they come to be individuated in the reader's memory
more by their names – admittedly Tolkien's expertise in nomenclature serves him well here – than by strongly differentiated features
of personality. All this is virtually inevitable, given the scale of the
legendary 'history', and the aspiration to produce a more or less
unified and consistent text: if the events of The Silmarillion were to
be narrated throughout with the intimacy of perspective of The
Lord of the Rings, the work would be several thousand pages long.

A further problem for The Silmarillion, as Tolkien himself was aware,
is the very completeness of the mythical and legendary structure,
the absence of the 'unattainable vistas',[9] glimpsed in the distance,
which are part of the expansive vision of The Lord of the Rings. In The
Two Towers Gandalf, thousands of years after the main action of The
Silmarillion, yearns in a brief moment of reflective nostalgia to use
the palantir 'to look across the wide seas of water and of time to
Tirion the Fair, and perceive the unimaginable hand and mind of

Fëanor at their work, while both the White Tree and the Golden were in flower!' (204). But the Fëanor of *The Silmarillion*, the subject of direct and explicit narrative, cannot remain 'unimaginable' and inevitably fails to live up to the expectation Gandalf's ancient memory arouses: that distance (in time and space) lends enchantment is an aesthetic as well as a psychological law. (Niggle, in the short story 'Leaf by Niggle', reflects that 'he had never... been able to walk into the distance without turning it into mere surroundings'.)[10] And there is no historical distance beyond *The Silmarillion*, which begins with the creation of the universe and traces the origins of all the speaking peoples (except Men, whose earliest, presumably Edenic, history remains off-stage).

The absence of the distinctive virtues of *The Lord of the Rings* – the exhilarating, expansive realisation of Middle-earth, the unified plot whose excitements are integrated with that realisation, the transparent prose which is the medium for both – has made *The Silmarillion* a confessed disappointment to many, perhaps most, of the admirers won for Tolkien by the earlier-published work. In view of the fact that its essential conception predates *The Lord of the Rings*, one is tempted to see its versions (up to 1937) as Tolkien's sketch-books, the evidences of his long and painful literary apprenticeship, through which he fumbled his way towards his true creative manner, that of *The Lord of the Rings*. According to this view, having accomplished *The Lord of the Rings* (for which *The Hobbit* is also an apprentice-piece), Tolkien proved incapable in his last years of bringing his mature mastery to bear upon transforming the recalcitrant material of 'The Silmarillion' into a comparably effective narrative.

There is some truth in this view: certainly at its weakest *The Silmarillion* (especially if we have *The Lord of the Rings* freshly in mind) reads like preliminary notes towards a much fuller narrative, written up in an exhausting 'high style' which proceeds in stilted paragraphs, linked by the formulaic conjunctions, 'And ...', 'Now ...', and 'For ...'. To find the strengths of *The Silmarillion* one must look to quite different qualities from those of *The Lord of the Rings*. And we should start by recognising that it is fundamentally different in mode and temper from that work: while *The Lord of the Rings* is a comedy, of which the keynote is joy enriched by regret, *The Silmarillion* is tragic, not to say bitter, in spirit. Its atmosphere comes as a shock to anyone who supposed (as it was natural to do before 1977) that Tolkien's entire literary career had been guided by the opinion, expressed in the essay 'On Fairy Stories', that 'Tragedy is the true form of drama, its highest function; but the opposite is true of Fairy-story.'[11] This assertion, written just as the early chapters of *The Lord of the Rings* were unfolding, can now be seen to represent a turning-point in Tolkien's reflection on his own creativity. *The Hobbit*, written in the early 1930s as a children's adventure story, had certainly culminated in what Tolkien in the essay calls 'eucatastrophe', a happy ending, against the odds, which has emotional intensity and moral fittingness. The passage in 'On Fairy Stories' thus signals Tolkien's intention to take *The Hobbit*, in this respect, as the prototype for *The Lord of the Rings* — not the tragic 'Silmarillion', which he had hitherto regarded as his serious work for adults.

It is true that *The Silmarillion* is as Augustinian in its theology as *The Lord of the Rings* — indeed the theology is fully explicit, as it is not in the latter work. But whereas in *The Lord of the Rings* the emphasis is ultimately upon the goodness of the created world, in *The Silmarillion* it falls upon the ubiquity of sin, the readiness with which created beings are deluded and corrupted, the tenacious power of pride, cupidity, and resentment, and the depths of cruelty and blasphemy to which they lead. The 'History of the Silmarils' ends with the overthrow of Melkor/Morgoth, but this is, significantly, one of the least developed parts of the narrative, and its final words are a reminder of the endurance of Melkor's lies, 'a seed that does not die and cannot be destroyed; and ever and anon it sprouts anew, and will bear dark fruit even unto the latest days' (S, 255). To a certain extent the difference of narrative mode is responsible for the contrast in mood (or conversely, the governing mood may be conceived as having dictated the level of narrative). The leisurely, cir- cumstantial manner of *The Lord of the Rings* is inseparable from its relish in the created world; the austere style of *The Silmarillion* reinforces the grimness of a narrative in which 'Then he put him cruelly to death' (S, 163) is a not untypical detail. But the darker atmosphere of *The Silmarillion* is more than a matter of narrative technique. Its plot seems often to be a catalogue of crimes and follies; and few of its characters can be called sympathetic. Its Elves, for example, are markedly less noble and serene than those of *The Lord of the Rings*, even allowing for the supposition that long ages of accumulated wisdom have intervened between the epochs treated in the two works. Few episodes are more impressive, or more characteristic, than that in which Fëanor, already stained with the blood of his kinsfolk as he pursues his reckless quest to regain the Silmarils from Melkor/Morgoth, is struck down in battle before the mountain range, Thangorodrim, which Morgoth has erected to protect his stronghold.

> Then his sons raised up their father and bore him back towards Mithrim. But as they drew near to Eithel Sirion and were upon the upward path to the pass over the mountains, Fëanor bade them halt; for his wounds were mortal, and he knew that his hour was come. And looking out from the slopes of Ered Wethrin with his last sight he beheld far off the peaks of Thangorodrim, mightiest of the towers of Middle-earth, and knew with the foreknowledge of death that no power of the Noldor would ever overthrow them; but he cursed the name of Morgoth thrice, and laid it upon his sons to hold to their oath, and to avenge their father. Then he died; but he had neither burial nor tomb, for so fiery was his spirit that as it sped his body fell to ash, and was borne away like smoke; and his likeness has never again appeared in Arda, neither has his spirit left the halls of Mandos. (S, 107)

Fëanor thus condemns his sons, already bound by a blasphemous oath, to a course of vengeance which he himself sees to be futile. If Tolkien felt the temptation to allow the gifted Fëanor a moment of sanity and repentance, he rightly resisted it, for this unflinching representation of the evil and misery to which powerful emotions can lead rational beings is of the essence of *The Silmarillion*. Its most memorable moments are those in which elemental motives (pride, vengefulness, jealous love, possessiveness) issue in tragic action, narrated in prose of the dignity and economy exemplified above. The most ambitious tale along these lines is that of Túrin Turambar (or 'The Children of Húrin'), on which Tolkien lavished much effort: in addition to the alliterative poem, and a chapter in *The Silmarillion*, there is a long version in *Unfinished Tales*. To my mind, however, Túrin's misfortunes (which include inadvertently killing his best friend, and inadvertently marrying and impregnating his own sister) are too complicatedly plotted to achieve the Sophoclean inevitability they require, and Túrin himself too simply headstrong, sullen and naïve to avoid inspiring a certain impatience. More convincingly tragic, because his own fate is simpler and his despair more clearly motivated, is the father, Húrin, imprisoned by Morgoth, compelled to be a helpless spectator of the sorrows, and suicides, of his children, and released only when his morale has been destroyed. His subsequent meeting with his wife (S, 229) must be the bleakest moment in the entire work: Tolkien again refuses to soften or reconcile, and briefly we are indeed in the world of Sophocles, or of *King Lear*. Almost equally powerful is the tale (apparently written later than *The Lord of the Rings*) of the introverted, embittered Dark Elf, Eöl, with its tragic properties of interfamilial hatred and murderous jealousy. A tyrannical but loving father, deserted by his wife and betrayed, even at his death, by the chilling silence of his son, Eöl is as hauntingly ambivalent a character as Tolkien created. In the figures of Húrin and Eöl the painfulness of paternal love − an important theme for Tolkien, treated through such contrasted characters as Denethor and Elrond in *The Lord of The Rings*, and handled with rather embarrassing directness in the unfinished time-travel story 'The Lost Road' of 1936–37[12] − is dramatised with operatic intensity.

In general the most convincing parts of *The Silmarillion* are those in which the mythical or legendary matter has a boldness and clarity of action, and a force of moral significance, that justifies the elevated style. The creation myth, *Ainulindalë*, which begins the volume; the presumptuous making of the Dwarves by Aulë, and Eru's compassionate conferral of independent life upon them (S, 43–4); the 'kinslaying' by the fugitive Noldor of their cousins the Teleri in the lamplit harbour of Alqualondë (86–7); the curse pronounced on the Noldor by the herald of the Valar, 'a dark figure standing high upon a rock that looked down upon the shore' (87); the journey of the betrayed host of Fingolfin across hills of ice, at last to blow their trumpets 'in Middle-earth at the first rising of the moon' (90); the deaths of Fëanor, of Beren, of Eöl, of Thingol; these episodes are memorable as tableaux: one can imagine them painted by a Blake or a Fuseli, with vivid figures against a dark, somewhat generalised background. For the most part they are narrated with spare dignity.

Above all *Ainulindalë*, the Elves' version of *Genesis*, seems to me a success both in literary and in philosophical terms. Its fundamental mythical conception, the world as a Great Music made visible, its history a fulfilment of creative purposes which proceed both directly from God and mediately from him, through the sub-creativity of created beings, dates from as early as 1918–20:[13] as I will show in chapter 5, it is the key to much else in Tolkien's religious, moral and aesthetic vision.[14] And its prose is at once appropriately 'scriptural' and distinctive of Tolkien.

> The Valar endeavoured ever, in spite of Melkor, to rule the Earth and prepare it for the coming of the Firstborn; and they built lands and Melkor destroyed them; valleys they delved and Melkor raised them up; mountains they carved and Melkor threw them down; seas they hollowed and Melkor spilled them; and naught might have peace or lasting growth, for as surely as the Valar began a labour so would Melkor undo or corrupt it. And yet their labour was not all in vain; and though nowhere and in no work was their will and purpose wholly fulfilled, and all things were in hue and shape other than the Valar had at first intended, slowly nonetheless the Earth was fashioned and made firm. And thus was the habitation of the Children of Ilúvatar established at last in the Deeps of Time and amid the innumerable stars. (S, 22)

If the cadences of the closing sentence are conventionally majestic, the rhythmically poised verbs earlier in the passage (*delved, carved, hollowed, spilled*) show Tolkien's visual imagination and tact, as well as his ear, at work; they render the perspective of the divine craftsmen (and craftswomen, for half of the Valar are female) upon their material, while leaving the Valar themselves, and Melkor, prudently unvisualised.

The *Silmarillion* concludes with two short works which deal with the Second and Third Ages respectively. The latter, *Of the Rings of Power*, is a dignified but somewhat dutiful retelling of the historical background of *The Lord of the Rings*. *Akallabêth* narrates the Atlantis-like downfall of the island realm of Númenor, established for Men after the overthrow of Melkor. The simplicity and grandeur of its themes – the rebellion of the Númenóreans against their own mortality, their regression to the worship of the exiled Melkor, their

impious assault on Valinor, the drowning of the island by the direct
intervention of Ilúvatar, the escape of an uncorrupted few from the
cataclysm – are preserved by the brisk and 'distanced' style, yet
there are enough vivid touches to save the narrative from aridity,
and to make one wonder whether a fuller version might not have
made the distinctive air of Númenor as imaginatively breathable as
that of Middle-earth. The lonely mountaintop temple hallowed to
Ilúvatar, 'open and unroofed' (S, 261), and Sauron's gigantic city-
centre shrine to Melkor, with its walls fifty feet thick and its silver
dome stained black by the smoke from human sacrifice (273), are
powerfully contrasted images. The Númenórean matter in Unfinished
Tales has similar unfulfilled promise: significantly, it includes both
a map and a seven-page geographical description of the island. But
the only extended narrative, the tale 'Aldarion and Erendis: The
Mariner's Wife', breaks off abruptly. Its theme of marital disharmony
– arising, not from ill-will, but from profound differences of
temperament and aspiration, and ending in bitter estrangement –
suggests that Tolkien might conceivably have found in Númenor a
setting in which the dark, disillusioned view of human experience
which dominates the later stages of The Silmarillion could have found
a more 'novelistic' embodiment. But The Lord of the Rings intervened,
and this can hardly be viewed as an accident: its completion, and
the neglect of Númenor, shows Tolkien moving decisively, in middle
age, towards a 'eucatastrophic' vision.

The miscellaneous texts collected in the volume Unfinished Tales
date from the last twenty-five years of Tolkien's life, and are
variable in quality and interest. They may be discussed alongside
the other unfinished narratives that did not find their way into
Unfinished Tales but surfaced later, in the closing volumes of 'The
History of Middle-earth'. These latter include two stories
abandoned because the projects they represent soon proved to be
unnecessary. 'The Notion Club Papers' (Sauron Defeated, 145–327),
written in 1944–45, labours abstrusely to use a fictionalised
version of Tolkien's own circle of friends and fellow-scholars as
a conduit into the matter of Númenor;[15] while 'The New Shadow'
(The Peoples of Middle-earth, 409–21), from the last years of Tolkien's
life, is a few exploratory pages of sequel to The Lord of the Rings,
hobbit-less and weighted with sententious dialogue. But many

other texts in these volumes are, in fact, not so much narratives as essays relating to the history, languages and metaphysics of Arda. In one series of reflections, for example (*Morgoth's Ring*, 408–24), Tolkien strives to resolve the problem of the apparently irredeemable wickedness of Orcs. What troubled Tolkien was not that their murderous sadism is incredible, for it is not. Given that they are a warrior horde, conditioned from birth to kill, their actions are consistent with what we know about the brutalisation of human children in sufficiently terrible circumstances, and the Orcs' deeds pale by comparison with the holocausts of Ruanda, Cambodia, or Hitler's and Stalin's death camps. The problem is that since only Ilúvatar can create, and 'Nothing is evil in the beginning' (FR, 281), the Orcs cannot be bad in their very nature, if they are living creatures; and in that case the narrative ought, arguably, to view them more sympathetically than it does, especially since – unlike, say, Gollum – they have not had the opportunity to live among the uncorrupted. Actually, there are intimations of this view in *The Lord of the Rings*, such as Gandalf's remark, in implied reproof of Denethor, that 'for me, I pity even [Sauron's] slaves' (RK, 87). But Tolkien, instead of trusting to such hints, struggled to perfect a retrospective solution, even toying with the idea that the Orcs were soul-less automata, directly moved by the will of Morgoth or Sauron – a theory that would in many ways have been consistent with his wider moral vision,[16] but can only unsettle, rather than enhance, our understanding of *The Lord of the Rings*.

Similarly, several of the *Unfinished Tales* are commentaries on plot-elements of *The Lord of the Rings* or *The Hobbit*, and are sometimes vulnerable to the objection that they do little more than pedantically clarify or make explicit features of the original story that are more than acceptable as they stand. The reader of *The Lord of the Rings*, for example, needs no explanation of why Sauron's Black Riders appear in the Shire precisely when they do. It is enough that pursuers from Mordor were bound to appear sooner or later: and indeed, the sense that the forces of evil are encroaching on the Shire, from a great distance and at a speed which cannot be predicted, driven by a malevolent mind whose knowledge and intentions are partly unknown, is integral to the literary effect. Tolkien's careful spelling out of Sauron's strategic judgements and

choices in 'The Hunt for the Ring' (UT, 337ff.) is therefore artisti-
cally redundant, and in fact disharmonious with the presentation
of Sauron in The Lord of the Rings, from a hobbit's-eye view, as a remote
though terrible Power. These supplementary texts are successful
only when (as is usually the case with the Appendices to The Lord of
the Rings) they add genuinely new material, expanding Middle-earth
rather than tidying it up. The detailed account of the powers and
attributes of the palantiri (UT, 409–11), in which Tolkien shows his
ability to take a rather shop-soiled item of mysticism and popular
fantasy (the magician's 'crystal ball') and transform it into a credible
property of a great culture, while leaving its mystery, if anything,
enhanced, is far more gripping than the preceding narrative, about
how and when precisely Denethor and Saruman fell under Sauron's
domination by using the stones – events which are sufficiently
hinted at in The Lord of the Rings. Even better, I think, is the treatment
of the Drúedain, the squat wood-dwellers all too briefly glimpsed
in The Return of the King; the two short, self-contained folk-tales about
them (UT, 379–82) have great charm and a truly authentic ring.

The most tantalising piece in Unfinished Tales is the first in the
collection, 'Of Tuor and his Coming to Gondolin', which
Christopher Tolkien ascribes to the year 1951. It has the lucid,
austere style of the later-written parts of The Silmarillion, but also, at
moments, a dream-like visual intensity and mystery largely absent
from that volume. It twice uses a landscape motif also employed
more than once in The Lord of the Rings: the journey, first through a
tunnel, then through a narrow ravine between towering hills, to a
place of awe and wonder. A post-Freudian reader may be strongly
tempted to interpret the imagery as symbolising birth: if this is so,
the experience appears as tremendous and exhilarating, rather than
traumatic. Tuor's journeys bring him, first to the Great Sea, and an
epiphany of Ulmo, the Lord of Waters; and then to Gondolin itself,
the hidden city and last stronghold of the Elves, with its seven
successive gates, miles apart, all elaborately described.

> Then Tuor passed through, and coming to a high sward that looked out
> over the valley beyond, he beheld a vision of Gondolin amid the white
> snow. And so entranced was he that for long he could look at nothing

else; for he saw before him at last the vision of his desire out of dreams
of longing' (UT, 50–1).

Like too many dreams, however, the story breaks off abruptly at
just this point. The subsequent history of Gondolin might well (if
the 1920 version is any indication) have provided further oppor-
tunities for visual splendour; and perhaps for counteracting the
main weakness of the 1951 narrative, the uninterestingness of Tuor
as an active character, as distinct from a consciousness to whom
extraordinary images are revealed. Tolkien's failure to proceed with
the tale suggests, either that his impulse to write it was essentially
an urge to deliver himself of these haunting landscapes, so that the
impulse expired once the narrative reached Gondolin; or that,
confronted with the task of re-narrating the entire Gondolin story,
with its interacting, passionately motivated characters and 'political'
complexities, he recognised the limitations of the elevated style and
distanced perspective of 'The Silmarillion' and its annexes. Twenty
years earlier he had, with the writing of The Hobbit, begun to evolve
a style altogether more intimate and flexible.

The Hobbit

Tolkien's first published work of fiction (1937) is in many respects
a dry run for The Lord of the Rings, though Tolkien of course did not
conceive it as such, and it is scarcely a fifth of the length of the later
work. Its hero Bilbo Baggins, like his nephew Frodo, is a hobbit
who becomes, only half-voluntarily, engaged in a quest: the
recapture of dwarves' treasure, stolen by the dragon Smaug, who
now hoards it in the Lonely Mountain far off in the East. After a
leisurely opening at Bilbo's home in Hobbiton, the narrative is
dominated by the journey to the Mountain (a series of largely
unconnected adventures), until in the final third of the tale several
of its threads come together in a relatively complex political and
moral entanglement. The dwarves reach the Mountain after escaping
from imprisonment by the Wood-Elves, into whose kingdom they
have trespassed, and obtaining hospitality from the Men of nearby
Lake-town under their cynical Master. The dragon, aroused from
his slumbers in the Mountain by the intrusion of Bilbo and the

dwarves, is killed after devastating Lake-Town. His death leaves the dwarves in possession of the Mountain, without having done much to earn it; but both Elves and Lake-men have claims for compensation from the dragon's hoard, and both send armies to the Mountain. The dwarves' leader, Thorin Oakenshield, refuses to negotiate under threat, and summons reinforcements to defend his patrimony. Bilbo alone recognises the need for compromise, and smuggles the dwarves' priceless Arkenstone into the elves' camp to be used in bargaining. This treachery to his friends marks a pointed rejection not only of the dwarves' obsessive lust for gold, but of the heroic self-respect which underlies Thorin's refusal to negotiate with armed men at 'his' gate: for Bilbo, the unheroic aim of avoiding bloodshed comes first, and he is prepared to humiliate himself in the attempt to achieve it. An attack by goblins (the 'orcs' of *The Lord of the Rings*) fortunately unites the disputing parties just as war seems on the point of breaking out. Thorin is mortally wounded in the battle, and forgives the 'traitor' Bilbo before dying.

> 'Farewell, good thief', he said. 'I go now to the halls of waiting to sit beside my fathers, until the world is renewed. Since I leave now all gold and silver, and go where it is of little worth, I wish to part in friendship from you, and I would take back my words and deeds at the Gate.'
>
> Bilbo knelt on one knee filled with sorrow. 'Farewell, King under the Mountain!' he said. 'This is a bitter adventure, if it must end so; and not a mountain of gold can amend it. Yet I am glad that I have shared in your perils – that has been more than any Baggins deserves.'
>
> 'No!' said Thorin. 'There is more in you of good than you know, child of the kindly West. Some courage and some wisdom, blended in measure. If more of us valued food and cheer and song above hoarded gold, it would be a merrier world. But sad or merry, I must leave it now. Farewell!'
>
> Then Bilbo turned away, and he went by himself, and sat alone wrapped in a blanket, and whether you believe it or not, he wept until his eyes were red and his voice was hoarse. He was a kindly little soul. (*The Hobbit*, 243)

As the close of this extract suggests, *The Hobbit* even in its most serious moments retains the self-conscious tone of a children's book: 'whether you believe it or not' is typical of the fireside intimacies to which the narrative is prone (and which Tolkien later regretted),[17] and the deliberately naïf diction and syntax of this and the final sentence seem to wrap Bilbo in a blanket of paternal tenderness. The anti-acquisitive moral, too, is spelt out more carefully and repeatedly than an adult reader, or possibly any reader, needs. (These shortcomings are further proof that the 1938 essay 'On Fairy Stories', with its vigorous rejection of any necessary association between children and fairy-tales, represents a turning-point in Tolkien's thinking.) Yet one reason that Thorin's words about food and cheer are superfluous is that the situation has taken on a realistic moral tension that requires no underlining. Bilbo has betrayed the dwarves for good reasons, and their prior debt to him is much greater than his to them, but he has nevertheless betrayed them, and Thorin's rage has been understandable. Bilbo's remark about his own deserts is a sufficient, though oblique, apology for his 'treachery'; Thorin repents his covetousness, and each forgives the other. The dialogue is effective because (as the occasion surely demands) the forgiveness is expressed with a minimum of explicit reference to the events which have divided them: Thorin's 'good thief' initiates this blend of bluntness and indirection. (The allusion to the Gospels which some readers will discern in these words is, so to speak, optional, or accidental: the phrase describes Bilbo quite literally, especially as he has been explicitly engaged by the dwarves as a 'burglar'.) The style of both characters' declarations is at once elevated and laconic, close to that of many dialogue passages in The Lord of the Rings in which the hobbits or other speakers adapt their normal discourse to a formal or solemn occasion. The success of the episode depends upon the reader's willingness to concentrate on the thoroughly imagined situation, to allow it to validate the momentarily dignified language, and to extend a certain indulgence to the lapses into sententiousness or chattiness. Indeed, this is true of the whole work.

Catharine Stimpson calls it 'a genial, attractive book ... . The whole narrative has the lilt and zest of fresh inspiration.'[18] Admittedly, for Tolkien's hostile critics, patting The Hobbit on the head has become something of a tradition: the critic indicates a benevolent receptiveness towards 'fantasy' (when confined to the marginal world of children's books) before proceeding to ridicule the ambitious scale and implied adult readership of *The Lord of the Rings*. *The Hobbit* seems to me, on the contrary, to be a likeable patchwork of accomplishments, blunders, and tantalising promises of the Middle-earth to come: flawed by inconsistencies of tone and conception, it is essentially a transitional work, a stopping-off point on Tolkien's creative journey from the exploratory forms of bedtime story-telling to the richly 'realistic' narrative of *The Lord of the Rings*, a journey that converges in that work with the progressive abandonment of the mannered archaism of the early mythical writings.

At one level, its most characteristic, *The Hobbit* functions extremely effectively as an adventure story for children that makes no particular bid for internal realism, or for emotional or moral depth. The delightful opening chapter, in which Bilbo is simply selected out of the blue as the burglar for the dwarves' expedition, makes no attempt to disguise the *deus ex machina* role of Gandalf in getting the adventure started. The thirteen dwarves' arrival at Bag End, in unannounced groups at more or less regular intervals, is a stylised effect (a kind of burlesque of the iterative structure of fairy-tale) which Tolkien is not above repeating several chapters later. Bilbo's wild shriek of terror at Thorin's remark that 'all of us ... may never return' (23) is a piece of comic business rather than a psychologically credible response. Several subsequent episodes, such as the encounter with three ill-bred trolls, or the battle with spiders, whom Bilbo taunts with insulting names, are gripping enough but leave no impression of a serious encounter with evil: the villains lack a moral history or distinctive motive, and the forces of good triumph through superior guile, energy and luck. Each conflict is essentially a battle of wits. Even Bilbo's confrontation with Gollum by his underground pool – rewritten for the 1951 second edition, to harmonise with *The Lord of the Rings* – is maintained at this stylised level by the ritual of the Riddle-Game the two characters play. Towards the end, as we have already seen, the story modulates into a more serious key. But it concludes with a conventional and unambiguous happy ending: Bilbo returns to Bag End enriched, with memories and with gold. He has lost nothing, except his spoons and his reputation for respectability.

At times *The Hobbit* falls below, or rises above, this level. The dialogue is often under-differentiated, with figures such as Thorin and Gandalf lapsing intermittently into a bourgeois banality more appropriate to Bilbo. There are occasional narrative contrivances which revision could easily have disguised, as when Dori tells Gandalf several things he knows already – 'All of a sudden you gave one of your blinding flashes ... . You shouted "Follow me everybody!"' (84) – for the benefit of an eavesdropping Bilbo and an eavesdropping reader. The humour sometimes cuts against, rather than functioning within, the integrity of the fictional 'history': there is, for example, a particularly incongruous and laboured joke about the invention of golf (24). The notion of 'magic', largely avoided in The Lord of the Rings in favour of a putatively consistent system of powers and 'lore', is too often invoked (sometimes in the vaguest terms) in the evident hope of lending colour to a prosaic episode or passage.

On the other hand, we find from the very beginning glimpses of an exhilarating temporal and spatial scope. The fifty-year-old Bilbo, we learn in the first chapter, 'had apparently settled down immovably' at Bag End. Then, 'by some curious chance one morning long ago in the quiet of the world, when there was less noise and more green ... Gandalf came by' (13). Both sentences imply the untroubled enjoyment of wide expanses of time, an impression reinforced by the prolonged, seemingly inconsequential conversation that follows.

> 'Good morning!' said Bilbo, and he meant it. The sun was shining, and the grass was very green. But Gandalf looked at him from under long bushy eyebrows that stuck out further than the brim of his shady hat. 'What do you mean by that?' he said. 'Do you wish me a good morning, or mean that it is a good morning whether I want it or not; or that you feel good this morning; or that it is a morning to be good on?'
>
> 'All of them at once', said Bilbo. 'And a very fine morning for a pipe of tobacco out of doors, into the bargain. If you have a pipe about you, sit down and have a fill of mine! There's no hurry, we have all the day before us!' Then Bilbo sat down on a seat by his door, crossed his legs, and blew out a beautiful grey ring of smoke that sailed up in the air without breaking and floated away over the Hill. (The Hobbit, 13)

As for space, Bilbo 'loved maps, and in his hall there hung a large one of the Country Round with all his favourite walks marked on it in red ink' (26). (Tolkien provided his own maps and illustrations for The Hobbit, and these are an important part of its charm.) The many windows of Bag End overlook Bilbo's garden 'and meadows beyond, sloping down to the river' (11). For Bilbo and his neighbours the features of the local landscape are simply 'The Hill', 'The Water', 'The Country Round': beyond them is the wide blue yonder into which only the reckless venture. Tolkien is, of course, in this opening chapter building a land of heart's desire by elaborating the fairy-tale formula 'once upon a time', and adopting the perspective formed in childhood (but deeply embedded in adult consciousness) of the world as concentric circles centred upon Home. As he observes in 'On Fairy Stories', 'If a story says, "he climbed the hill and saw a river in the valley below" ... every hearer of the words will have his own picture, and it will be made out of all the hills and rivers and dales he has ever seen, but specially out of The Hill, The River, The Valley which were for him the first embodiment of the word.'[19] The insight is not especially original. What is important is the conviction with which the compositional project is carried out. Through writing The Hobbit, initially for his own children, Tolkien discovered not only the hobbit's-eye-view which humanised (if one can put it that way) his mythical vision in The Lord of the Rings, but also the concretely imagined Middle-earth of the later work, though he did not yet call it by that name and though its realisation was as yet rudimentary. The two qualities are in fact connected: the hobbits' grateful and unassuming pleasure in life, which gathers value and significance as the narratives of The Hobbit and The Lord of the Rings proceed, requires the texture of experience to be evoked as compellingly as possible. That in turn requires a plain and transparent, but flexible and sensuously alert, prose style. The simple and direct, even at times naïve and homespun, style of The Hobbit was an indispensable rehearsal for the huge narrative labour of The Lord of the Rings. The 'old castles with an evil look, as if they had been built by wicked people' which Bilbo sees on the 'dreary hills' of the Lone-lands (34) may represent only the faintest inkling of Isengard or the tower of Minas Morgul;

but in phrases and sentences a paragraph later the mature style can be seen beginning to emerge.

> It was after tea-time; it was pouring with rain, and had been all day; his hood was dripping into his eyes, his cloak was full of water; the pony was tired and stumbled on stones ... . Somewhere behind the grey clouds, the sun must have gone down, for it began to get dark as they went down into a deep valley with a river at the bottom. Wind got up, and willows along its banks bent and sighed. (The Hobbit, 34–5)

Later Poetry

Just as the development of Tolkien's fiction has two starting-points – in the mythical and legendary matter developed during his twenties, and in the intimate paternal story-telling of his thirties – so there are two dominant strands to his work as a poet. The ambitious introspective lyricism of his youth soon gives way to a modest willingness to turn out relaxed, homely verse, often marked by what he himself called 'a very simple sense of humour, which even my sympathetic critics find tiresome'.[20]

> The lonely Troll he sat on a stone
> and sang a mournful lay:
> 'O why, O why must I live on my own
> In the hills of Faraway?
> ('Perry-the-Winkle', ll. 1–4)

This is a long way from the 'golden-rondured moons with glorious face' of the early 'Kortirion among the Trees'. But the convergence of two styles into a mature masterpiece never happened with the poetry – or rather, it is only within, and in sub-servience to, the fiction that the verse achieves complete effectiveness. Most of Tolkien's best verse after 'The Lay of Leithian' – as well as a little of his worst – is in the songs and rhymes of The Lord of the Rings itself. In context, experienced strictly as the utterances of characters, or of cultures, these are generally apt and sometimes moving; they are, nevertheless, a second-order achievement. To speak bluntly of 'pastiche' would be unfair, since whatever the debt owed by Rohan to Anglo-Saxon culture (not least for alliterative verse), or by the Shire to a half-remembered, half-idealised rural England, Tolkien himself created, through the prose narrative, the imaginary cultural traditions to which the verses are assigned. But the outstanding feature of the verse in The Lord of the Rings is the individuation of poetic styles to suit the expressive needs of a given character or narrative moment: the Barrow-Wight's bleak incantation; the comic-funereal rhythm of Gollum's 'The cold hard lands / They bites our hands' (TT, 227); the Ents' marching song; the Eagle's psalm-like song of rejoicing after the fall of Sauron; the Elves' hymns and Dwarves' chants; the robust spondees, and sprightly trochees and dactyls, of Bombadil's song-speech; the variously comic and ruminative and joyful verses of the hobbits. Tolkien's romantic lyricism finds, at times, memorable outlets.

> O slender as a willow-wand! O clearer than clear water!
> O reed by the living pool! Fair river-daughter!
> O spring-time and summer-time, and spring again after!
> O wind on the waterfall, and the leaves' laughter!
>
> (FR, 135)

> O stars that in the Sunless Year
>   With shining hand by her were sown,
> In windy fields now bright and clear
>   We see your silver blossom blown!
>
> (FR, 89)

Geoffrey Russom has shown how Tolkien, by avoiding iambic pentameter, the staple of modern English verse, in favour of an extraordinary diversity of rhythmical structures, creates one distinctive characterising or lyrical effect after another.[21] Even the best passages, however, would hardly stand displacement from their narrative context: we need first to imagine a world in which they might be sung, or exclaimed, with complete fitness and without irony. Indeed of all the poems in The Lord of the Rings, only one, Bilbo's 'I sit beside the fire' (FR, 291–2) would, I think, survive independently.[22] A serene, understated poem about old age and the regretful acceptance of transience, it would be a better candidate for the role of 'Bilbo's Last Song' than the banal, technically inept verses published under that title after Tolkien's death. Other verses in *The Lord of the Rings* are less persuasive, even in context: at times an incongruous suggestion of popular-song cliché intrudes. The lowest point (perhaps) is reached with the Ent Bregalad's

> O rowan mine, I saw you shine upon a summer's day …
> Your crown is spilled, your voice is stilled for ever and a day.
>
> (TT, 87)

Tolkien excels, as I argued in chapter 2, in restoring vitality to simple phrases, but in the absence of sharp ambient detail to give the image of 'a summer's day' definition (all we are offered is the equally routine 'your rind so bright, your leaves so light, your voice so cool and soft'), the phrase simply appears as a predictable sequel to the reach-me-down rhyme that precedes it. 'For ever and a day' is a scarcely redeemable cliché, and its woolliness is a misjudgement in a work which seeks to make imaginatively plausible long expanses of time: compare Legolas' 'beneath the Sun all things must wear to an end at last' (FR, 405).

The Adventures of Tom Bombadil, the 1962 collection in which 'Perry-the-Winkle' appears, is further evidence of the dependence of Tolkien's best verse on a fully developed narrative setting. The poems, with one exception, are effective only in so far as one can imagine them (as a brief, mock-scholarly Preface suggests) as hobbit verse, the product of a rustic culture. (Three of the sixteen poems are in fact reprinted unaltered from *The Lord of the Rings*.) 'Perry-the-Winkle', the unserious tale of a hobbit's instruction in cooking by an avuncular Troll desperate for company, is quite enjoyable in that light, especially in the unabashedly comic reading recorded by Tolkien towards the end of his life; the title poem also fares well in his own performance.[23] It is much harder to imagine the hobbits relishing the encounter of 'Little Princess Mee' with her reflection ('Princess Shee') in a poem technically fluent but indebted for its imagery to the conventional fairyland of the nursery. 'Cat' ('The fat cat on the mat / may seem to dream / of nice mice that suffice / for him, or cream') is even more plainly an alien creature introduced by the scruff of its neck. Both poems are self-enclosed by an all too obvious 'point', whereas the charm of 'Perry-the-Winkle' is its inconsequential detail, its quality of being an anecdote from a wider history.

'The Sea-Bell', praised by Auden though not by Tolkien himself,[24] is a success of a different kind. Several of Tolkien's poems, from the early 'Eärendel' verses, through 'The Happy Mariners' (published 1923, revised about 1940) to 'Imram' (published 1955),[25] deal in various guises with the theme of a sea-voyage which brings a glimpse, but only a glimpse, of a paradisal realm. 'The Sea-Bell' is the most memorable of them, as well as the darkest. The solitary narrator travels eagerly in an enchanted boat to a remote, beautiful land, is shunned by its mysterious people, brings disaster on himself by hubristically proclaiming himself 'king' of the land, and returns home in despair and bereavement, to find himself shunned by his fellow men as well. The poem may be read as an allegory of the loneliness and discouragement which are the destiny of a fallen (and therefore imperfectly creative) being who aspires to full creative power, and is ultimately stranded between two worlds, that of the fulfilled imagination and that of the earthbound multitude. Technically the poem is one of Tolkien's most distinctive, drawing upon his skill in both stress-based alliterative verse and rhymed stanzaic structures: there is a regular pattern of end-rhyme and internal rhyme in groups of four four-stress lines, a fluid mix of end-stopping and enjambment with caesuras, and occasional grace-notes of alliteration or additional internal rhyme.

> There was echo of song all the evening long
>   down in the valley; many a thing
> running to and fro; hares white as snow,
>   voles out of holes; moths on the wing
> with lantern-eyes; in quiet surprise
>   brocks were staring out of dark doors.
> I heard dancing there, music in the air,
>   feet going quick on the green floors.
> But wherever I came it was ever the same:
>   the feet fled, and all was still;
> never a greeting, only the fleeting
>   pipes, voices, horns on the hill.
>   (ll. 45–56)

The poignant incompleteness of our perception of beauty, intimated at moments in The Lord of the Rings, is suggested with unusual directness here, and still more in the despondent final lines of the poem. If the allegorical reading is correct, imagination (that of the ordinary person as well as that of the creative writer) appears rather as a curse than as a gift. However, Tolkien at other times viewed the human imagination more positively. 'The Sea-Bell' might be seen as a melancholy counterpart to 'Mythopoeia', begun in 1931 and first published in full in 1988, in which Tolkien robustly justifies myth-making as a right retained by human beings despite their fall:

> Though all the crannies of the world we filled
> with elves and goblins, though we dared to build
> gods and their houses out of dark and light,
> and sowed the seed of dragons, 'twas our right
> (used or misused). The right has not decayed.
> We make still by the law in which we're made.
> ('Mythopoeia', ll. 65–70, Tree and Leaf, 99)

Our creative work may be 'impure and scanty', but it partakes of truth because the capacity for 'sub-creation' is among the Creator's endowments out of himself to men: this lesser creativity, which cannot give being to its productions, just as the Ainur of The Silmarillion need Ilúvatar's 'Let these things Be!' to give life to their vision of the unfolding World, is still in its essence divine. The poem concludes with a vision of Paradise, where

> though they make anew, they make no lie.
> Be sure they still will make, not being dead,
> and poets shall have flames upon their head,
> and harps whereon their faultless fingers fall:
> there each shall choose for ever from the All.
> (ll. 144–8)

For all the transcendental vision, and occasional lyricism, of 'Mythopoeia', its iambic couplets suggest Pope, and in more discursive parts of the poem the resemblance is clearer: once again, there is at least a suggestion of pastiche. Outside Middle-earth,

Tolkien never found a distinctive personal voice for poetry, and a collection of his more attractive poems would be stylistically very diverse. To those already mentioned one might add two short poems which are, in slightly different senses, translations: 'To W.H.A.', the modern English version of his own Anglo-Saxon poem in celebration of Auden's sixtieth birthday, a warm and dignified piece;[26] and 'Gawain's Leave-taking', an affecting and grateful farewell-to-life adapted from an anonymous fourteenth-century poem, and appended in 1979 to Tolkien's translations of 'Sir Gawain and the Green Knight', 'Pearl' and 'Sir Orfeo'.[27]

Two longer poems are in the nature of pseudo-translations. 'The Lay of Aotrou and Itroun', published in *The Welsh Review* in 1945, tells of a Breton king tormented by his childlessness. He resorts to the aid of a witch's potion; after his wife gives birth to twins, he is ensnared by the witch (now an alluring fay) while hunting in the forest, and she demands his love as the reward he has promised. He rejects her, despite a threat that he will die within three days if he returns to his castle. He does die, after a hideous dream-vision of the witch, and his wife dies of grief. The moral, evidently, is the necessity of accepting even bitter disappointment at the hands of God's providence. Technically the verse is well executed, though it has little of the lyrical sweetness achieved in parts of 'The Lay of Leithian'. Its greatest strength is its sympathetic evocation of the troubled Aotrou's changing moods.

> At last he slept in weary sleep
> beside his wife, and dreaming deep,
> he walked with children yet unborn
> in gardens fair, until the morn
> came slowly through the windows tall,
> and shadows moved across the wall.
> Then sprang the day with weather fair,
> for windy rain had washed the air,
> and blue and cloudless, clean and high,
> above the hills was arched the sky,
> and foaming in the northern breeze
> beneath the sky there shone the seas.
> (ll. 99–110, *Welsh Review*, IV, 4, p.256)

The poem could easily stand alongside Tolkien's version of the late medieval poem 'Sir Orfeo', which deals more optimistically with a theme of marital love and bewitchment, and is similar in length and versification: one would hardly know which was the translation and which the original poem, except for a certain sensuous precision, distinctive of Tolkien, in 'Aotrou and Itroun', and exemplified by the moving shadows and rain-washed air of the passage just quoted. Its devout conclusion – a prayer to be kept 'from evil rede and from despair' until we come 'to joy of Heaven where is queen / the maiden Mary pure and clean' – is precisely comparable to those of 'Sir Orfeo', 'Pearl' or 'Sir Gawain'. Pastiche though it be, 'Aotrou and Itroun' deserves a more accessible and appropriate setting: its tetrameter couplets, in the style of 'The Lay of Leithian', look rather incongruous amid slice-of-life narratives and articles on the economic development of Wales. But its deliberate medievalising gives it a certain impersonality. Similarly, the alliterative dialogue 'The Homecoming of Beorhtnoth Beorhthelm's Son' (published in 1953 in *Essays and Studies*) is a kind of annex to the unfinished Anglo-Saxon poem' The Battle of Maldon' – indeed it is enclosed within a prose commentary on that poem and its implications. The historical Duke Beorhtnoth, facing a Viking host across a river with an easily defensible causeway, chivalrously allowed the enemy to cross unhindered, in order to fight on equal terms. As a result, he and the greater part of his army were slaughtered. Tolkien's essay highlights the lines in which the poem rebukes Beorhtnoth for his 'overmastering pride': only for the defence of his people against a savage enemy, he suggests, could Beorhtnoth have justified risking his subordinates' lives. His heroic gesture was reprehensible in a leader, however much the last stand by his bodyguard (after he himself had been killed) is to be admired. 'It is the heroism of obedience and love not of pride or wilfulness that is the most heroic and the most moving ... even if it is enshrined in verse no better than "The Charge of the Light Brigade"' (*Essays and Studies*, 1953, p.16). In Tolkien's verse dialogue, two Saxon soldiers arrive late at the battlefield, and bear away Beorhtnoth's huge (though headless) body; the younger, Torhthelm, breaks into elegiac chanting, but soon finds the weight of Beorhtnoth's corpse oppressive.

Torhthelm: Now mourn ever
Saxon and English, from the sea's margin
to the western forest! The wall is fallen,
women are weeping; the wood is blazing
and the fire flaming as a far beacon.
Build high the barrow his bones to keep ...
Glory loved he; now glory earning
his grave shall be green, while ground or sea,
while word or woe in the world lasteth ...

Dead men drag earthward. Now down a spell!
My back's broken, and the breath has left me.

      Tidwald: If you spent less in speech, you would speed better.
                           (ll.132–7, 145–7, 159–61)

The older Tidwald keeps rubbing in the disparity between the idealised heroism of the lays and the brutishness of battle itself. As for the great Beorhtnoth, Tidwald breaks the news of his folly to Torhthelm, who expects to find a pile of slain Northmen at the river-crossing. 'He let them cross the causeway, so keen was he / to give minstrels matter for mighty songs' (ll. 254–5). 'The Homecoming of Beorhtnoth', at times almost as difficult to obtain as 'Aotrou and Itroun',[28] likewise deserves to remain in print, for it illuminates Tolkien's complex and ambivalent attitude to heroism, though it belongs, with the accompanying prose commentary, rather among the monuments of his distinctively humane scholarship than among his important works as a creative artist.

Shorter Fiction

At various times Tolkien produced fiction which lies outside the narrative history of Middle-earth. The earliest examples arose, like *The Hobbit*, in the context of family story-telling: indeed, so personal are they that they only appeared after Tolkien's death, when the insatiable public appetite for his work made even the publication of his 'Father Christmas Letters' to his children (with expensively reproduced illustrations) commercially viable.[29] Not that the *Letters* (written between 1920 and 1939, and published in 1976) lack charm, but it is at least partly derived from the reader's awareness that publication was never intended: we look through both text and pictures, and participate vicariously in the delight of the original recipients, and of the author. The experience could have been an embarrassment, but for the Letters' absolute freedom from Wendyish sentiment or moral earnestness: the personages of Father Christmas's household and workshop are comically ineffectual and obstreperous, and one feels that the infant readers are expected to recognise this: there is no smiling over the heads of the children. The later Letters reach out occasionally and tentatively towards Middle-earth: tunnel-dwelling, bat-riding goblins attack the North Pole, and one of Father Christmas's elves is called 'Ilbereth', but both elves and goblins are conventionally diminutive.

The playful tone is shared by a more complex story, *Roverandom*, conceived on a family holiday in 1925, developed in 1927 and again in the mid-1930s, and finally published in 1998.[30] One can see why the story was rejected by Allen & Unwin in 1937: this tale of the adventures of a toy dog, lost on a beach by Tolkien's five-year-old son, is ramblingly digressive and episodic, and as diversely allusive as 'The Waste Land'. (The Isle of Dogs, for example, appears in both.) One is initially tempted simply to quarry it for hints of Tolkien's other writings: its various crotchety wizards or near-wizards; its dragons and spiders; its dream-travel; its sudden epiphanies of enchanted flora and fauna and 'faint thin music' (28), reminiscent of 'The Sea-Bell', Lúthien's glade, or the woods of Lothlórien. Roverandom himself is the earliest of Tolkien's reluctant travellers: unlike Bilbo Baggins, however, he remains predominantly passive, a lonely consciousness to whom (mainly) alarming and (occasionally) delightful things happen. This unexpectedness is also a feature of the prose: individual passages spring too many surprises, of image, language or logic, for fluent bedtime reading, and an attempt to digest the whole 80-page narrative at a sitting can lead to weariness. Yet there is an underlying *Odyssey*-like structure of exile, wandering and return, and there is also a pervasive mood which continually comes through the jokes and the stream-of-consciousness invention: the mood of the truthful parent, conscious of the need both to remind the children that the world is a dangerous, baffling place, governed by severe necessities and by the caprice of the powerful, and to reassure them.

> They saw all kinds of queer things, and had many adventures – perfectly safe, of course, with the Man-in-the-Moon close at hand. That was just as well, as there were lots of nasty creepy things in the bogs that would otherwise have grabbed the little dog quick. The dark side was as wet as the white side was dry, and full of the most extraordinary plants and creatures, which I would tell you about, if Roverandom had taken any particular notice of them. But he did not; he was thinking of the garden and the little boy.
>
> At last they came to the grey edge, and they looked past the cinder valleys where many of the dragons lived, through a gap in the mountains to the great white plain and the shining cliffs. They saw the world rise, a pale green and gold moon, huge and round above the shoulders of the Lunar Mountains; and Roverandom thought: 'That's where my little boy lives!' It seemed a terrible and enormous way away.
>
> 'Do dreams come true?' he asked.
>
> 'Some of mine do', said the old man. 'Some, but not all; and seldom any of them straight away, or quite like they were in dreaming them.'
> (*Roverandom*, 46)

Mr Bliss, written and drawn in the mid-1930s, has greater economy and a more euphoric atmosphere, as well as a greater degree of independence from the family Tolkien (though one suspects certain characters of being derived from living, or stuffed, models). None of the characters is virtuous or dignified. Mr Bliss keeps the house-high Girabbit in his garden a secret because he does not want to pay the licence money. Herbert Dorkins swallows a beetle in his soup. The three bears are hospitable, but light-fingered and greedy: they eat all the Dorkins' cabbages, and play alarming practical jokes. The story is replete with collisions, breakages, and public disputations. The humour has the quality of self-confident absurdity which is achieved by subjecting adult practices to a child's perspective, and a child's freedom in narrative sequence.

> After breakfast Mr Bliss put on his green top hat, because the Girabbit said it was going to be a fine day.
>
> Then he said: 'I will go and buy a motor-car!'

So he got on his bicycle, and rode down the hill to the village.

He walked into the shop, and said: 'I want a motor-car!'

'What colour?' said Mr Binks. 'Bright yellow', said Mr Bliss, 'inside and out.'

'That will be five shillings', said Mr Binks.

'And I want red wheels', said Mr Bliss.

'That will be sixpence more.'

'Very well', said Mr Bliss; 'only I have left my purse at home.'

'Very well, then you will have to leave your bicycle here; and when you bring your money you can have it back.'

It was a beautiful bicycle, all silver – but it had no pedals, because Mr Bliss only rode down hill. (Mr Bliss, 7–8)

At least half the effect of Mr Bliss is derived from the author's quaint, amateur, occasionally beautiful drawings. Tolkien's limited skill in depicting the human figure leads him in many of his pictures and illustrations to a somewhat apologetic marginalisation of figures, in favour of landscape. But in the comic context of Mr Bliss, the awkward postures become almost a virtue: Mr Bliss's stiff-jointed grasp of his steering-wheel matches his dialogue, suggests his insecure control of the machine, and forms a satisfyingly oblique angle with his absurdly tall, backward-tilted hat.

In Farmer Giles of Ham, written in the mid-1930s and finally published after some revision in 1949, Tolkien maintains a more sophisticated comic tone, though there are traces of the deliberately abrupt simplicity of Mr Bliss. ('Farmer Giles had a dog. The dog's name was Garm' (p. 2).) The plot, recounting Giles's reluctant defence of his neighbours against a giant and a dragon, is handled with scholarly irony: there are learned jokes, including an attributed quotation from the 'Four Wise Clerks of Oxenford' (i.e. the OED). Where The Hobbit hesitates at times, especially in dialogue, between anachronistic humour and an approach to high seriousness, the shorter Farmer Giles is more consistent: the dragon Chrysophylax talks throughout like a shifty businessman, and never switches, as Smaug memorably but anomalously does, into heroic diction. Both Giles' antagonists are easily cowed, and his own heroism consists mainly in being not quite such a coward as everyone else. Indeed the tale's perception of human nature is, throughout, that of comedy: Giles' neighbours eagerly load all responsibility on to his shoulders, the King pays his bills in promissory notes and then devalues them, and his knights, who avoid serious fighting and prefer discussing the latest fashion in hats, pretend not to notice the compliments Giles receives. This consistency of tone and perspective makes *Farmer Giles* a more completely accomplished work than *The Hobbit*, but its world lacks the amplitude and openness of the latter's: the text is well matched by Pauline Baynes's stylised, fluid, mock-medieval drawings, with their flattened planes and compressed perspectives. Only at the margins of the work can one discern the Tolkienian yearning for space.

> People were richly endowed with names in those days, when this island was still happily divided into many kingdoms. There was more time then … . The time was not one of hurry or bustle. But bustle has very little to do with business. Men did their work without it; and they got through a great deal both of work and of talk. (*Farmer Giles*, 1–2)

Actually the story itself bustles, or at least speeds, along, as its comic mode requires, and there is a minimum of lingering over landscape, over dialogue, or over the detail of village or court life. Perhaps this nostalgia for a supposedly leisured past is an occupational hazard for busy writers, especially when engaged on huge projects: George Eliot in an early chapter of *Middlemarch* looks back to the days of Fielding, 'when summer afternoons were spacious, and the clock ticked slowly in the winter evenings';[31] and John Fowles in *The French Lieutenant's Woman* makes a similar comment about the days of George Eliot.[32] At all events, the insufficiency of time for the creative artist is a principal theme of Tolkien's next story, 'Leaf by Niggle', written around 1943. The story is a Christian allegory with a strong element of autobiography. Niggle is an amateur painter, conscious that he will soon have to make a long and alarming journey. He resents the distractions (especially the moral obligation to assist his lame neighbour, Mr Parish) which delay progress on his huge canvas, an elaborate painting of a Tree amid a wide landscape. But his own fits of idleness, his ever-expanding design, and his tendency to dwell lovingly on the details of individual leaves, also contribute to his failure to finish the picture. Fairly obviously, the Tree is The Lord of the Rings (or perhaps the whole history of Arda), the dilatory and unsystematic working habits are Tolkien's, and the feared journey is death. (Tolkien would have been a little over fifty at the time of composition.)

The later part of the story accepts the likelihood of temporal failure, and affirms the hope that the incomplete sub-creation may be fulfilled in heaven. When Niggle, having caught a fever while performing an errand for Parish, is whisked away on his journey (leaving his uncompleted canvas to be requisitioned for patching flood-damaged houses) he finds himself in a purgatorial 'Workhouse Infirmary', where he expiates the niggling reluctance of his moral life by hard work, bitter medicine, and contemplation in the dark. He is released at last into a beautiful countryside, which he comes to recognise as his own painting, complete with Tree, Forest and Mountains, and given reality, though requiring further touches to complete it. Parish arrives with his gardening skills (previously scorned by Niggle, as Parish scorned Niggle's art) and the two collaborate in perfecting the landscape. Loving one's neighbour and creating beauty, activities disjoined in the fallen world, are united.

The execution of 'Leaf by Niggle', especially the management of the allegory at a local level, is at times laboured or ingenuous. The doctors in the Workhouse Infirmary, we learn, keep Niggle at his work of carpentry and painting boards for a long time. 'They may have been waiting for him to get better, and judging better by some odd medical standard of their own' (Tree and Leaf, p. 84). The word 'odd' draws attention to a non-literal intent which is all too obvious anyway; and the quibble on 'better' suggests lack of confidence in the vehicle of the allegory. Lying in the darkness of the Workhouse, Niggle, not unlike the Ancient Mariner, hears a severe 'First Voice' and a gentle 'Second Voice' (God the Father and God the Son?) discussing his fate. Later, when Parish thanks Niggle for putting in a word for him and hastening his liberation from the Workhouse, Niggle says 'No. You owe it to the Second Voice. ...We both do' (p. 91). It is all a little pious and self-conscious. A coda, in which the insignificance of the late Niggle is discussed by Messrs Tompkins, Atkins and Perkins, gives Tolkien the opportunity for some robust, but decidedly unsubtle, satire against utilitarian, and totalitarian, attitudes.

> 'I think he was a silly little man', said Councillor Tompkins. 'Worthless, in fact; no use to Society at all. ... I dare say he could have been made into a serviceable cog of some sort, if you schoolmasters knew your business. But you don't, and so we get useless people of his sort. If I ran this country I should put him and his like to some job that they're fit for, washing dishes in a communal kitchen or something, and I would see that they did it properly.' (Tree and Leaf, 93–4)

Atkins demurs, but half-heartedly. Irritation, even despondency, are detectable not far below the surface. 'Leaf by Niggle', like 'Mythopoeia' and 'On Fairy Stories' with which it is combined in Tree and Leaf, shows Tolkien doggedly thinking through the difficulty, given his own temperament and the conditions of modern life, of realising his creative vision, and determining nonetheless to press on, in the belief that authentic sub-creation must have spiritual value even if it turns out to be, in the temporal world, defeated by circumstance or rejected by an inhospitable culture. ('I bow not yet before the Iron Crown / nor cast my own small golden sceptre down', as he puts it rather too grandly in 'Mythopoeia'.) Thinking is perhaps the operative word: the intellect predominates in these texts, and deeper imaginative resources are scarcely tapped. The composition of 'Leaf by Niggle', Carpenter points out,[33] coincided with a barren period during work on The Lord of the Rings; after finishing the story, Tolkien recovered confidence, and moved on to write the powerfully imagined journey of Frodo and Sam to Mordor.

None of the shorter works of fiction so far discussed can compare in interest with The Hobbit, let alone The Lord of the Rings. In 1965, however, at the age of 73, Tolkien produced his last complete story, Smith of Wootton Major, in which many of the themes and images of his work converge. Despite its brevity (fewer than 10,000 words) it is arguably his best work, apart from The Lord of the Rings, and his most nearly perfect. Neither paraphrase nor quotation can really begin to suggest its beauty – it must be read through, preferably at a sitting, and preferably in an edition using Pauline Baynes's illustrations which, especially in facial expression and gesture, evoke a grave, tender and melancholy mood far removed from that of *Farmer Giles of Ham.*

Smith deals, like some earlier works, with the acquisition, and then the loss, of imaginative power and joy. The boy Smith (as he will be called) swallows at a Feast, without knowing it, a 'fay-star', which has been introduced into the Great Cake, baked every twenty-four years in Wootton Major, by the mysterious apprentice the Master Cook has brought back from a journey. His enchantment recalls Tolkien's earlier attempt, in the contemporary setting of the unfinished 'The Lost Road', to evoke an adolescent's rapturous vision of the sanctity of the world; but whereas in that work the presence of the sympathetically observing father engenders a certain self-consciousness ('young Alboin' is seen through a sophisticated, donnish intelligence), in *Smith* the boy is alone: and the style is serenely simple.

> The Feast had been in mid-winter, but it was now June, and the night was hardly dark at all. The boy got up before dawn, for he did not wish to sleep: it was his tenth birthday. He looked out of the window, and the world seemed quiet and expectant. A little breeze, cool and fragrant, stirred the waking trees. Then the dawn came, and far away he heard the dawn-song of the birds beginning, growing as it came towards him, until it rushed over him, filling all the land round the house, and passed on like a wave of music into the West, as the sun rose above the rim of the world.
>
> 'It reminds me of Faery,' he heard himself say; 'but in Faery the people sing too'. Then he began to sing, high and clear, in strange words that he seemed to know by heart; and in that moment the star fell out of his mouth and he caught it in his open hand. It was bright silver now, glistening in the sunlight; but it quivered and rose a little, as if it was about to fly away. Without thinking he clapped his hand to his head, and there the star stayed in the middle of his forehead, and he wore it for many years. (*Smith of Wootton Major*, 19–20)

Smith becomes a maker of beautiful objects, for use and for ornament; and the star gives him entry to the regions of Faery, conceived here as a great continent of inexhaustible scope (especially by comparison with the mortal world, which is essentially represented simply by the village, and that in turn largely by the Hall, the Kitchen and the Forge). In brief but poignantly imagined episodes we are given the impression of a world of heart's desire (and terror) wide as Middle-earth: the Tree of 'Leaf by Niggle' is here, 'springing up, tower upon tower, into the sky, and its light was like the sun at noon; and it bore at once leaves and flowers and fruits uncounted, and not one was the same as any other that grew on the Tree' (28); and Smith's encounter, in the Vale of Evermore, with a young maiden with flowing hair and kilted skirt distantly recalls the meeting of Beren and Lúthien. 'There they danced together, and for a while he knew what it was to have the swiftness and the power and the joy to accompany her. For a while' (33). The nostalgic erotic suggestion is delicate, but it is unmistakeable. The Faery of Smith of Wootton Major is more than an allegory of the creative imagination – or, if you prefer, it is a more complete allegory thereof: it represents, in sad but grateful retrospect, the inner emotional life, of youthful hope and yearning, and mature energy and passion, out of which art is born. At the same time creative vision is ideally reconciled with moral value ('Leaf by Niggle' having explored the implications of a conflict between them). Smith serves the village, as artist and toolmaker, the more effectively because of his 'gift'; and he is a loving husband and father: his dalliance with the kilted maiden in Faery (who turns out also to be the Queen of Faery) is not perceived as infidelity to his wife Nell in Wootton, for the former, in both her incarnations, represents the inward images of the feminine (the *anima*, to borrow a Jungian term) which are both drawn from, and inform, a man's relationships with women. The keynote of Smith's behaviour to women is 'courtesy' (understood as an emotional, in the deepest sense erotic, disposition, not as a matter of formal gestures): his awed and blissful deference to the Queen, in an encounter which suggests at once the intimacy of mother and child and the epiphany of a goddess before a mortal, is consistent with his first action in the story, when as a boy at the Feast he gives the girl Nell beside him the silver coin he has found in his slice of Cake, because 'she looked so disappointed at finding nothing lucky in hers' (19).

In Wootton Major, we are told in the first paragraph, 'a fair number of folk lived, good, bad and mixed, as is usual' (5). Unlike the Shire, whose inhabitants are human beings morally enhanced ('no hobbit has ever killed another on purpose in the Shire'), and unlike the Little Kingdom of *Farmer Giles of Ham*, whose inhabitants, Giles and the parson apart, are human beings with their wisdom and heroism left out, Wootton is to be taken, morally speaking, as our own human world. The sceptical view of human insight and motive which the earlier stories reveal is given expression here too, in the figure of the self-promoted Cook Nokes, with his contemptuous tinselly notions of the 'fairylike'. And Smith says little, except to his family, of his journeys into Faery, because 'too many had become like Nokes' (22). The Great Hall in which meetings, feasts and family gatherings take place – not merely, I think, a narrow allegory of the Church, but a material and aesthetic symbol of a community's sense of itself as belonging to a history which transcends individual lives – is used by most of the villagers, but restored and preserved in its full beauty only by a few. However, the underlying exasperation of *Farmer Giles* and 'Leaf by Niggle' has given way to benevolent acceptance: Nokes is allowed to dismiss as a dream his terrible confrontation with the King of Faery, who grants his wish to be made thin again; and it is Nokes's great-grandson who inherits the star when Smith relinquishes it. For the story ends in 'bereavement': the word itself is used (39), and Tolkien used it again in a letter about the work to Roger Lancelyn Green.[34] Returning from his last journey into Faery, Smith tells his son he has walked 'all the way from Daybreak to Evening' (49), and a little later remarks of his grandson that 'his time has not yet come for the counting of days … and of weeks, and of months, and of years' (51). In this last work, Tolkien reaches back to the youthful source of his own vision, the perception of a world opening inexhaustibly before us in space and time.

FOUR

Tolkien and the Twentieth Century

I

A t the beginning of 1900, John Ronald Reuel Tolkien, aged exactly eight, was living with his widowed mother and younger brother in a brick cottage in Sarehole, a tiny Warwickshire village. Though it was only four miles from the industrial centre of Birmingham, Sarehole, with its nearby farms, its mill by the riverside, its willow-trees, its pool with swans, its dell with blackberries, was a serene, quasi-rural enclave, an obvious model-to-be for certain aspects of Hobbiton and the Shire. The Tolkiens had been there for three and a half years – a long age from the perspective of a young child. In many respects it might be called a pre-modern world: the mill was driven by a water-wheel (though it also contained a steam-engine) and, as Tolkien recalls in the Foreword to *The Lord of the Rings*, 'motor-cars were rare objects (I had never seen one)' (FR, 8). But 1900 saw an important, and disruptive, change in Tolkien's life. In September he became a pupil at a school in the city centre, and as a result the family moved shortly afterwards to the inner district of Moseley, conveniently near to the tram route. It would have been too difficult, and too expensive, for Tolkien to travel daily from Sarehole.

King Edward's School, Birmingham was (and is) a day school with a scholarly tradition, not the residential hothouse sometimes represented by the English 'public school' and experienced and loathed by Tolkien's friend C. S. Lewis. It stood close to the railway station, New Street. Unlike many twentieth-century English writers, educated in the country, or at least amid secluded courtyards, gardens and playing fields, Tolkien acquired his first ten years of formal education (for he remained at King Edward's, with a brief intermission, until 1911) in a soot-blackened building with a prospect of railway lines and factory chimneys. When the house in Moseley was scheduled for demolition, to make way for a new fire-station, the Tolkiens moved to another house, in Kings Heath: it too overlooked a railway line.

Much has been made, rightly, of the significance of the idyllic Sarehole years for Tolkien's imaginative development; Sarehole Mill houses a small museum, from which the determined tourist can pursue a 'Tolkien Trail'.[1] But it is at least of symbolic interest (and easily overlooked by readers determined to detach Tolkien from his times) that his intellectually formative years were spent in the busy, noisy, polluted, capitalist-nonconformist atmosphere of Joseph Chamberlain's Birmingham; it is as if an American writer of the same generation had been schooled and domiciled in, say, Chicago. If Tolkien was hostile to industrialism, and to the lifestyles and landscapes it generated, it was at any rate a hostility based on a reasonable degree of acquaintance. One American critic writes of Tolkien as belonging to the 'aristocratic academic conservative tradition';[2] but 'aristocratic' is a retrospective distortion, based perhaps on a misguided notion of the social exclusivity and prestige of Oxford professorships. Tolkien's social origins were (impover-ished) middle-class; and the circumstances of his upbringing and education were poorer and more dispiritingly 'urban' than those of almost any, except D. H. Lawrence, of the major English-language writers of the first half of the century.

In *Remembrance of Things Past*, Proust's boy-narrator imagines his favourite novelist, Bergotte (partly based on Anatole France) to be, as the cadences of his prose seem to imply, a frail, melancholy old man, 'the sweet singer with the snowy locks'; he is later discon-certed to encounter a youngish, black-haired, garrulous man with a nose like a snail who turns out to be none other than – Bergotte.[3] Those (like myself) who encountered *The Hobbit* and *The Lord of the Rings* during the years of the author's retirement, and associated the pre-modern world of Middle-earth only with photographs of an elderly Oxford professor, are liable to a similar misconception. Tolkien's very success in giving imaginative authenticity to Middle-earth has encouraged a perception of its author as an unworldly figure, eternally aged like Gandalf, brooding over his creation and possessed of no additional interests, except the study of Anglo-Saxon. (Which of us, for example, until it was revealed in a recent biography, would have imagined 'The Master of Middle-earth' playing squash?)[4] Tolkien's 'life and times' spanned almost three-quarters of the twentieth century: if we dispassionately reflect upon them, the grounds of his modernity, as well as his anti-modernity, may gradually come into view.

Tolkien was born on 3 January 1892, in Bloemfontein, South Africa. Despite the vaguely Dutch (or Afrikaans) appearance of his name to uninstructed English eyes – especially when misspelt as 'Tolkein', a common error – his parents were recent English émigrés from Birmingham. Arthur Tolkien, the writer's father, was a bank manager, who had taken up a post with the Bank of Africa in 1890; Mabel Tolkien, née Suffield, had arrived in Bloemfontein for her marriage in March 1891. The Tolkien family, clock-makers and piano manufacturers, had been in England since the eighteenth century. 'I am not a German', Tolkien wrote in his early sixties, 'though my surname is German ... I have inherited with my surname nothing that originally belonged to it in language and culture, and after 200 years the 'blood' of Saxony and Poland is probably a negligible physical ingredient.'[5] On another occasion he declared that he was more a Suffield, in other words, an Englishman of the West Midlands, than a Tolkien.[6] Nevertheless the exotic quality of both name and birthplace are not entirely irrelevant to his work: the imaginative potency of names, and the emotional impact of powerfully contrasted landscapes, are essential to his literary achievement. He created, on the one hand, an idealised rural middle England in the 'Shire'; but on the other, and beyond the boundaries of the Shire, a polyglot world wider and stranger than Europe.

The Tolkiens' residence in South Africa was brief. Within four years of her arrival Mabel Tolkien had returned on 'home leave' with her two small sons; her husband ought to have followed within months, but in February 1896 he died, still in Bloemfontein, following rheumatic fever. Mabel Tolkien lived with her sons for eight further years, in Sarehole and then Birmingham; but she too died, of diabetes, in 1904, when Tolkien was twelve. Love for a beloved person, especially for a mother in the case of a small child, and love for the place which for both of you is home, may be indissolubly associated: or so Wordsworth and Proust suggest. Tolkien's work, with its richly imagined locales, also draws profoundly upon the delight and consolation which for many people is to be found in the sense of place. Revering his mother's memory as that of a 'martyr'[7] (she had become a Catholic during her widowhood, and had suffered hostility and neglect from her Protestant family on account of this apostasy) Tolkien invested it with something of the numinous intensity which radiates from the adored, benevolent, intimately present or achingly distant, feminine figures of his work: Galadriel, Arwen, Goldberry, and, most remote of all, Varda (or Elbereth Gilthoniel), the Queen of Heaven worshipped by the Elves. The hymns they sing to her from their exile in Middle-earth, in the Elvish tongues Quenya and Sindarin, are a kind of consummation of the love of languages initially fostered in Tolkien by his mother's teaching of Latin, in the years before school and the loss of Eden.

After Mabel Tolkien's death, Tolkien and his younger brother were taken under the guardianship of a priest, Father Francis Xavier Morgan. During his teens Tolkien formed friendships with three fellow-pupils at King Edward's School: they became a self-conscious, if light-hearted, fraternity, a 'tea club' devoted to boyish intellectual discourse and debate after the school day ended. At sixteen, unknown to his schoolfriends, he formed a romantic attachment to a fellow orphan, Edith Bratt, who lived in the same Birmingham lodging-house. The romance was interrupted by the scandalised intervention of Tolkien's guardian: after enduring a three-year prohibition on all contact with Edith ('I owe all to Fr. F and so must obey')[8] Tolkien, now an Oxford undergraduate, wrote to her at midnight on his twenty-first birthday, received a reply telling him of her engagement to another man, and travelled in haste to her home in Cheltenham to win her back. Their marriage, though at times troubled, was to last fifty-five years, from 1916 until her death in 1971. If its difficulties are dimly discernible in his work, in a recurring theme of estrangement of interests between husband and wife (the Ents and Entwives in The Lord of the Rings; the late, bleak, unfinished tale 'Aldarion and Erendis'), the romance in which it was founded is also commemorated, in the tale of Beren and Lúthien (whose names appear on the Tolkiens' tombstone), and in a number of shorter works, from early poems such as 'You & Me' to the last story, Smith of Wootton Major. It undoubtedly surfaces also in The Lord of the Rings, where Elrond (in the Father Francis role) forbids Aragorn to marry Arwen unless and until he achieves the kingship: Sam Gamgee's delayed marriage to Rosie Cotton duplicates the theme at a homely level.

It was in 1911, at the mid-point of his separation from Edith, that Tolkien went up to Oxford to read Classics. After a year, his enthusiasm for the study of the northern tongues diverted him into the 'English' school, with its strongly historical and philological emphasis. The analytical skill and mastery of philological detail which gained him a First in 1915 were accompanied by an unusual emotional and imaginative response to language – or more exactly, perhaps, to languages. His belief in 'linguistic esthetic' – in the existence of distinctive qualities of beauty in the styles, especially the phonological styles, of languages, such that a person might, irrespective of his own mother-tongue, prefer one to another, as he himself preferred Finnish to French or Greek to Gaelic – sprang from his own earlier experiences: of the inexplicable fascination of Welsh place-names, glimpsed on coal-trucks in railway sidings; of the rapture induced by a first encounter with Joseph Wright's Primer of the Gothic Language. Though it may strike later linguists as an eccentric obsession, Tolkien's belief finds support in the pleasure taken by many readers in the fictional languages of Middle-earth, whose styles he evolved, in a half-intuitive, half-systematic fashion, alongside, and in intimate connection with, the development of the narrative 'history'. The oddly authentic ring of these inventions, which appear in the personal and place-names of the major works, as well as in quoted fragments, and which retain distinctive and consistent styles notwithstanding their debts to Welsh, Finnish, and other natural languages, reflects Tolkien's formidable range of philo-logical knowledge, consolidated, after his graduation, by two years' work on the New English Dictionary (1918–20). A long and distinguished academic career was to follow: five years as Reader in English Language at Leeds (1920–25); and at Oxford, twenty as Rawlinson and Bosworth Professor of Anglo-Saxon (1925–45), and fourteen more as Merton Professor of English Language and Literature (1945–59).

A further impetus to the creation of Middle-earth and its myths was given by the experience of war. Tolkien enlisted in the Lancashire Fusiliers in 1915, after taking his degree. From July to October 1916 he served, as a signalling officer, through the battle of the Somme; at length he fell victim to 'trench fever', and returned to hospital and a long convalescence in England. The ineradicable memory of a land pulverised by 'total war' is evident (though combined with images suggestive of industrial pollution, and fully absorbed into the wider imaginative geography) in the most hauntingly repellent landscapes of his work – less, perhaps, in the desert plains of Mordor than in the Dead Marshes, with their preserved corpses, half-real, half-hallucinatory, staring out of deep water; and the 'obscene graveyard' before the gates of Mordor, with its 'gasping pits and poisonous mounds', and 'pools … choked with ash and crawling muds, sickly white and grey' (TT, 239). At a still deeper level, the mingled relief and regret of the war-survivor may have played some part in reinforcing the emotional ambivalence that is so marked a feature of Tolkien's fiction. The earlier mythical writings have, as we have seen, an insistent, almost pagan, pessimism, and a surprisingly grim level of violence, which darken, indeed come close to undermining, the affirmative theistic universe they postulate. In the later work, as if a trauma has been worked through, joy and grief are more evenly and subtly interfused. Victories over the forces of evil are real victories, though rarely final; the survivors rejoice, though they do not display triumph, and we are likely to leave them, as in The Lord of the Rings, not in uncomplicated bliss or comfort, but 'filled with a sadness that was yet blessed and without bitterness' (RK, 309), as they foresee departure from a world which is at once profoundly beloved and full of peril. In a rare half-concession to the relevance of autobiography to literary creation, Tolkien acknowledges, in the Foreword to the second edition of The Lord of the Rings (FR, 7), the influence of wartime bereavement on the content of that work. It might indeed be seen in certain respects as the last work of First World War literature, published almost forty years after the war ended.

Tolkien had retained, into the period of his war service, close contact with his three schoolfriends: their genial fellowship took on a sober, eventually tragic, tone as they communicated across the theatres of war. Robert Gilson and Geoffrey Bache Smith were killed in 1916. Tolkien was later to write the Introduction to a posthumous edition of the latter's poems; and a letter from Smith to Tolkien, quoted in Carpenter's biography, in effect hands on to Tolkien the responsibility for literary creativity in the event of Smith's being 'scuppered'.[9] All four members of the group had had artistic ambitions, of varying kinds; and the deaths seem to have acted for Tolkien as an additional, quasi-moral spur to the decades-long effort by which he transformed his art from the naïve and derivative manner of the early mythological writings into the distinctive achievement of *The Lord of the Rings*. Not that Tolkien lacked ambition on his own account: as early as 1916 he had submitted a volume of poems, unsuccessfully, to the publishers Sidgwick and Jackson. In 1937, following the success of *The Hobbit* (which, ironically enough, he had not himself prized particularly highly), he submitted a variety of manuscripts to Allen & Unwin; and he was later to engage in some rather unedifying manoeuvres with the aim of inducing a publisher to take on *The Silmarillion* as part of the same package as *The Lord of the Rings*. These considerations ought finally to lay to rest the once-popular view of Tolkien as a professional scholar who stumbled, in a fit of absence of mind, into writing fiction in middle age: a view which readily leads to the tendency to interpret the fiction as a version of the scholarship. The evidence suggests that Tolkien's literary ambitions were at least as deep-rooted as his academic ones. *The Lord of the Rings* was no bolt from the blue: the writer who began it a fortnight before his forty-sixth birthday had already a quarter-century of work behind him. If long perseverance in solitude, without public encouragement, is any proof of resolute ambition, no twentieth-century literary career was more ambitiously planned than Tolkien's.

In his productive middle years, his forties and fifties, Tolkien led a busy and demanding life. He was a family man, the father of four children (the youngest born in 1929), and (as C. S. Lewis put it, though this to some extent reflects Lewis's particular perspective) 'a man of cronies rather than general society'.[10] He belonged to the 'Inklings', the informal circle of mainly Christian scholars and writers, centred on Lewis himself, which met twice weekly in Oxford through much of the Thirties and Forties. The Tuesday lunchtimes and Thursday evenings evidently contributed something to the tension within Tolkien's marriage, a tension further complicated by Edith Tolkien's hostile attitude to her husband's Catholicism, which may have featured to her – as Lewis clearly did – as emotionally isolating Tolkien from her. She was not highly educated, and felt socially insecure in Oxford: conversely, Lewis lacked the ability or willingness to conciliate her, and encouraged Tolkien to compartmentalise domestic life and intellectual discourse – the more pressingly, one suspects, since Lewis's own unconventional ménage (he lived with an older married woman who may well at some stage have been his mistress) was one he preferred to keep in the background and discuss with no one. (It was rather through family friendships with a number of his female pupils that Tolkien achieved a measure of integration between his domestic and professional lives.) Equally, it is apparent from Humphrey Carpenter's illuminating book on the Inklings,[11] and from A. N. Wilson's biography of Lewis, that Tolkien was intellectually something of a loner within the group, more ambivalent towards some of its members, including Lewis himself of whom he was often privately critical, than Lewis might have wished, or than subsequent commentators, postulating a 'school' of Oxford Christian writers, have supposed. Lewis admired Tolkien's work, and encouraged him to persevere with The Lord of the Rings; but it is not so clear that he fully understood the aesthetic and formal, as distinct from the ethical and religious, foundations of Tolkien's work. His own fiction, though it has distinctive merits, is only superficially influenced by Tolkien's: the underlying cohesiveness, rigour, and amplitude of conception are missing. Temperamentally the two writers were quite different. Tolkien was a careful, single-minded literary artist whose work is essentially one great project; Lewis was a prolific and versatile man of letters whose work is always readable but not always carefully considered. (He published no fewer than twenty-five books during the eighteen years it took

Tolkien to see *The Lord of the Rings* through to publication.) Tolkien's admiration for Lewis's writings, and for those of Charles Williams, who came to Oxford during the Second World War, was, to say the least, selective: he was particularly ill-at-ease with Lewis's combative, often facile, contributions to popular theology (though he himself had been partly instrumental in Lewis's conversion to Christianity around 1931) and by his appropriation of some of Tolkien's own themes and devices in the 'Narnia' tales. At a personal level, Lewis's hero-worship of Williams, and much later his unannounced marriage to the formidable Joy Davidman, had an alienating effect on Tolkien. Towards the end of their lives there was a virtual estrangement between the two men, with an uncomfortable final meeting not long before Lewis's death.[12] It is plainly impossible (as well as impertinent in both senses of the word) for anyone not closely involved to pass judgement on Tolkien's success, in middle life, in reconciling the moral obligations of marriage, paternity and friendship – though one or two academic commentators, in a spirit less 'feline' than canine (though Tolkien would perhaps have called it 'Dantean')[13] have had no hesitation in doing so. At all events, it was against the background of this complex emotional economy, in the times, often late at night, spared by professional duties and by domestic and social commitments, that *The Lord of the Rings* was written.

Tolkien was sixty-three when the third and last volume of *The Lord of the Rings* was published, and its unparalleled commercial success only really began after his retirement, at the age of sixty-seven, in 1959. By 1968 three million copies of *The Lord of the Rings* had been sold.[14] The late 1960s especially saw the worldwide Tolkien cult, of which the more absurd manifestations (the badges and the T-shirts and the graffiti, the comically inapt equation with the values of 'hippiedom') are too well known to dwell on. Tolkien viewed this international celebrity with mixed feelings. Success on such a scale brought him financial security, a sense of achievement, the affection and admiration of countless readers, and pleasure at the discovery that so many others responded to the feelings and values that pervade his writings; it also brought him unwelcome attention from the press, from would-be biographers and collaborators, and from importunate visitors, as well as bewilderment at naïve misconstructions of his work. 'Art moves them,' he said of his youthful American devotees, 'and they don't know what they've been moved by and they get quite drunk on it'.[15] His years of retirement produced one marvellous but brief work, Smith of Wootton Major, and a variety of mostly unfulfilled projects, including the revision of the much earlier 'Silmarillion' and its associated texts. Secluded, so far as possible, from the public gaze, and for four years exiled from Oxford to the south coast (partly for privacy, partly out of consideration for his wife's health), he experienced some frustration and depression: it is a melancholy thought that even the admiration of millions could not prevent – may even indirectly have increased – for Tolkien the intermittent loneliness of old age. A large extended family, and a number of devoted friends and correspondents, alleviated it. After Edith Tolkien's death in November 1971, Tolkien returned to Oxford, to accommodation provided by Merton College. He was awarded the CBE in 1972. On 2 September 1973, at the age of eighty-one, he died in Bournemouth, of pneumonia, following treatment for a gastric ulcer.

Published photographs of Tolkien show a man of medium height and slender build, with a sensitive, slightly anxious, often humorous expression: in earlier photographs the anxiety tends to predominate, in later ones the humour. He is always a little more elegantly dressed than one quite expects of the reclusive professor, or the affectedly 'masculine' anti-aesthete he has sometimes been portrayed as by critics determined to conflate him with the notoriously shabby Lewis and to caricature them both. (The tailor-made suits and Japanese prints which, as Carpenter tells us, Tolkien improvidently purchased as an undergraduate also suggest aesthetic tastes subsequently reined in by financial prudence.) Recordings of his voice in interviews and recitations, made comparatively late in life, reveal a smoker's throatiness, an admirably varied intonation and rhythm in reading poetry, and a crisp articulation – though in conversation, with sudden *accelerandos* and elisions which can be hard to construe on a first hearing. It is the voice of a well-educated twentieth-century Englishman, but is otherwise curiously hard to place, socially or geographically: it is free from those nasal or drawling or 'plummy' tones which have marked out the fashionably upper-class (or would-be upper-class) voice in its numerous shifting manifestations, and though the vowels do not precisely suggest any specific provincial accent they have a purity (assisted by the full value given to medial and final consonants) uncharacteristic, to a layman's ear, of 'received pronunciation'. 'Jewel' is 'jewil'; 'curtained' almost 'curtinned'; the vowel sounds in 'pool' and 'pipe' are not diphthongs; in 'fair' and 'hair' the r is lightly trilled. It is an idiosyncratic voice, that of a man who has, no doubt largely unconsciously (though few men can have been in a better position to do it consciously), developed his own nuances within the variety of the given speech of a given time and place.[16]

In his letters, and in the recollections of acquaintances, Tolkien appears as courteous, modest, humorous and affable, though defensive of himself and his work, in his later years, against intrusion and against the follies of insensitive translators, would-be adaptors and fanciful biographical commentators. He lived in conventional and unassuming style, occupying undistinguished suburban houses, and even when he became famous and highly taxable showed little inclination to leave England. He was no ascetic, and enjoyed the pleasures of the table, as well as the comforts of domestic life. (Asked in a radio interview whether, as his books suggested, he attached importance to 'home, fire, pipe, bed', he replied, with apparently genuine surprise, 'Don't you?')[17] Holidays with his young family were often taken at conventional seaside resorts like Sidmouth and Lyme Regis. In early and middle life he enjoyed tennis and swimming, as well as country rambles (tending to dawdle, to the irritation of strenuous walkers like the Lewis brothers). In the 1930s he drove a car. During the Second World War, in which two of his sons were in the armed forces, he served for a spell as an air-raid warden. He read newspapers, possessed a radio (and even broadcast once or twice), and visited the theatre and the cinema, even as an undergraduate – though he did not know who Ava Gardner was, when introduced to her by Robert Graves in 1965.[18] He worried about the state of the world ('The news today about Atomic Bombs is so horrifying one is stunned'),[19] about the inadequacy of his pension (until the royalties of *The Lord of the Rings* began to accumulate), about the increasing prevalence of 'haute cuisine' at Oxford dinner-tables.

This last prejudice, against French cooking, might be seen as epitomising an obstinate and self-conscious, not to say hidebound, English ordinariness. Tolkien on this view would be an 'Anglo-Saxon professor' in a punning as well as a literal sense. But the more one glimpses of Tolkien's interior life, as distinct from his social persona, the less compelling appears this impression – which he himself undoubtedly did something to encourage – of the professor as plain man, this 'image of a fuddy not to say duddy old fireside hobbitlike boozer', as he himself expressed it in a wry comment on a television programme which he felt had misrepresented him.[20] He was passionate and (by English standards) demonstrative in his emotional attachments, and earnest in his beliefs, especially about religion. 'Out of the darkness of my life, so much frustrated, I put before you the one great thing to love on earth: The Blessed Sacrament. There you will find romance, glory, honour, fidelity, and the true way of all your loves upon earth …',[21] he wrote, in his late forties, in a long and confessional letter to one of his sons. His published letters often display sadness, anger or pessimism, but never sophisticated cynicism. Like his fellow-Midlander and fellow-Catholic, the composer Edward Elgar, he was in many ways temperamentally the opposite of the plausible stereotype of the phlegmatic, unintrospective Englishman: in both men, one might suggest, we can discern in the work a tension between 'English' values of restraint, understatement and good humour, and an emotional ardour springing from inner sources scarcely touched by cultural influences.

As for professorial myopia, Tolkien's intellectual and cultural life extended well beyond his academic specialism. He had an interest in some of the sciences, especially in the branches of natural history (Carpenter records him, on a walking holiday with the Lewis brothers, discoursing on the formation of the Spanish chestnut),[22] and in astronomy: the calendar he ascribes to his Elves is, as he gleefully points out,[23] slightly more astronomically accurate than the Gregorian, and he took elaborate care to co-ordinate the phases of the moon with the chronology of his narrative in *The Lord of the Rings*. A number of episodes in that work benefit from the added level of realism which comes from a 'scientific' understanding expressed unobtrusively in non-scientific language: one thinks of the plain of Gorgoroth, 'pocked with great holes, as if, while it was still a waste of soft mud, it had been smitten with a shower of bolts and huge slingstones' (RK, 211), and of the time-lapse between sight and sound as Sam witnesses the collapse of Barad-dûr from the slopes of Orodruin (RK, 224). He read a good deal of science fiction: we find him, in 1967, praising the work of Isaac Asimov, as well as Mary Renault's novels on the Theseus myth.[24] He was responsive to music and painting, attending performances of operas by Wagner and Verdi (though he did not much admire the former), declaring a liking for Weber in a television interview,[25] and devoting a longish footnote in his essay 'On Fairy Stories' to Surrealism. His own illustrations and designs show skill and taste: and he provided Donald Swann with the Gregorian-chant-like theme for his setting of Galadriel's farewell song from The Fellowship of the Ring. He travelled little, but for all the ardent 'northernness' of spirit imputed to him by Auden and others (wrongly, as he insisted)[26] relished his experience of Italy, especially Venice ('incredibly, elvishly lovely'),[27] loved modern Spanish and Italian as well as the classical tongues, and valued the literature and culture of the ancient world. Minas Tirith, as he pointed out, is at roughly the latitude of Florence; and the history and culture of Gondor owes something to ancient Rome, and even to ancient Egypt.[28]

In short, Tolkien was in many ways an even more ordinary man than is commonly supposed, precisely because he was a more complex personality than the tweedy and cerebral academic of sentimental or contemptuous legend. He was distinguished from other ordinary men by his particular gifts, intuitions and experiences, and especially by that integration of them within his inner life which is accessible to us only through his works. There is a temptation – even Carpenter's imperturbable biography briefly succumbs to it – to find the elements of suburban ordinariness in Tolkien's life paradoxical in the inventor of an extraordinary fictional universe. But the sense of paradox is based partly on the Proustian illusion, the expectation that an artist's exterior personality will body forth the essence of his art, and partly on the presupposition that Tolkien's invented world has nothing to do with the world in which he lived for eighty-one years.

II

'Though Tolkien lived in the twentieth century he could scarcely be called a modern writer', Carpenter suggests in The Inklings.[29] In earlier chapters I have sought to emphasise the modernity, in the chronologically widest sense, of Tolkien's best work: its affinities to the traditions of the novel, its marked elements of realism, its predominantly non-archaic diction and syntax. Tolkien's evolution as an artist, I have suggested, is precisely an evolution from a derivative archaism, rooted not so much in medieval literature proper as in a nineteenth-century romantic antiquarianism, towards a narrative design, and a range of stylistic resources, which proved their accessibility to a twentieth-century readership. Nevertheless, Carpenter's implication that Tolkien's work is in some sense incompatible with, or antipathetic to, the twentieth-century literary mainstream needs to be examined, especially as others have expressed the point less neutrally than Carpenter. John Carey, for instance, deplores Tolkien's lack of interest in 'the writers who were moulding English literature in his own day – Eliot, Joyce, Lawrence'.[30] Even if we reject Carey's vision of English literature as a single substance, appropriated for a definite period, like the only blob of Plasticine in the classroom, by an exclusive group (however gifted), it is clear that Tolkien's relation to twentieth-century literary history is a problematical one. Tolkien lived through, and beyond, at least two important movements in the development of English literature: the great age of cosmopolitan modernism, which reached its apogee in the 1920s, the decade of 'The Waste Land', Ulysses, To the Lighthouse, 'Ash Wednesday'; and the quite different and more diffuse tendency, or cluster of literary attitudes and practices, which can best be summarised as contemporary social realism, and which in England seems to have come in two waves in Tolkien's lifetime, roughly in the 1930s (Orwell, Greene, Waugh, Isherwood, some aspects of the early Auden, and a host of minor figures) and the 1950s (Snow, Amis, Braine, Osborne, Larkin and others). Tolkien was somewhat younger than the principal figures of modernism, and somewhat older than the 'Thirties' generation: he was, for example, ten years younger than Joyce, but eleven years older than Orwell. Indeed he belongs to something of a lost, or at any rate depleted, generation: the killed war poets, Owen and Rosenberg, and his fellow war-survivors, Graves and Blunden, are his closest contemporaries. When he was beginning *The Lord of the Rings* in 1937, Lawrence was already dead, and Joyce was finishing *Finnegans Wake*; as the composition of the work progressed, Joyce, Yeats and Woolf died, and Eliot produced his last important work, *Four Quartets*. By the time *The Lord of the Rings* was published in 1954–55, on the other hand, the second wave of anti-modernist social realism had set in. 'I have no belief in "tradition" or a common myth-kitty or casual allusions in poems to other poems or poets', wrote Philip Larkin;[31] among novelists, William Cooper promised to 'run Experimental Writing out of town',[32] and Snow and Amis made similar statements. Poets, novelists and playwrights examined contemporary urban life, often in styles of calculated plainness. It was noticed that *The Lord of the Rings* did not do so. Tolkien's age made it easier to dismiss his work as the prank of an elderly don: he was more than a generation older than, say, Kingsley Amis or John Wain, both of whom had encountered him as a lecturer at Oxford.[33] Readers living in the 1950s, in a world reconstructing itself after the Second World War, might be forgiven for missing the emotional depth of a work whose origins lie, far below its surface, in private and public events of a much earlier date; or for misconstruing the work as an allegorical commentary (unaccountably inflated in scale) on the recent events which for them were formative: the war against Hitler, the encroaching 'shadow of the Bomb'.

Few would now press, even against Tolkien, the necessity for literature of any merit to depict 'contemporary realities' with naturalistic directness. Nor, if we really must conceive literary history as a Darwinian struggle, do the writers fashionable in the 1950s, on the whole, present very formidable opponents for Tolkien. After the 1960s, the directness of social realism went out of fashion for a generation. Ironically enough, the very transparency, literalness and interior consistency of the narrative of *The Lord of the Rings*, the features which paradoxically cause it to resemble realist fiction in spite of its setting in an imaginary world, were just the qualities which set it apart from the allusive and self-conscious post-modernist metafictions of the final quarter-century: its failure to be *That Uncertain Feeling* or *Saturday Night and Sunday Morning* was succeeded by its failure to be *The Name of the Rose* or *A History of the World in 10½ Chapters*. The still fashionable 'magic realism' sounds like the appropriate category for Tolkien, but actually relates its two elements quite differently, making (one might crudely say) the historical magical rather than the magical historical. Yet somehow *The Lord of the Rings* went on being read by millions of educated readers, in spite of the fact that the only fashion which could accommodate it (and even this categorisation is misleading) is the downmarket fashion it created itself, for 'fantasy fiction'.

Tolkien's relation to modernism is more complex. Even if the historical term 'modernism' itself loses currency (and there are some signs that this is happening), there remain discernible family resemblances among a range of important works produced in the first half of the century: stylistic and structural innovation; anxious scepticism about the possibility of making sense of human experience; exploitation of myth, symbolism, literary allusion; complex irony about value. Proust, Mann, Joyce, Kafka, Rilke, Eliot, Faulkner and others (every critic will have a slightly different list) occupy in relation to twentieth-century literature roughly the position of the Romantic movement in relation to that of the nineteenth century: a position of prestige founded on the originality of their achievements, and further guaranteed by lasting and widespread influence. Indeed many modernist features reappear (often handled rather playfully, in confirmation of Marx's dictum that history repeats itself, first as tragedy, then as comedy) in the sophisticated and reflexive narratives of the last quarter-century, as well as in major postmodernist figures, closer in age to Tolkien, such as Beckett and Nabokov. There must be a presumption, as with Romanticism, that so dominant a literary tendency is grounded in, and expressive of, fundamental cultural developments. A twentieth-century work which showed no relation whatever to modernism, which might so far as conception and style are concerned have been written in a literary world to which modernism had not happened, would then be a genuine anomaly.

Actually, *The Lord of the Rings* is not such a work. Its relation to the values and practices of modernism is in many ways – indeed, in crucial ways – antagonistic; yet it is easy to point to respects in which it participates in the shifts of taste and sensibility which characterise the early twentieth century. Like many modernist texts, for example, it makes creative and adaptive use of myth. I am thinking less of the ironic-parodic transformations of myth in *Ulysses* or 'The Waste Land' than of the serious reconceptions of mythical elements in such works as Mann's *Joseph and his Brothers*, or in Rilke's poetry. Tolkien's Elves, like Rilke's Angels in the *Duino Elegies*, represent a reworking of a familiar mythical archetype: that of an order of beings close in nature to humankind, and yet sundered from it by some fundamental metaphysical fact. Different though the two cases are in almost every respect, both inventions serve the purpose of expressing, by imagining the human condition from a perspective outside itself, a perception of the essential transitoriness, insufficiency and pain of human experience. Like Rilke's Angels, the Elves throw human mortality into relief, and help to exhibit Death as a necessary and fitting, as well as a tragic, completion of our destiny. Unlike them, the Elves, fated to deathlessness (within time), are themselves laden with a distinctive burden. Tolkien made the point explicit in letters. 'Of course, in fact exterior to my story, Elves and Men are just different aspects of the Humane, and represent the problem of Death as seen by a finite but willing and self-conscious person. ... Elves are certain aspects of Men and their talents and desires, incarnated in my little world. They have certain freedoms and powers we should like to have, and the beauty and peril and sorrow of the possession of these things is exhibited in them.'[34]

More generally, like many modernist texts, *The Lord of the Rings* is informed by a highly eclectic awareness of the literature of the past: and not merely the remote past. Tom Shippey, who persuasively catalogues Tolkien's likely sources in folk-tales and in medieval literature, also points out his numerous echoes and half-echoes of Shakespeare, of which the most striking are the transformations of motifs from *Macbeth*: the march of the tree-like Ents on Isengard, and the discomfiture and destruction of the Witch-king ('not by the hand of man shall he fall', RK, 92), by the woman Éowyn and the hobbit Meriadoc.[35] Certain other episodes recall, faintly but discernibly, nineteenth-century novelists whom we know Tolkien had read. The river-journeys prompt occasional reminiscences of Mark Twain (*Huckleberry Finn*) and, as Shippey again notices, of Fenimore Cooper. The episode at Rivendell (FR, 231ff.) in which

Frodo awakes from sickness and delirium to find he has been tended for days by the devoted Sam reminds one of a similar moment in *Great Expectations*, where Joe Gargery plays the Sam Gamgee role; the very names are similar, though the much more restrained sentiment in the Tolkien is a further index of his modernity. The image of the Witch-king 'trampling the fallen' as he approaches the gates of Minas Tirith looks to me like a verbal echo of Shelley's poem 'The Mask of Anarchy',[36] though both have a clear common source in the Apocalypse. The arrows that onomatopoeically fall 'clinking and glancing on the stones' in the battle of Helm's Deep (TT, 138) suggest that the mature Tolkien had not entirely jettisoned the Tennysonian poetic of his youth. One could go on – but perhaps we are drawing dangerously close to the territory of Robert Giddings and Elizabeth Holland, who convince themselves that the Old Forest is derived from the Wild Wood in *The Wind in the Willows*, on the grounds that characters get lost in both of them, and that Lorna Doone is to be connected with the *Akallabêth*, the chronicle of Númenor, because 'Lorna' suggests 'lorn', which means lost, and Númenor is a lost land, 'Dûn' (meaning 'west' in Elvish) suggests 'Doone', and 'both Saruman and Counsellor Doone have remarkable hair-styles'.[37] These absurdities bring home the danger of attributing a fictional conception to a single, chronologically recent, influence when we are much more likely to be dealing with the fresh embodiment (it is never simply the repetition) of a motif or archetype which has recurred a number of times in literary history.

Philip Larkin may have had no time for 'tradition' or a 'common myth-kitty', but it seems that Tolkien did. His own relation to past literature does not yield to a nineteenth-century, evolutionary model of continuous development, in which each generation of writers is perceived as modifying the techniques of its immediate predecessors: rather it is a relation which, in the approved modernist fashion, cuts right across chronological sequence. One of the salient features of twentieth-century literary, and for that matter musical and artistic, culture is this unprecedentedly rich and versatile historical awareness: if Tolkien drew some inspiration from historically remote literary models, this, so far as it goes, aligns him with, rather than distancing him from, the culture of Picasso and Stravinsky and T. S. Eliot. Eliot claims, in a famous essay, that 'the historical sense involves a perception, not only of the pastness of the past, but also of its presence; the historical sense compels a man to write not merely with his own generation in his bones, but with the feeling that the whole of the literature of Europe from Homer and within it the whole of the literature of his own country has a simultaneous existence and composes a simultaneous order'.[38] Few writers, except Eliot himself and Joyce, even come near this supposed ideal, but Tolkien (if we defer for the moment the question of his relation to his own generation) comes closer than many of his contemporaries, and far closer than almost any pre-modernist writer. His range of interests is different from Eliot's, but it is hardly less wide, at least so far as the Eliot of 'The Waste Land' is concerned. Not that Tolkien's use of past literature remotely resembles the bold explicit allusiveness of 'The Waste Land': he neither imitates nor steals, nor parodies earlier writing. It is much closer to that of Four Quartets, in which the echoes of other writers are for the most part implicit, evanescent, absorbed into a self-sufficient text.

Finally, like many modernist writers – and here again one thinks of Rilke and Eliot – Tolkien constructs a vision informed by what can only be called religious intuitions, yet does not begin from any foundation of assumed dogma. In this respect the modernist writers themselves are continuing a development which pre-dates the twentieth century. Until the late eighteenth century, virtually all European writers could assume that, if they wished to write in a religious spirit (that is, if they did not belong to the minority of freethinkers), the appropriate way to do so was through explicit reference to the doctrines of Christianity. But the decline of Christian belief among the intelligentsia over the last two centuries has abolished this assumption. With the young Wordsworth, for example, we find, for almost the first time, a writer imbued with a religious vision eschewing explicit reference to Christianity, and instead exploring what seem to him the most valuable and fundamental human experiences in order to reconstruct, on experiential grounds, the basis for a religious faith. (Earlier writers such as Traherne and Vaughan, who covered some of the same ground as Wordsworth, nevertheless employed a Christian frame of reference. The older Wordsworth, of course, reverts to a much more deferential conformity, but it is the earlier work, culminating in The

Prelude, which is universally valued.) By the twentieth century there is a background cultural assumption of unbelief, or at least a disturbed scepticism: where writers move, tentatively or decisively, towards a religious vision, they do so under the compulsion of experience, ecstatic (like Proust's involuntary memory) or terrible (like the profound abasement of Eliot's 'The Hollow Men'). The existence of a transcendent order giving value to the world can no longer credibly be propounded as a datum, but must be glimpsed, as a possibility, or a hope, through a persuasive evocation of human experience. Even the particularist Catholic novelists – Greene, Waugh, Mauriac – proceed in this way, focusing on human crises and dilemmas and inviting the reader, more often by implication than by direct appeal, to recognise an interpretative power in religious faith which supposedly eludes secular ideologies. And it is open to the reader to be moved by the authenticity with which the humane is explored, yet to reject any transcendental interpretation, to find in *Duino Elegies* or in *Four Quartets* or in *The Power and the Glory* an existential, not a religious vision. Where Christian writers have explicitly pressed the doctrinal point, as Chesterton and C. S. Lewis sometimes do in their fiction, they inevitably tend to forfeit the sympathy of the unconverted majority, except to the extent that Christian apologetics can, even for a non-Christian reader, locate weak points in fashionable secular beliefs. But Tolkien was not interested in this gadfly role.

It is natural enough, then, that the Christian religion in which Tolkien was so orthodox a believer is firmly excluded from *The Lord of the Rings* – so firmly that at least one reviewer expressed puzzlement at the alleged absence of 'religion' (in the sense of formal worship and doctrine) from so elaborately developed an imaginary world as Middle-earth.[39] Not only is Christianity not literally present; there is no surrogate for it, or allegorical structure suggestive of it. Instead, as we have seen, Tolkien sets out to 'amuse' readers, to 'delight them, and at times maybe ... move them deeply';[40] or to express the point less modestly, to create a world, and a narrative history, which are imaginatively compelling, and which answer to the heart's desire. Drawing, in the act of composition, upon his own feelings, his own intuitions of value, his own perceptions and notions of coherence in the real world, he inevitably conceived an imaginary world partly conditioned by the Augustinian Christianity in which he believed. That is not to say that the work makes sense only to a fellow-believer: indeed it is obvious that this is not the case, since only a small minority of the work's appreciative readers can have consciously made the connection with Christian doctrine. (A larger minority may actually be Christians of one sort or another, but that does not mean that the connection is made by them at a sophisticated, or even a conscious, level.) The virtual suppression, in The Lord of the Rings, of the theogonic and teleological myths central to The Silmarillion, so that the reader must intuit for himself, through imagined experience, the possibility of a religious order underlying Middle-earth, marks a huge stride into the world of modernism. The effectiveness of the work is founded, not upon the presumed truth of Christian doctrine, but rather upon the emotional appeal of a powerfully realised imagining of the world, which affirms its essential goodness, locates evil in negation, and relates ethical and peri-ethical values to this fundamentally affirmative conception. The reader's invited response is, 'If only it were so!' The recognition of this response within oneself is a recognition of an aspect of human desire, brought vividly to the surface of awareness. Whether one actually believes 'it is so' is a matter for a different kind of judgement.

In a number of respects, then, Tolkien's work shares qualities with modernism, as well as having elements of novelistic 'realism' which are modern in a broader sense. For all that, The Lord of the Rings could not plausibly be called a modernist work, because it lacks a crucial quality universal within modernism: irony. The term is an ambiguous one in literary criticism, but as it happens most of its senses are applicable here. Occasionally in minor works of Tolkien's there is irony in the sense of the transparent expression of a meaning by its opposite (Atkins in 'Leaf by Niggle' 'was nobody of importance, just a schoolmaster');[41] and the narrative of Farmer Giles of Ham can be called ironic in that it maintains a gently mocking, unheroic view of human motive. There are some traces of this tone in The Hobbit and in Smith of Wootton Major, and just a few in The Lord of the Rings, notably in the treatment of the gossipy and narrow-minded populace of Hobbiton. However, the keynote of both Smith and The Lord of the Rings, Tolkien's finest works, is a profound earnestness. I do not mean humourlessness (though that might be alleged against some of the earlier mythical writings). But it is notable that the characters whose ready humour we are likely to admire – Gandalf, Sam, Tom Bombadil, Treebeard – rarely if ever employ irony. Their humour is benevolent or bantering, and when they denounce others they do so with deadly seriousness: there are no Wildean quips at the expense of Saruman or Sauron, or even Gollum. It is, on the contrary, Saruman who attempts irony as he taunts the hobbits on the doorstep of Bag End (RK, 298).

More important for our present purpose is the absence of irony of two kinds which have a specific relevance to modernism: irony about value, and irony about the literary text itself. In 'East Coker' II Eliot follows an incantatory passage of astounding imagery with the lines

> That was a way of putting it – not very satisfactory:
> A periphrastic study in a worn-out poetical fashion,
> Leaving one still with the intolerable wrestle
> With words and meanings.

And the next section (III) concludes with the paradoxical affirmation that

> what you do not know is the only thing you know
> And what you own is what you do not own
> And where you are is where you are not.

Modernist texts deal in instability of value, uncertainty of knowledge. Proust's narrator asks whether the deceased Bergotte is 'dead forever' and replies, 'Very possibly';[42] the exalted passage that follows affirms the tentative possibility, but no more, of a world of eternal value. Mann, in The Magic Mountain, plays off ideologies against one another in a strenuous and unresolved dialectic. Kafka's heroes strive to discern meaning and a source of indisputable authority, but fail: the stories are like religious parables, but the god does not come. Rilke couches much of the Duino Elegies in the form of passionate questions. Beckett's Estragon and Vladimir wait in vain for Godot. Nabokov's John Shade writes that

> I think I understand
> Existence, or at least a minute part
> Of my existence, only through my art ...[43]

But his poem is left incomplete, to be edited by a monomaniac. The modernist irony, at the expense both of the text itself and of the values the text calls into play, is not a nihilistic scepticism – the texts remain ambitious, and the quest for values urgent – but it does express a deep pessimism about the ability of human beings to understand themselves and their place in the universe. (Though this pessimism is itself, of course, a proposition about human nature and the human predicament.)

Tolkien's major work has none of this irony about value or about its own literary processes. The Lord of the Rings exhibits an acute sense of the moral and intellectual imperfection of human beings, and even the wisest of its characters have a restricted understanding of their universe, but this is a different matter from a radical pessimism about the possibility of knowledge. In 'On Fairy Stories' Tolkien speaks of the power of art to help us in the 'regaining of a clear view'.

> I do not say 'seeing things as they are' and involve myself with the philosophers, though I might venture to say 'seeing things as we are (or were) meant to see them' – as things apart from ourselves.[44]

The objectivism here is clearly founded in a conviction that God does not deceive, though it could be rephrased as a proposition about the fit between human and non-human nature. (Despite the disclaimer about philosophers, Tolkien is perhaps hinting at Berkeley's theory that the world of our experience is immediately given by God.) The literary text, on this account, must be a clear lens. There is a playful element in the composition of The Lord of the Rings: the Appendices, especially, could hardly have been written had Tolkien not taken an almost Joycean pleasure in pursuing the game of fiction with pedantic precision. But the objective of Tolkien's ingenuity is to sustain the authenticity of the imagined world: the aesthetic force of the work would be severely damaged if any part of it appeared to be inviting an ironic smile at the enterprise itself (or even to be drawing attention to it as a literary enterprise at all). Transparency, not ironic self-reference, is essential to *The Lord of the Rings*.

It is a mark of the continued influence of modernist values on our literary culture that to say of a work that it is not characterised by irony or self-reference might be assumed to be a way of disparaging it. If we step back to the Romantic period, by contrast, we are hard pressed to find a work which is not essentially earnest: where we do find irony, as in Byron's *Don Juan* or Goethe's *Faust* or Peacock's novels, we question the work's unequivocal affiliation to romantic values. In a long retrospect such as we can now enjoy on to Romanticism, we are more likely to be grateful for the presence of these works than to deplore their resistance to the romantic *Zeitgeist*, their harking back to an eighteenth-century rational temperateness of expression and to neo-classical poetics. I do not compare Tolkien to Goethe, whose greatness incorporates both much of the essence of romanticism and a classical spirit which is fused with it, nor to Byron who manages to be an arch-romantic and an anti-romantic at once (or in succession). But I cannot help feeling that as modernism fades into historical perspective, the elements of neo-romantic earnestness in Tolkien may, like the neo-classical restraint and irony of Peacock, come to seem a welcome variant, rather than a lamentable failure of adjustment to the dominant cultural trend.

FIVE

Tolkien in the History of Ideas

I

Much depends, of course, on what precisely Tolkien's work is earnest about. In the three sections of this chapter, which examines Tolkien as a thinker, and a figure in the history of ideas, I want to consider how his writing responds to its time; to examine and evaluate some applications, or appropriations, of his work for particular ideological purposes; and to show that there is an underlying coherence in his thought.

The idea that as a literary artist he should be required to 'respond to his time' is one that Tolkien himself might have questioned, for all his admission of certain influences from personal experience in the Foreword to *The Lord of the Rings*. One reason is that he was unsympathetic to many preoccupations of the modern world, and disinclined to serve its agenda. A number of commentators have complained, for example, that his work ignores or underplays the role of the erotic in human life.[1] Actually his work is not quite so indifferent to the erotic as may be supposed, though it may involve a different conception of the erotic from that of Joyce or Lawrence (see, for example, my discussion of *Smith of Wootton Major* in chapter 3 above); but in any case, since the role of the erotic in human life is fairly extensively explored by other twentieth-century writers, one should not be too disappointed to find a writer who deals with something else. A second reason is that Tolkien disclaimed, at least for his fiction, any attempt to expound or promulgate explicit ideas, rejecting any suggestion that the events of *The Lord of the Rings* offer a comment on twentieth-century history, and remarking in connection with *Beowulf* that 'a myth … is at its best when it is presented by a poet who *feels rather than makes explicit* what his theme portends' (italics added).[2]

Perhaps the deepest reason, however, is that Tolkien's most earnest commitments were to values which he believed to be independent of specific historical circumstances. By conceiving for his major works of fiction a historical situation quite different from that of the twentieth century, and expecting his readers to be moved, if they were moved, without having to translate the action into twentieth-century correlatives, Tolkien signalled his conviction that the most fundamental psychic and moral values are not relative to particular societies or periods of history. When Éomer, in *The Two Towers*, asks 'How shall a man judge what to do in such times?', Aragorn replies, 'As ever he has judged. … Good and ill have not changed since yesteryear; nor are they one thing among Elves and Dwarves and another among Men. It is a man's part to discern them, as much in the Golden Wood as in his own house' (TT, 40–1). It is one of Aragorn's more stiltedly priggish speeches, but it does serve to make explicit (given Aragorn's authoritative status and the fact that Éomer equably answers 'True enough') Tolkien's rejection of the moral relativism which became increasingly fashionable during his lifetime. (It emphatically does not follow from this view of Tolkien's – though this is what a belief in moral absolutes is sometimes imagined to entail – that exactly the same behaviour is called for in any society or at any period. It merely follows that right conduct, whatever varied forms it may take in different contexts, must be traceable back to certain fundamental principles.)

The literary-critical equivalent of this confusion so far as Tolkien is concerned is the attempt to deny the imaginative autonomy of Middle-earth by translating Sauron as Hitler or Stalin, the Nazgûl as the Nazis, the Shire under Saruman as the post-war Labour government, and so on: interpretations which infuriated Tolkien, the more justifiably since these are essentially conjectures about covert intentions on the author's part. His narrative is not a kind of coded satire or polemic: its aim is to present certain essentially desirable and undesirable forms of life with maximum imaginative lucidity for a modern readership. In particular, the war against Sauron is not intended to represent any real war, least of all those against Germany in which Tolkien and his country were engaged during his lifetime. To spell out a necessary distinction which many critics ignore: *influence by X* is one thing; *representation of X* is another. That Tolkien drew on the private soldiers he commanded in the First World War for some aspects of Sam Gamgee, or on his experience of battle for some images of the Dead Marshes, does not mean that the imaginary war is supposed to *represent* either of the real world wars. That his letters show he detested Hitler does not mean, as Colin Wilson and Martin Dodsworth suggest, that the forces of Sauron are designed to represent those of Nazi Germany, pitted in a patriotic allegory against plucky little Britisher-hobbits.[3] Quite apart from his general repudiation of topical allegory in his Foreword, Tolkien's statements elsewhere show that such an application would have been unacceptable to him. 'I've never had those feelings about the Germans', he protested to Philip Norman in 1967. 'I'm very anti that sort of thing.'[4] His comments in letters on the international politics of the 1940s are anything but chauvinistic ('I know nothing about British or American imperialism in the far East that does not fill me with regret and disgust');[5] and in an incomplete, posthumously published essay he shows a mature understanding of the moral complexities of war, and of the distinction between the justice of a cause and the justice of the actions used to further it.[6] For similar reasons it is superfluous for J. R. Watson to protest that 'the unassuming good are as likely to be found among the slag-heaps of Mordor-Leeds as in Minas Tirith'.[7] Mordor is not Leeds, which Tolkien, as it happens, seems to have liked – certainly he respected the Yorkshire students, from 'home backgrounds bookless and cultureless' he taught there – and the orcs are not industrial workers in disguise.[8]

If even a basically sympathetic reader like Colin Wilson is tempted to look for topical allegory, unsympathetic commentators on Tolkien, sensing his non-subscription to the secular-left consensus, and indifferent to his declared purposes, have found construing his work as a coded right-wing polemic even more helpful. To Nick Otty, for example, Mordor simply is 'Wigan or Sheffield in the

1930s', while Aragorn is 'like a Tory cabinet minister'.[9] To John Carey, as we have seen, the hobbits are 'gentlemen' and the orcs 'working-class'.[10] Germaine Greer picked this theme up in her televised outburst with her assertion that the villains of *The Fellowship of the Ring* (movie version) are 'the dwarves', who live in mines and 'actually do the work', while the hobbits are 'a leisured class'.[11] All these 'readings' exemplify a tendency endemic in twentieth-century literary criticism, with its unresolved confusions over meaning and authorial intention: the tendency to use the licence of the critical reader ('what it means to me') to assign a crass and reductive meaning to a text, and then to hold the author responsible for having written a crass and reductive work.

Greer's remark is particularly sad; not so much because, after seeing the film and (presumably) reading the book, she still confuses mine-working dwarves with mine-wrecking orcs, as because so ideologically aware a critic ought to be capable of recognising in Tolkien's invention, even if she disagrees with it, an attitude to work which is close to John Ruskin's, and not too remote from Marx's. All the benign peoples in Tolkien have a distinctive kind of productive work. The hobbits are essentially farmers; the fact that Bilbo and Frodo have no occupation – except 'burglary' and writing books, neither of which ties them to one place – is a narrative convenience, like their being bachelors. The Dwarves are essentially miners and craftsmen, the Elves are essentially creative artists. In every case, work is inseparable from enjoyment, and from love and respect for the materials of the world. Orcs, in contrast, do not in this sense *work* at all: what they typically do is destroy the products of other people's work, and if they and Sauron's other servants sometimes labour, it is as slaves under threat of death or torture. There is no evidence in Tolkien of the aristocratic idea that a life of idleness is to be commended, and much evidence of the more modern view, a dominant one since the Romantic period, that expressive work (as contrasted with alienated labour) is a basic fulfilment for human beings. Ruskin remarked that 'it may be proved, with much certainty, that God intends no man to live in this world without working: but it seems to me no less evident that He intends every man to be happy in his work. It is written, "in the sweat of thy brow," but it was never written, "in the breaking of thine heart," thou shalt eat bread.'[12] Freud said that psychological health was the ability to love and work; Marx that we should not be reduced to the condition in which we work only in order to live.[13] And a recent exponent of Marx summarises his view – with a slightly Ruskinian gloss, I think – as follows:

> A living being which has once begun to make nature his own through the work of his hands, his intellect, and his imagination, will never stop. Every achievement opens the door to unconquered territory ... . But when labour is destructive, not creative, when it is undertaken under coercion and not as the free play of forces, when it means the withering, not the flowering, of man's physical and intellectual potential, then labour is a denial of its own principle and therefore of the principle of man.[14]

Lest there be any doubt about Tolkien's adherence to this tradition, two other stories, 'Leaf by Niggle' and Smith of Wootton Major, have the joy of productive work at their very centre: only the centrality of war in The Lord of the Rings pushes it to the margins. Where Tolkien's view of work diverges very drastically from Marx's is in the morally inert role Marx assigns to the natural world, as the material of human self-realisation through labour.[15] To Tolkien the coercion of nature was as suspect as the coercion of people – a point which both section II and section III below will revisit.

The temptation to seek in The Lord of the Rings direct allusion to contemporary events and conditions, as if only such allusion could give it moral credibility, is itself a symptom of the disbelief in lasting values to which the work is implicitly a reply. For Tolkien himself, such values were ultimately grounded in God: there existed, in fact, eternal moral values, as well as eternal principles governing eudaemonia, the sources of possible happiness. Of course he would not have suggested, and no critic should suggest on his behalf, that his works embody such values perfectly. It is sufficient, for the works to be aesthetically effective, that they should evoke the kind of emotional response in readers which indicates that some widely shared values have been powerfully tapped. Those of us who have no religious beliefs may still take the view that moral and 'eudaemonic' values can be derived from the unchanging elements of human nature:[16] such as reflective self-consciousness, the capacity to imagine and to reason, susceptibility to pleasure and pain, interdependence with other persons, interdependence with a non-human environment; or from elements which, if not invariable, represent such strong general dispositions that they can weigh heavily in moral and practical reasoning. Values so derived may not, on a humanist view, be eternal, but they are lasting for all practical purposes, however varied the circumstances of their possible embodiment.

The modernity of Tolkien's work, from the point of view of its content, lies not in coded reference to specific contemporary events or phenomena, but in the absorption into the invented world – no doubt a partly unconscious absorption – of experiences and attitudes which Tolkien would scarcely have acquired had he not been a man of the twentieth century. Some are obvious enough. *The Lord of the Rings* describes a continental war, in which the survival of whole peoples and cultures is at stake. The undertow of apocalyptic dread is familiar to anyone who has lived in the nuclear age, but its primary biographical source must greatly pre-date Hiroshima: almost certainly it lies around 1914–15 when Tolkien, in common with millions of young men, discovered that he would have to go to war. The successive international crises of the Thirties and Forties can only have reinforced this impression of secular imperilment. Naturally Tolkien would have been more aware than most people of pre-modern analogies: the fall of the Roman Empire, the bare survival of Christian civilisation in the age which produced *Beowulf*, the lively expectation of world's end that obsessed some medieval and Reformation believers. But that historical awareness is itself a modern, even a modernist, attribute.

At a deeper level, there are in Tolkien's 'political' vision, especially in *The Lord of the Rings*, elements which are markedly modern. So far from attempting to resurrect in the twentieth century the heroic ethic of *Beowulf*, Tolkien explicitly warns against it in his 1936 lecture on the poem, making, indeed, what looks like an allusion to the revival of a pagan warrior-ethic in contemporary Germany.[17] His fiction reiterates an anti-'heroic' theme. The sorrows of the Elves in Beleriand, in *The Silmarillion*, stem from Féanor's vengeful decision to pursue the crimes of Melkor with war. 'The Homecoming of Beorhtnoth' criticises the sacrifice of military prudence to the heroic code. Bilbo Baggins and Farmer Giles are reluctant – in effect, conscripted – heroes, and as much stress is laid on their fear as on their courage. The warmly sympathetic Smith (of Wootton Major) falls on his face in terror before elvish warriors. In *The Lord of the Rings*, for all its pre-modern setting, only Gimli and Éomer could be said, at moments, to rejoice in battle, the former because of the long-standing hatred between Dwarves and Orcs and the latter because Rohan is indeed a 'heroic' culture of sorts (and to that extent inferior to Gondor, with its inheritance from the Elves and from Númenor). None of the other principal antagonists of Sauron, not even Faramir or Aragorn, is interested in warfare for its own sake, or as a sphere in which to win 'honour': for Aragorn, as for Sam (and for Tolkien in 1915–16) war is a necessary evil which delays, and threatens to forestall, marital happiness; Faramir too finds a partner in Éowyn, who renounces her warrior role. Above all, the hobbits are embroiled in war against their own wishes, and fight only when immediately attacked. They are essentially 'civilian' temperaments, unsuited to combat and danger yet forced into them by circumstance: a common twentieth-century fate. They are, precisely, anti-heroes, in the pointed sense that their deeds of physical courage do not express their intrinsic characters (which are pacific and self-effacing) but are performed in spite of them. We admire them for their aversion to fighting, not their love of it. Sam is tempted by the Ring to imagine himself as 'Samwise the Strong, Hero of the Age' (RK, 177): but he resists. Frodo's salvation is achieved by sparing Gollum's life, and by abstaining from the use of the potentially most powerful weapon of all, the Ring. By the time of his return to the Shire he has renounced the use of force: though the other hobbits do fight to expel Saruman's Men, and there is an implication that Frodo's renunciation is untenable for others, a personal privilege earned by his earlier sacrifice, his pacifism expresses a yearning to have done with the taint of bloodshed which innumerable men and women returning from war in 1918 or 1945 must have felt. The failure of the Shire-folk to honour Frodo – and the sense that this does not ultimately matter

– rings far truer than the songs of praise to him performed by the minstrel on the field of Cormallen.

These preoccupations are inseparable from Tolkien's historical period: an English writer even a few years older, or a couple of generations younger, would be very unlikely to have had Tolkien's military experiences, or his perception of the virtual normality of total war. That Tolkien absorbed these ingredients into 'fantasy' rather than the social-realist novel might seem remarkable or idiosyncratic, were it not for the fact that, as Tom Shippey has recently demonstrated, several of Tolkien's contemporaries did the same: George Orwell, William Golding, Kurt Vonnegut, T. H. White, C. S. Lewis.[18] The thrust of Shippey's argument is that the problem of 'how one resists evil without becoming it' presented itself with such hideous directness to these writers – of whom all but White were combat veterans – that they were obliged to construct new myths to articulate it: neither social realism nor the existing 'myth-kitty' (to borrow Larkin's phrase) seemed adequate. One's first response is that the concept of fantasy has to be stretched a bit to accommodate the diversity of Shippey's examples. But there are indeed some similarities of theme and approach among these writers. A contemporary political dystopia like Nineteen Eighty-Four seems a long way from the Arthurian makeover of The Once and Future King; but as a matter of fact, White's romance does contain a very Orwellian episode, in which the communications within an ant nest suggest the mind-numbing, language-perverting propaganda system of a totalitarian state. Merlyn's education of Arthur through exposure to other species, like Golding's dislocating shift from Neanderthal consciousness to homo sapiens consciousness half-way through The Inheritors, shows us a writer making sense of the configuration of human nature by imagining a perspective from outside it, as Tolkien also does.

Shippey has also pointed out that the central donnée of the plot of The Lord of the Rings – the comprehensively corrupting power of the Ruling Ring, so infallibly effective in the long term that even benevolent leaders such as Galadriel and Gandalf dare not possess it – implies a distinctively modern view of the psychology of political power.[19] Earlier writers had distinguished good rulers from bad, strong from weak, legitimate from illegitimate. Nero and

Caligula, everyone agreed, were evil rulers, but Julius and Augustus Caesar, no less powerful, were virtuous. In Shakespeare, Macbeth and Richard III are bad kings because they are usurpers, who persist, in power, with the methods by which they gained it; Lear and Richard II are bad kings because they exert their power insufficiently or misguidedly. There is little trace of the notion that power is in itself prone to corrupt; as for truly absolute power, it was scarcely conceivable (in practice, as distinct from constitutional fiction) until relatively modern times. Lord Acton's assertion, five years before Tolkien was born, that 'absolute power corrupts absolutely' has a compelling resonance, after a century of totalitarian dictatorships ruling through systematic terror, that Acton himself can scarcely have foreseen: the disparity between the reality of these regimes and the ostensibly altruistic principles on which many were founded could hardly be better symbolised than by the Ring's power to bring forth tyrannical evil out of good intentions.

This suspicion of the corrupting effect of power might be expected to suggest to a twentieth-century mind a liberal-democratic theory, of constitutional checks and balances, individual rights, and so forth, designed to restrict the accumulation of power in one or a few hands; and I imagine that many readers assimilate *The Lord of the Rings* to this view. They are not wholly wrong, for the work has a liberal temper: it invests high value in the joyful acceptance of diversity, in the contemptuous tearing up of unnecessary Rules, in resistance to those who 'like minding other folk's business and talking big' (RK, 281). And by comparison with many twentieth-century writers, from Pound on the right to Brecht and Sartre on the left, to say nothing of the massed ranks of minor intellectuals sneering at 'bourgeois' liberal humanism, Tolkien himself can be acquitted of admiration for illiberal causes – though he did, when presented with a choice between two ultimately illiberal forces in the Spanish civil war, sympathise with Franco, not as a Fascist but as the protector of the Catholic Church and clergy. Tolkien's own political attitudes have, indeed, to be understood as conditioned by, and integrated with, his religious convictions. Tolkien would almost certainly have reflected that Acton's maxim is implicit in the myth of the Fall: that created beings are always liable to abuse whatever power is given to them, and that the distinctive feature of the twentieth century is simply that the technological resources available to the abusers of political power have been unprecedentedly great. 'I am not a democrat,' he wrote, 'if only because humility and equality are spiritual principles corrupted by the attempt to mechanize and formalize them, with the result that we get not universal smallness and humility, but universal greatness and pride.'[20] On this view, only personal moral action, founded on self-effacement rather than the competitive assertion of one's own interests, can create the society of free and equal beings to which democracy aspires: and in a fallen world such a society cannot actually be attained, though fiction, with its distillation of values, can give us a glimpse of the realised ideal. It is a view not far removed from Tolstoy's; and in the final section of this chapter I will return to it, and will try to show how consistent, and how fundamental, is the integration of religious, moral, political and aesthetic values in Tolkien's thought.

II

If Tolkien was unwilling to assume the mantle of a prophet for the twentieth century, he did recognise and accept that what he had written would be applied by others to their own experiences and perceptions. In the Foreword to the revised edition of *The Lord of the Rings* (1966), he addressed himself as follows to the commentators who had read his work as an allegory on contemporary events.

> I cordially dislike allegory in all its manifestations, and have always done so since I grew old and wary enough to detect its presence … . I think that many confuse 'applicability' with 'allegory'; but the one resides in the freedom of the reader, and the other in the purposed domination of the author. (FR, 7)

The idea of *applicability* is not quite as transparent as it looks. With a very simple narrative, such as the traditional tale of the shepherd boy who cried 'wolf!', one can see how different readers might find applications of it in their own experiences. A parent might apply it to a child who repeatedly faked illness at school-time, for example. For the thought to be an application of the tale, however, it must be an application of a correct memory of the tale, not of a distorted memory of it. If a politician campaigning against the admission of foreign refugees said, 'The time has come to cry "wolf!" before we are overrun', he would have missed the point of the tale, and could not be said to be applying it. If another politician said of his opponents, 'they are like boys crying "wolf!"', this would only be an application of the tale if there were in fact some correspondence between the pattern of his opponents' utterances and the pattern of the boy's utterances in the tale; if there were no such correspondence, he might be said to be *appropriating* rather than applying the tale, enlisting the prestige of its supposed wisdom on behalf of his own views.

With a much more complex narrative like *The Lord of the Rings*, it is harder to draw such a clear line between application and appropriation. Precise applicability of the entire narrative seems impossible, since nothing outside *The Lord of the Rings* could match every detail of it (what would be the equivalent of Will Whitfoot's transformation into a floured dumpling?),[21] or even every detail of one of its main themes or plot-lines. (A reader might, for example, find herself as she reads 'applying' the story of Éowyn to the progress of her own emotional life, but this 'application' would be unlikely to involve an exact equivalent to all such details as, say, Aragorn's departure on the Paths of the Dead, or the intervention of the Warden of the Houses of Healing in Minas Tirith. Only a reader very confused about the role of fiction in human life would then start hunting for equivalents of those missing elements in order to make the application work. The relationship in such a case between the reality and the fiction might more often, perhaps, be expressed the other way round: the reader's personal experiences are part of what enables her to respond to this element in the story.) The application, then, must at best be of some selected part of the narrative, or aspect of it, and it is difficult to say in an absolutely determinate way when precisely such selectiveness amounts to distortion, and leads to mere appropriation or enlistment.

When it comes to political applications, the search for direct equivalents is even more likely to degenerate into appropriation, based on false or partial readings. As Tolkien himself pointed out, the fact that he did not intend to represent the closing phases of the

Second World War in *The Lord of the Rings* could be seen from the fact that the story could not even be *applied* to it: in order to do so, it would have had to show Gondor and its allies using the Ring to defeat Mordor with the aid of Saruman, who would then forge a Ring of his own, so dividing Middle-earth between two superpowers.[22] It is of course always possible to think of oneself and one's friends or political allies as being like the good guys in a novel or romance, but the supposed resemblance cannot be pressed without an element of arbitrariness becoming apparent, quite apart from the distorting effect of one's own interest in appropriating the most favourable role. (Tolkien hints at this when Sam, discussing the tale that may be made of the hobbits' exploits, wonders whether Gollum thinks of himself as the hero or the villain.)[23] All applications to definite moral or political contexts exterior to the work itself are likely to be, at best, the selection of some reasonably suitable element of the narrative as the text for a sermon.

Nevertheless, we can distinguish differing degrees of fidelity to the original along this application/appropriation spectrum. Tolkien's fiction is not a blank page on which anything can be written: there are ideas implicit, and occasionally explicit, within it. The central conflict within *The Lord of the Rings* is not between two morally or politically undifferentiated sides, and there are, as I tried to show in my analysis in chapters 1 and 2, values embodied within that work that are inseparable from its aesthetic and emotional power. Some of the shorter works are in part satirical or allegorical; various characters in the fiction express opinions, with more or less authority. A number of recent commentators have built intellectual edifices upon these elements, though with different resources of ingenuity, boldness and architectural skill, and I will devote the rest of this section to discussing three examples.

Of these, Joseph Pearce's *Tolkien: Man and Myth* (1999)[24] is the most fluent and well-organised, and in some ways the most convincing in that it focuses on the elements that are traceable to, or at least consistent with, Tolkien's Catholicism, the importance of which in forming his imagination cannot be doubted. Pearce points up well, for example, the Christian elements implicit in some of the shorter fiction, from the Purgatorial allegory of 'Leaf by Niggle' to the mockery of sceptical secularism in the figure of Nokes in *Smith of*

Wootton Major. However, Pearce's strategy of specific Catholic applications is less convincing when applied to the far more complex, and
at the same time more self-sufficient, world of *The Lord of the Rings*.
Some of these seem to assimilate Tolkien to an implausibly specific
polemical agenda. Pearce claims, for example, that Sam's reflection,
as he approaches the Tower of Cirith Ungol, that 'the one small
garden of a free gardener was all his due ... his own hands to use,
not the hands of others to command' (RK, 177), succinctly expresses
'the Distributist *credo* that private property should be enjoyed by as
many of the population as possible, so that people could be freed
from the wage slavery of Big Business or State Monopoly'[25] –
Distributism being the early twentieth-century alternative to
socialism espoused by the polemical Catholic writers Hilaire Belloc
and G. K. Chesterton, on whom Pearce has also written. Here one
can seriously question whether the text contains the materials for
the application. Conceivably Tolkien would have sympathised with
the Distributist theory – his writings are silent on the matter – but
we need to remind ourselves that in its context in *The Return of the
King* the point of Sam's reflection is to resist the megalomaniac
visions induced by the Ring, which he has just been wearing: the
moral point of the passage concerns the refusal of power, not the
superiority of an economic system. Similarly Charles Coulombe,
quoted approvingly by Pearce, says that the Shire 'expresses perfectly
the economic and political ideals of the Church, as expressed by
Leo XIII in *Rerum novarum*, and Pius XI in *Quadragesimo anno*. Traditional
authority ... popular representation ... subsidiarity ... minimal
organization and conflict.'[26] Here we need to recall that the 'half
republic half aristocracy of the Shire', as Tolkien called it,[27] is only
one, and not necessarily the most admired, community of Middle-
earth (are we sure that the Elves, for example, have private property,
or popular representation?), and that its harmony is a consequence
of its sheltered prosperity and of the virtue of its inhabitants.[28]

Pearce is on safer ground in suggesting that the sacrificial element
in Frodo's quest is Christian in spirit. Tolkien's remark in 'On Fairy
Stories' that the prototypes of 'eucatastrophe' are the incarnation
and resurrection of Christ provides additional encouragement to
this application.[29] Even here, though, one can have reservations
about the fitness of the fictional text to the analogy suggested for

it. Frodo is not the Son of God, but an originally much more insignificant person: his (and Sam's) indispensable role in saving Middle-earth is an ennoblement rather than a condescension. And it is difficult to think of Frodo as imitating Christ, since the myth of Arda does not really contain any comparable element: if Frodo is imitating anyone, it is Bilbo. As for the authorial sources of the hobbits' heroism, these may be traceable not so much in Tolkien's Catholicism as in a more secular observation he once made. 'I've always been impressed that we're here, surviving, because of the indomitable courage of quite small people against impossible odds: jungles, volcanoes, wild beasts. They struggle on – almost blindly, in a way ... . I thought that the wisest remark in the whole book was that where Elrond says that the wheels of the world are turned by the small hands because the great are looking elsewhere, and they turn because they have to, because it's the daily job.'[30] When Pearce says, 'the parable of Frodo's burden may even lead us to a greater understanding of Christ's burden',[31] one notices that the literary text has become subservient to the sacred one, and that the reader's assent to the latter is being tacitly assumed. Such an approach leaves us with the puzzle of Tolkien's profound appeal for the non-Catholic, and indeed for the unbeliever, who tends eventually to sense himself excluded by Pearce's analysis.

Christopher Garbowski's *Recovery and Transcendence for the Contemporary Mythmaker* (2000) lacks Pearce's unified focus, but it is an important example of the response to Tolkien outside the Anglo-American mainstream of critical commentary. (Garbowski is a Polish-Canadian living in Lublin, Poland.) The reception of Tolkien in Poland has, naturally enough, been influenced by the Christian elements in his work: essays by writers such as Tadeusz Olszański and Garbowski himself take the theology of Arda with absolute seriousness, but are more willing than Pearce to treat it as an exploratory discourse, rather than moving swiftly to resolve it into Catholic doctrine. They probe, in particular, its treatment of the nature of evil: as understandable a preoccupation, perhaps, for a post-holocaust, post-Stalinist society as for Shippey's combat veterans. Olszański's paper, in fact, gives some support to Shippey's view that a hint of a dualistic, Manichaean element can be traced in Tolkien's conception of evil: he points out that before the Creation begins in *Ainulindalë*, there exists not only God (Eru), but 'the Void … a "space" where objection to God, a seed of evil, could appear and develop'.[32] The Void is not nothing, since Melkor (Morgoth) is able to go into it, and it is there that his estrangement from Eru and from the other immortals begins. While evil remains negation, and God does not create evil, it is not incomprehensible that good should become evil when God countenances the existence of a state outside himself. Olszański also suggests that in an ultimately abandoned element of his mythology, the 'Second Prophecy of Mandos' (see *The Lost Road*, p. 333) Tolkien toyed with the idea of universal salvation.

In his monograph Garbowski deploys a complex and eclectic apparatus of explanation and application of Tolkien, drawing especially on the psychological theory of the concentration camp survivor Viktor Frankl. Frankl explains human motivation primarily as a quest for meaning, a response to the 'pull' of discerned values, rather than as determined by the 'push' of instinctual drives to sex or power: through this quest, human 'growth' is possible even in the most dire circumstances. Such features of Tolkien's work as his theory and practice of 'eucatastrophe', and his conception of art as a mode of 'recovery', whereby the too-familiar known world is seen afresh 'as we were meant to see it',[33] are assimilated to this ethic of growth, as is the exploratory, 'dialogic' quality Garbowski finds in Tolkien's myth-making. Though the line of Garbowski's argument is often circuitous, its effects are clear enough: without doubting Tolkien's orthodoxy, to free his vision from any strict reduction to Catholic doctrine, bringing out its general human persuasiveness, and to offer the *evangelium* of his later work as an alternative to Adorno's post-holocaust pessimism about the possibility of art.

There is also an important political element to Garbowski's commentary. Unlike Patrick Curry, whose work I will discuss in a moment, he avoids any explicit 'application' of the conflict in *The Lord of the Rings* to the impact of Soviet communism in Eastern Europe, and focuses instead on the general characteristics of Tolkien's vision of the good social life.

In *The Hobbit*, along with its residents, Tolkien discovered the Shire, the almost archetypal small homeland, a geographical unit that adorns the entire Middle-earth of the Third Age from the Grey Havens to Fangorn Forest and beyond. The geographical distances may be reminiscent of Europe ... but the social geography is based on what the Germans call *Heimat* ... . Large as the Kingdom of Gondor is, it actually constitutes a federation of small states rather than a uniform one. The only large state can be said to be Mordor, which is centralist to say the least ... . Miłosz writes that 'in comparison with the state, the homeland is organic, rooted in the past, always small, it warms the heart, it is as close as one's own body' ... . Different homelands introduce genuine diversity, while the large state, whether benign or threatening imposes uniformity.[34]

A lot depends here on the validity of the claim about Gondor, which might perhaps be under suspicion of being a large nation-state. And there is evidence to support Garbowski's view. When the forces of the outlying regions troop in to Minas Tirith in *The Return of the King*, they do so under their own captains, and are markedly differentiated from one another by their dress and gear: the people of the city hail them as friends, rather than taking their conscription for granted (RK, 43–4). The ability of Denethor to command their allegiance perhaps owes more to feudalism than to 'subsidiarity', but it is true that Gondor is much more like the Polish-Lithuanian republic, say, than it is like the bureaucratic state of the nineteenth-century Tsars, or the Soviet Union.

A great strength of Garbowski's analysis is that (in contrast here to Pearce) he can see the limitations of the small homeland as well, and since these are also intimated in Tolkien's story, the application of the latter seems entirely appropriate.

Not that the small homeland is without faults. A well-known example is the all too familiar division of orbis-interior/orbis-exterior, where those who are from outside the community are frequently the unwanted *other*, to be treated with suspicion ... . Even within the Shire there is a mistrust of citizens from far flung parts; Breelanders consider hobbits from Hobbiton strange and vice versa ... . Much of the conflict between elves and dwarves can be considered along this orbis-interior/orbis-exterior fault line ...

> A journey develops, or at least requires, openness and brings with it the risk of change ... The journey [in *The Lord of the Rings*] often leads from one small homeland to another. The Heimats of the *other* are the repositories of values that often challenge cherished beliefs of the traveller, and lead to an awareness unavailable from the limited perspective of home ... . Dialogue is in fact a precondition for the survival of the free peoples who must overcome their isolation if they are to adequately deal with the danger facing them.[35]

Another commentator who has pointed out the 'multicultural' diversity of the benign peoples in *The Lord of the Rings* is Patrick Curry.[36] But Curry is best known for his combative appropriation of the 'green' elements in Tolkien's work, and the radical anti-modern agenda he constructed around them in his *Defending Middle-earth: Tolkien, Myth and Modernity* (1997).[37]

> There are (mainly) young people trying, as I write, to defend the remaining countryside outside Newbury, Berkshire, against yet another destructive, expensive and futile bypass. Their principal means of resistance is to put themselves, with extraordinary skill, determination and humour, up trees, underground, and literally in the way of an army of security guards, bailiffs and police, not to mention bulldozers and chainsaws. And among them, I found only one person out of dozens who hadn't just read *The Lord of the Rings* but know it, so to speak, inside out ... . It is no coincidence, then, that an early supporter of one such bypass, running through Dartmoor, slammed his opponents as 'Middle Earth hobbits'! Nobody can tell me that Tolkien's books do not encourage such ecological activism; nor, for that matter, that he himself would not have been firmly on the side of the trees and their protectors.[38]

One should perhaps be more cautious about presuming the support of an author for specific actions in specific historical circumstances twenty years after his death, but in substance Curry is right on both his final points. Not only did Tolkien personally criticise a bypass proposal in the early 1950s, and repeatedly complain about the impact of new roads on the landscape,[39] but in the march of the Ents on Isengard in *The Two Towers* his work dramatises the retribution of trees against their assailants. Indeed of all the sceptical responses to the modern world which are manifest in Tolkien's work, this romantic protest against the despoliation of nature is the one which has gained greatest retrospective force since his death, as well as the one which has the deepest roots in his personal life, and the one which most comprehensively informs his work. Gandalf's advocacy of 'uprooting the evil in the fields that we know, so that those who live after may have clean earth to till' (RK, 155) is at once metaphorical (Sauron's tyranny threatens to blight the freedom of speaking-peoples throughout Middle-earth) and literal (Sauron and Saruman actually pollute the soil, poison watercourses, pour smoke into the atmosphere, cut down trees, create deserts where grass once grew). It rejects the defeatism which regards such developments as irreversible, affirms the resilience of the earth (the physical aspect of that Middle-earth which is at once the unifying conception of *The Lord of the Rings* and the most general object of the reader's quickened desire), and calls on the present generation to take thought for the generations that are to come.

No doubt this aspect of Tolkien's work has biographical origins in the move of 1900 from Sarehole to Moseley, and in subsequent involuntary experiences of the contrast between urban squalor and green fields: but it is precisely characteristic of Tolkien's response to modernity that he should not directly and literally record private experience, but should move ambitiously towards conceptions which may incarnate lasting values. On this point at least, history seems to be (for the moment) on his side. Even at the end of Tolkien's life, it seemed more plausible than it does now to stigmatise his firm repugnance against the environmental damage caused by industrialism as a quietistic retreat into Edwardian nostalgia, or as politically 'reactionary' in terms of a historical model which identifies industrialisation as 'progressive'. J. R. Watson comments on the chapter 'The Scouring of the Shire' that 'our preference for the little houses with thatched roofs and bulgy walls is taken too much for granted',[40] as if some obligation of even-handedness (or modern-mindedness) required us to see the virtues of grassless fields, treeless roads, piles of refuse and stinking effluence. John Carey complains that Tolkien shows 'a childish identification of heavy industry with wickedness'.[41] I am not sure what purpose 'childish' serves except to intimidate the reader, but if the claim is that, in Tolkien's view, some forms of heavy industry were quite a good way of polluting the earth, Tolkien would no doubt plead guilty. Certainly he shows Saruman using that means to achieve that end: what other means could have been made credible? In *The Hobbit*, too, the narrator attributes to the goblins the invention of 'the ingenious devices for killing large numbers of people at once' (60). There is, however, no reason to suppose that Tolkien deplored industry for any other reason than that it scarred and poisoned the natural world, including (through pollution, and by mechanising labour) the natural life of human beings: in 'Leaf by Niggle', indeed, Niggle actually enters his paradise by a 'pleasant little local train'. ('The sleepers gave off a delicious smell of fresh tar in the warm sunshine.')[42] Needless to say, both Watson (implicitly) and Carey (explicitly) draw the inference that Tolkien was prejudiced against the industrial working class, but it is hardly a logical inference from the condemnation of an environmental affliction to the condemnation of its most immediate victims, and neither critic brings forward any evidence to support it.

The worldwide decline of heavy industry in the last quarter of the twentieth century, and the contemporaneous rise of 'green' movements, have done much to counteract the prestige of modernity once enjoyed, if I can put it this way, by the Moseleys at the expense of the Sareholes. A world in which 'there was less noise and more green' (*The Hobbit*, 13) has become a live contemporary aspiration which it is no longer fashionable to sneer at. (One explanation of Tolkien's rapidly burgeoning popularity in the 1960s may be his appeal to 'green' values at a time when these were somewhat disdained: literary fashions, especially fashions which bewilder the critics, may paradoxically be grounded in what is unfashionable and therefore repressed.)

Where Curry's own anti-modern polemic can be mapped fairly closely on to statements by Tolkien himself, it is generally plausible both in its own terms, and as an 'application'. For example, Curry rightly distinguishes between the purely scientific impulse to understand the world for its own sake (an impulse which Tolkien grouped with the artistic and the aesthetic, as the three principal motives of the Elves), and the impulse to use the findings of science to coerce the world in the service of one's own power, through technological warfare, reckless consumption of natural resources, misuse of advanced methods of communication, or 'brainwash-ing'. As Curry says, Tolkien sometimes equates the latter with 'magic', a term which Galadriel notes the hobbits apply to 'the deceits of the Enemy' (FR, 377). In contrast, Tolkien gives the name 'enchantment' to the 'Art, delivered from many of its human limitations' achieved by the Elves.[43] Many of the evils of the modern world, for both Tolkien and Curry, arise from the rampant power of coercive technological 'magic'. The problem is that Curry now embarks on a series of improvisations around the idea of *enchantment* which lose touch with Tolkien's fundamental point: that enchantment belongs to the secondary world of imagination, in which our deepest desires can be realised; the attempt to actualise desires in the primary world is precisely what leads to coercion.[44] Perhaps, as 'Leaf by Niggle', the Epilogue to 'On Fairy Stories' and – as we shall see – the creation myth of *The Silmarillion* imply, in Eternity the enchantment of art can become actual, but this possibility only makes sense if one retains a sense of the categorical difference between the two worlds, the actual world which is the object of pure science, and the imaginative world of art. The post-modernist dictum that 'we can be sure of nothing but story' (which Curry quotes from Brian Attebery with apparent approval) fogs this distinction, and I can find nothing in Tolkien's writing which suggests that he would have accepted it.[45] With Curry one is left with an uncomfortable sense that 'enchantment' denotes a practical mode of life, or social being, proposed for this world, in which case it needs a lot of explaining.

Invoking Tolkien's idea of 'recovery', Curry calls for the 'rekindling of the wonder of the natural world' and 'a resacralization of nature'. This sounds an attractive idea, but one asks whether – setting aside the power of art to defamiliarise one's perceptions – we can have that sense of rekindled wonder without accepting some definite religious view which justifies us in seeing natural things as more than material objects. Curry, however, wants 'collective spiritual-ity', rather than a new (or old) religion. Attacking Cartesian science, rationality and 'humanist utilitarianism' on the basis of their worst perversions, he laments 'the modern loss of myth-consciousness', but does not explain what a revival of myth-consciousness would be like (over and above the appreciative reading of Tolkien).[46] In short, Curry is sweeping in his critique of 'modernity', but less successful in bringing into focus his ambitious alternative. Tolkien's critique is more cautious in what it rejects – as an orthodox Catholic, Tolkien is never less than respectful towards rationality, or science as a mode of knowledge, whatever its abuses – and much more cautious in what it proposes.

III

Tolkien did, nevertheless, give voice to some surprising opinions for a man widely regarded as 'conservative' in temperament. On 29 November 1943, he wrote to his 18-year-old son Christopher, then serving in the Royal Air Force,

> My political opinions lean more and more to Anarchy (philosophically understood, meaning abolition of control not whiskered men with bombs) or to 'unconstitutional' Monarchy. I would arrest anybody who uses the word State (in any sense other than the inanimate realm of England and its inhabitants, a thing that has neither power, rights nor mind); and after a chance of recantation, execute them if they remained obstinate! If we could get back to personal names, it would do a lot of good .... If people were in the habit of referring to 'King George's council, Winston and his gang', it would go a long way to clearing thought ...
>
> The most improper job of any man, even saints (who at any rate were at least unwilling to take it on) is bossing other men. Not one in a million is fit for it, and least of all those who seek the opportunity .... The medievals were only too right in taking nolo episcopari as the best reason a man could give to others for making him a bishop. Give me a king whose chief interest is in stamps, railways, or race-horses; and who has the power to sack his Vizier (or whatever you care to call him) if he does not like the cut of his trousers. And so on down the line. But, of course the fatal weakness of all that – after all only the fatal weakness of all good natural things in a bad corrupt unnatural world – is that it works and has worked only when all the world is messing along in the same good old inefficient human way. The quarrelsome, conceited Greeks managed to pull it off against Xerxes; but the abominable chemists and engineers have put such a power into Xerxes' hands ... that decent folk don't seem to have a chance. We are all trying to do the Alexander-touch – and, as history teaches, that orientalised Alexander and all his

generals ... . The Greece that was worth saving from Persia perished anyway, or became a sort of Vichy-Hellas ... . There is only one bright spot, and that is the growing habit of disgruntled men of dynamiting factories and power-stations; I hope that, encouraged now as 'patriotism', may remain a habit. But it won't do any good, if it is not universal.[47]

This is as much an outburst as an argument, with more than a trace of mischievous overstatement (at least one hopes that Tolkien did not literally wish to execute anybody); and we have to remember that it is a private letter, written probably in haste at the end of a long day, and that Tolkien is not offering a considered summary of his political ideas. Nevertheless, the letter seemed to me, when I first came upon it, to make explicit certain attitudes to power that are also embodied in Tolkien's fiction. The sympathy towards 'Anarchy' it expresses corroborates a view I've already hinted at, that Tolkien belonged to a type of Christian quasi-anarchist who rejects the claims of secular politics, even 'liberal' or 'democratic' politics, because he believes that political institutions are intrinsically coercive, and that only uncoerced obedience to the will of God by individuals can produce a good society. The best-known, greatest and most persuasive example is Tolstoy, but I think there are traces of this attitude in partially secularised form in Dickens and perhaps other English writers such as D. H. Lawrence.

In Tolkien's fiction this 'anarchist' suspicion of political processes and institutions manifests itself in a number of hostile portrayals of smooth-talking demagogues and political operators (Wormtongue and Saruman in The Lord of the Rings, the Master of Lake-town in The Hobbit, Sauron in 'Akallabêth' are examples); and more significantly in the way his benign imaginary societies are conceived. The Hobbits' rustic homeland, 'The Shire', for example, has virtually no government, apart from an elected mayor whose main duty is to preside at banquets; the rudimentary police force is 'more concerned with the strayings of beasts than of people' (FR 18). However, this Arcadian society is possible because hobbits are better (uncoerced) than most of us: if we are not told in so many words that hobbits freely obey the will of God, we are told that they 'attributed to the king of old all their essential laws, and usually they kept the laws of free will, because they were the Rules (they said), both ancient and just' (FR 18). Other benign societies of Middle-earth tend to be what Tolkien calls 'unconstitutional monarchies', that is systems of direct personal rule, but their command structures seem to be largely confined to military purposes, and to depend in any case on personal loyalties and on oath-keeping rather than on any formalised apparatus of government. Malign societies – Mordor, Saruman's rule at Isengard, and the Shire under occupation by Saruman's agents – are, of course, brutally and comprehensively coercive in intent: their objective is a state whose subjects cannot make any free choices at all.

According to Christopher Tolkien,[48] Tolkien several times expressly said that one of the underlying themes of *The Lord of the Rings* was 'the machine', a term which Tolkien used in an extended sense to signify the attempt to actualise our desires by coercing the world, and other wills, into satisfying them. In this sense the technological 'machines', alluded to in Tolkien's advocacy of the universal dynamiting of factories and power-stations, are simply a special case of such coercion. Christopher Tolkien's formulation enables us to see the harmony between the 'anarchism' of Tolkien and his more widely recognised 'green' sympathies, his repugnance at the damage inflicted on the earth by human attempts to transform it to serve the actualisation of impious human desires, such as the desire to travel at very high speed or to have limitless supplies of luxury goods or to destroy one's enemies in large numbers.

The use of both literal and extended senses of 'machine' here, though confined in Tolkien's case to letters and private conversation, reminds us of Matthew Arnold's use of 'machinery' to disparage not only his Victorian contemporaries' over-valuation of technological progress but their faith in instrumental political devices such as the extension of the franchise. While Arnold opposes 'machinery' to 'culture', in Tolkien there is a more emphatic sense that the impropriety of the attempt to enforce one's will by means of the machine lies in the fact that it refuses submission to limitations that Nature (or the will of the Creator) imposes on human fulfilment. The machine is contrasted with the other characteristic product of human labour: art, which gives expression to those desires which transcend the possibilities of human life, but holds back from the hubris of seeking to realise them; God, it is implied, retains, and might exercise, the power to *realise* human, or mortal, imagination.

As Christopher Tolkien again says, the supreme 'machine', in the extended sense, in Tolkien's fiction is the Ring of Power itself: 'it is the ultimate machine, because it is made for coercion'. Not only does it empower its owner to coerce others, it slowly – but the more quickly the more it is used – seduces its owner into the nihilistic pride and malice which is the defining quality of its maker. It cannot therefore be used against Sauron, since to be used with the necessary force to overthrow Sauron would suffice to turn its owner into something just as bad as Sauron himself, or worse. The Ring therefore embodies the insight Tolkien expresses in his letter through the example of Alexander: in assailing the Persian tyranny to defend Greece, Alexander, according to Tolkien, degenerated into a tyrant himself, and contributed in the process to the cultural and political degeneration of Greece (much as, Tolkien believed, the coercive triumphs of British and American imperialism, to say nothing of Soviet imperialism, would deteriorate the world in the process of overthrowing the Nazi tyranny). Tolkien's implied position here is not far from that of Tolstoy, who rejected violence even when used in defence of innocents: for Tolstoy a good person would cease to be good in and by acting violently, and only the example of submission to the (pacific) will of God could lead the world towards salvation.[49] Tolkien in fact drew back from Tolstoy's conclusion. He did not reject war against Germany, and in *The Lord of the Rings* he gives an anti-pacifist speech to an authoritative character ('It needs but one foe to breed a war, not two ... and those who have not swords can still die on them' says the warrior princess Éowyn (RK, 236), though her interlocutor is allowed to sigh and shake his head.)[50] Tolkien recognised that a very heavy price would be paid for failing to organise efficient political and military power against aggression, but also recognised the moral price of using such power, and came close to regarding both outcomes as equally lamentable. *The Lord of the Rings* dramatises this tragic dilemma, but whereas in the real world Tolkien despaired of a solution, in the fiction he allows a (partially) happy ending: the benign forces use some violence in self-defence, but hold back from the ultimate coercive act of wielding the Ring, and indeed achieve their triumph by renouncing and destroying it.

In the first edition of this book in 1992 I treated what I called Tolkien's 'theological anarchism' somewhat apologetically and marginally, as if it would be better cut away, but I now believe that it is essentially related to Tolkien's overall ethical vision, and that that vision is a compelling one. Explaining it will also, perhaps surprisingly, help to resolve another puzzle which has troubled a number of Tolkien's readers: what was Tolkien doing, as a believing and practising Christian, in writing a version of the myth of the creation of the world which diverges in some respects from that of Christianity?

In the previous chapter I made the general point that, since around the eighteenth century, Christian writers have been increasingly unable to assume a readership ready to take for granted explicitly Christian doctrines or myths. Tolkien aims to achieve an expression as a literary artist which is *compatible* with Christian doctrines, but which can speak persuasively to readers without actually invoking those doctrines. He certainly believed that if the deliverances of his imagination had value it would be derived from their underlying 'truth', even if readers whose responses showed that they recognised that truth would not necessarily assent to a Christian formulation of it. 'The LOR is of course a fundamentally religious and Catholic work' (he wrote to Robert Murray, S. J. in 1953); 'unconsciously so at first, but consciously in the revision. That is why I have cut out practically all references to anything like "religion", to cults and practices, in the imaginary world. The religious element is absorbed into the story and the symbolism.'[51]

In *The Lord of the Rings*, God is mentioned a couple of times in the Appendices to the main narrative (as 'the One'), but the firmly terrestrial perspective of that work, set in a pre-Christian era, makes it relatively easy for Tolkien to avoid contact or direct comparison with the Judaeo-Christian myths and scriptures. In other writings, however, he aims to present an account of 'the beginning of days' – indeed of the origins of the world itself – and cannot avoid writing, for the Elves who are his main protagonists in these texts, an equivalent of the opening chapters of the Book of Genesis. This is 'Ainulindalë' or 'The Music of the Ainur', which we will revisit and consider in more detail in a moment.

The Creation and maintenance of the World by God can be conceptualised in at least two ways: as an exercise of power, or as a creative process. (It is, of course, both, but its rhetorical and imaginative presentation can emphasise one or the other aspect.) Before looking at *Ainulindalë*, I want to set up for purposes of comparison another text in which the creation and maintenance of the world are firmly conceptualised as an exercise of power. This is chapter XXXI of Hobbes's *Leviathan* (1651).

Hobbes, one can safely say, was not an anarchist. In *Leviathan* he argues that human beings in civil society are obliged to obey the actually existing Sovereign authority, because they may be supposed to have made a pact or contract with one another to surrender their individual rights in favour of that authority. (Hobbes does not, of course, literally claim that such a pact has historically been made in his own or any other society, but he believes that given the conditions of human existence on earth, it would be rational for human beings to have made it.) For Hobbes, the state of nature, that is, human existence without an acknowledged sovereign power, would be incomparably worse than the rule of even the worst sovereign: it would be a condition of perpetual war by every man against the lives and property of every other.

Like many political philosophers, Hobbes uses the concept of a natural Right in order to give a moral, and ultimately religious, foundation to his theory of just government. (By a natural right we mean a right that is not conferred by any human law, but is possessed by its owner simply by virtue of his or her natural being.) Hobbes's Sovereign is shown to have, and retain, the right to govern, and where necessary to punish or otherwise coerce his subjects; while the subjects themselves, according to Hobbes' theory, originally *had* natural rights, which they all surrendered when they contracted among themselves to obey the Sovereign.

What is the ontology of these natural rights? Where do they come from? Lesser philosophers than Hobbes prefer not to answer this question. Hobbes's answer is a very clear and rather chilling one, and it directly connects the human right to power with the creation and maintenance of the world conceived as acts of power. He begins by rejecting the idea that God's rights over his creatures are grounded upon their debt of gratitude to him.

> The Right of Nature, whereby God reigneth over men, and punisheth those that break his Lawes, is to be derived, not from his Creating them as if he required obedience, as of Gratitude for his benefits; but from his *Irresistible Power* … . Seeing all men by Nature had Right to All Things, they had Right every one to reigne over all the rest. But because this Right could not be obtained by force, it concerned the safety of every one, laying by that Right, to set up men (with Soveraign Authority) by common consent, to rule and defend them: whereas if there had been any man of Power Irresistible; there had been no reason, why he should not by that Power have ruled, and defended both himselfe, and them, according to his own discretion. To those therefore whose Power is irresistible, the dominion of all men adhaereth naturally by their excellence of Power; and consequently it is from that Power, that the Kingdome over men, and the Right of Afflicting men at his pleasure, belongeth Naturally to God Almighty; not as Creator, and Gracious; but as Omnipotent …
>
> This question, *Why Evill men often Prosper, and Good men suffer Adversity*, has been much disputed … Job, how earnestly does he expostulate with God, for the many Afflictions he suffered, notwithstanding his Righteousnesse? This question in the case of Job, is decided by God himselfe, not by arguments derived from Job's Sinne, but his own Power. For whereas the friends of Job drew their arguments from his Affliction to his Sinne, and he defended himselfe by the conscience of his Innocence, God himselfe taketh up the matter, and having justified the Affliction by arguments drawn from his own Power, such as this, *Where wast thou when I layd the foundations of the earth*, and the like, both approved Job's Innocence, and reproved the Erroneous doctrine of his friends. Conformable to this doctrine is the sentence of our Saviour, concerning the man that was born Blind, in these words, *Neither hath this man sinned, nor his fathers; but that the works of God might be made manifest in him*. And though it be said, *That Death entred into the world by sinne*, (by which is meant that if Adam had never sinned, he had never dyed, that is, never suffered any separation of his soule from his body,) it follows not thence, that God could not justly have afflicted him, though he had not Sinned, as well as he afflicteth other living creatures, that cannot sinne.[52]

In brief, Hobbes is saying that natural right simply *is* power, or rather power rationally understood. God has the right to afflict us, however innocent we are, because he has the power to do so. God could justly have afflicted Adam, even if Adam had not sinned. Equally, every human being has (in the state of nature) the natural right to afflict anyone else to the full extent of his or her power. (And Hobbes might have added that the spider has the right to afflict the fly, the lion the lamb, and so on.) But because this world in which everyone has a right to afflict everyone else is a nightmare, it is rational for us to establish civil society, in which almost all of us lay down this right and only one person or agency retains it.

Whether Hobbes's analysis is good theology or good politics is unimportant for our present purposes. The relevant point is that the universe it presents to us is a deeply unattractive one to most present-day sensibilities: it is a universe in which moral value is not (as we generally like to think) something which questions and limits power, but is itself ultimately derived from, or at least closely implicated with, power. And the God who says to the unfortunate Job *Where wast thou when I layd the foundations of the earth?* is the Creator God conceptualised merely as irresistible power (so far as Hobbes's use of the quotation is concerned).

One difference between presenting the Creation as power and presenting it as creativity is that the former emphasises the dependence of the thing or person created, and the latter its independence. (Again, it is necessarily both, since any created thing or person is both initially dependent and ultimately at least to an extent independent, but the relations between creator and creature can be presented with different kinds of emphasis.) If you conceptualise the Creation as power, and if your political vocabulary is based on rights derived from Nature, that is from God, you move easily with Hobbes to the vindication of a coercive politics. 'To those therefore whose Power is irresistible, the dominion of all men adhaereth naturally by their excellence of Power.'[53] It is true that Hobbes strongly upholds such traditional non-coercive virtues as justice, gratitude, mercy, modesty and equity, since these are conducive to 'peaceable, sociable and comfortable living', and any action which so tends is *ipso facto* virtuous.[54] But most conducive of all to peace, and so pre-eminently virtuous according to the logic of Hobbes's argument, is the surrender of one's rights in favour of the Sovereign's, and an obedience to him which is qualified by little more than the right of self-preservation in extremis.[55]

I would like to be able to show that Tolkien read and criticised Hobbes, but unfortunately I know of no evidence that he did. However, I think we have seen enough of Tolkien's political views to prepare us to recognise the legitimacy of the contrast I am now about to draw. In Hobbes, a vindication of the authoritarian state is derived, by logical steps, from a conception of God as original Power: the fundamental currency of political legitimacy is the Right, and the fundamental Right is the Right to use one's power. The Sovereign must be obeyed because he is the only human being who remains in possession of that Right once civil society has been established. In Tolkien, a deep suspicion of the state, a near-anarchist attitude towards political power, is connected to a conception of God not as original Power but as original Artist: an essential feature of an artist, on Tolkien's conception, being the renunciation of power over one's creatures, the delegation of power to others. In Ainulindalë he preserves the essential features of an Augustinian Christianity, while pulling the basic myth of creation firmly towards the 'creative' pole. Moral value will be seen to have its origin, or at least prototype, in the renunciation of power. And in certain later episodes of the mythical and legendary narrative set out in The Silmarillion, Tolkien follows through with impressive consistency his prioritisation of creativity over power.

'The Music of the Ainur' was one of the earliest components of Tolkien's mythical narrative to achieve a more or less stable form, around 1920: its foundational role for the subsequent narratives is indisputable.[56] In the published Silmarillion, Ainulindalë begins with God (Eru Ilúvatar) creating the Ainur, the 'offspring of his thought', and causing them to sing before him.

> For a long while they sang only each alone, or but few together, while the rest hearkened; for each comprehended only that part of the mind of Ilúvatar from which he came, and in the understanding of their brethren they grew but slowly. Yet ever as they listened they came to deeper understanding, and increased in unison and harmony. (S, 15)

At length Eru declares a 'mighty theme' to the Ainur, and calls upon them to create a Great Music around it. In a passage reminiscent of the Psalms, this is magnificently evoked, until

> it came into the heart of Melkor to interweave matters of his own imagining that were not in accord with the theme of Ilúvatar … . He had gone alone often into the void places seeking the Imperishable Flame; for the desire grew hot within him to bring into Being things of his own, and it seemed to him that Ilúvatar took no thought for the Void, and he was impatient of its emptiness. Yet he found not the Fire, for it is with Ilúvatar. But being alone he had begun to conceive thoughts of his own unlike those of his brethren. (16)

Melkor's discords disrupt the Music, which Ilúvatar restores to euphony with two additional themes. Finally, after silencing the Music with one tremendous chord, Ilúvatar takes the Ainur out into the Void, and shows them their Music in visible form, as a spherical world. It begins to unfold its history; and the Ainur see, arising from the third theme of Ilúvatar, Elves and Men, the 'Children of Ilúvatar', entering the World which their own Music has formed. Perceiving the joy of the Ainur at this vision, Ilúvatar says 'Let these things Be!' (20), the World comes into existence, and many of the Ainur, including Melkor, descend into it to fulfil their part in the realisation of its history.

The structural resemblances here to the Christian myth are already clear enough: Eru Ilúvatar is God, the Ainur are like angels, and Melkor is clearly shaping up for the role of fallen angel, Satan or Lucifer. The basic Augustinian apparatus in which nothing is created evil, but evil arises from the free will of created beings, is in place. But the differences are equally striking.

Firstly, in this myth the Creation of the World is carried out partly through intermediaries. The world is not (directly) God's music, but the music of his creatures, the Ainur, composed by them, though based upon the themes He propounds and given being – that is, translated from imaginative conception into historical reality – by Him. And the Ainur are not simply tools or extensions of God's power, as puppets or zombies or machines would be: as independent minds, they have to learn gradually what to do and how to collaborate (hence the emphasis on the slow growth in understanding of their brethren). Though each of them is invested with native powers by Ilúvatar, their music is not a product of the aggregate of those powers, but of the synthesis of their powers which they achieve. Their function is therefore deliberately made to resemble human creativity, with its requirements of learning and discipline and intuition as well as direct divine 'inspiration', and its necessarily collective and traditional aspects. They are in fact 'sub-creators', to use Tolkien's own term for human artists.

One consequence of the use of intermediaries is that highly specific features of the world are conceived as the outcome of both intentional and unintentional collaboration among sub-creators.

> And Ilúvatar spoke to Ulmo, and said: 'Seest thou not how here in this little realm in the Deeps of Time Melkor hath made war upon thy province? He hath bethought him of bitter cold immoderate, and yet hath not destroyed the beauty of thy fountains, nor thy clear pools. Behold the snow, and the cunning work of frost! Melkor hath devised heats and fire without restraint, and hath not dried up thy desire nor utterly quelled the music of the sea. Behold rather the height and glory of the clouds, and the everchanging mists; and listen to the fall of rain upon the Earth! And in these clouds thou art drawn nearer to Manwë, thy friend, whom thou lovest.' (19)

The distinctive feature of Tolkien's myth here is that, from the point of view of Ulmo and Manwë, the first snowflake is at once a product of their own actions and a delightful surprise, and this is a deeply attractive picture of creation – more attractive, I think, than the production of the snowflake by God's immediate *fiat* would be.

Secondly, the media of creation, or the metaphors for Creation, are themselves artistic. The process begins as music, is converted into a vision (and initially it is an imaginative vision) of the world 'globed amid the void' – one imagines something like the outer panels of Bosch's *Garden of Earthly Delights* – and it finally realises itself as a narrative. The Ainur are called upon to enter into the world, and to fulfil, with others, the unfolding history that is their 'minstrelsy'. Later there is a certain amount of forceful engineering of the physical universe (see the passage from the end of *Ainulindalë* quoted in chapter 3), but this is delegated to the Ainur rather than carried out by Ilúvatar. As readers of *The Silmarillion* and *The Lord of the Rings* will know, Eru takes a back seat from this point onwards: if he retains overall narrative direction – and there are a few very elusive and delicate hints to this effect – his creatures do not perceive it, and independently act out the history as free agents, God intervening directly only on extremely rare occasions. This is like a consummation of the fiction-writer's ideal: the author maintains overall supervision, but enjoys a sense of delighted discovery as characters act for themselves.

Thirdly, we should note the role played by the Imperishable Flame or 'secret Fire' in giving reality to what was previously merely art. Here, if you like, God's supreme power is manifest – no one else can give Being to the imagined. But this function is not only separated out from the imaginative work, but placed chronologically later. The artistic creativity comes first: the making real comes later.

Fourthly, it is worth remarking that even Melkor's rebellion is initially creative in nature ('desire grew hot within him to bring into being creatures of his own … it seemed to him that Ilúvatar took no thought for the Void, and he was impatient of its emptiness'). Arguably, indeed, this has to be the case given the artistic nature of the angelic culture Ilúvatar has created. Melkor cannot 'make war' against God – for how can he know that there is such a thing as war? Milton's Satan can do so, and can speak in metaphors of warfare, because Milton's heaven is militarised. We notice too that in Tolkien's version Melkor's rebellion is as much a rebellion against the harmony and unison of his peers as against Ilúvatar directly. Milton's Satan can plausibly conceive God as a tyrant; Melkor cannot.

The spectacle of Melkor as frustrated genius points us to an important qualification of the simple polarity 'Power Bad, Creativity Good'. Melkor begins as an impatient creative spirit; as the myth proceeds, his activity becomes progressively more destructive, because it has been tainted from the beginning with pride of power and self-glorification: his desire to create other beings for his glory rather than for delight in their independent life degenerates into the desire for servants of his own will, and finally into hatred of all other wills and all products of others' creativity.

This theme of the temptations of creativity is sustained later in the narrative through such figures as Fëanor, who becomes enamoured of the Silmarils he has created, and leads his entire people into an unwinnable war when they are stolen from him by Melkor. Indeed both the Elves, who are superhuman artists, and the Dwarves, who are superhuman craftsmen, are characterised in the tragic narratives of *The Silmarillion* by their inability to let go of the products of their skill: this is, if you like, their distinctive way of sinning. The crucial distinction between good and bad attitudes to creativity is spelt out in a particularly moving episode in *The Silmarillion* which seems designed to stand as a benevolent counterpart to Melkor's rebellion. The Ainu Aulë, whose special talent is for working with the mineral world, secretly fashions the Seven Fathers of the Dwarves in a hall under the mountains. Ilúvatar reproves his blasphemy, pointing out that these creatures lack independent life, and only move when Aulë thinks to move them: they are machines, wholly subservient to his will. (Only God can create new living beings.) Aulë replies that 'I did not desire such lordship. I desired things other than I am, to love and to teach them' (43); and, weeping, he takes up a hammer to destroy them. But the Dwarves flinch from the hammer, and beg for mercy. The Dwarves' actions show, of course, that Ilúvatar has conferred independent volition upon them, and this is the consummation of Aulë's desire. In contrast, when at the end of *The Lord of the Rings* Sauron is overthrown, the dependence of his creatures, and the reduction of his servants to 'machines', is, as we have seen, vividly displayed:

> His armies halted, and his captains, suddenly steerless, bereft of will, wavered and despaired ... the creatures of Sauron, orc or troll or beast spell-enslaved, ran hither and thither mindless; and some slew themselves, or cast themselves in pits, or fled wailing back to hide in holes and dark lightless places far from hope. (RK, 223, 227)

To summarise, then, we have a God who acts through the direct exercise of power to the absolutely minimum possible extent, who creates a universe of independent beings for freedom not for domination, and expects them in turn to sub-create in the same spirit. Those who do so may have reality conferred on what they imagine; conversely those who seek power over their creations (or others' creations), who treat created things and persons as 'machines' in the extended sense, are themselves diminished.

Tolkien's sympathy for 'Anarchy, meaning abolition of control' is therefore rooted in his moral conception of the universe itself. Contrary to Hobbes's view, the natural right to power is precisely what we do not have, and if God has it, his natural inclination is to forgo it as far as a benign Creator can. There is a text – the discursive poem 'Mythopoeia' – in which Tolkien seriously uses the concept of a God-derived right, and the relevant lines run as follows:

> Though all the crannies of the world we filled
> with elves and goblins, though we dared to build
> gods and their houses out of dark and light,
> and sowed the seed of dragons, 'twas our right
> (used or misused). The right has not decayed.
> We make still by the law in which we're made.[57]

For Tolkien the fundamental derived human right is the right to create. The idea, with its romantic exaltation of the creative artist, its implied rejection of the classical notion of art as imitation, has its immediate roots in Coleridge, whose celebrated but cumbrous jargon of Fancy and Imagination Tolkien makes a bold attempt to improve upon in 'On Fairy Stories'.[58] But Tolkien saw perhaps more clearly than Coleridge that creative power was as capable of corrupting its owner as any other gift. His view of artistic 'sub-creation', both as a self-conscious artist himself and as a depictor of artists in his work, is at once a continuation of the romantic tradition and a critique of it.

What difference does all this make to our understanding, or evaluation, of Tolkien?

Firstly, and speaking for myself, I now view the 'anarchist' elements more sympathetically than in my earlier work on Tolkien. I still regret Tolkien's expressed indifference to what I called in 1992 'the necessity of those unaesthetic political structures which, however imperfectly, curtail the concentration of power', but I can see that his anti-political stance, like Tolstoy's, rests on a considered and consistent metaphysic, and is more than just the indulgence of a pious wish that everyone would act rightly without any need of politics.

Secondly and conversely, I feel better placed to explain to the sceptical why 'The Music of the Ainur' is more than a mere pastiche, an exercise in 'playing at the Old Testament'. I hope to have shown that the metaphorical structure it employs is neither arbitrary nor merely ornamental, but motivated by an expressive purpose of considerable seriousness.

Finally, I believe the analysis harmonises closely with Tolkien's best-known statement of what he was doing in his fiction. If I am right, his rejection of the author's 'purposed domination' over the responses of the reader is much more than an acceptance of the modernist truism that a literary text, once published, becomes an item of 'public property' which anyone can interpret or misinterpret; rather, it is an intentional adoption of the creative ethic of Ilúvatar himself, and is in absolute harmony with the moral and political values which pervade Tolkien's work.

SIX

The Cultural Phenomenon
Relabelling, Assimilation, Imitation, Adaptation

Tolkien knew that his work would have an afterlife that he could not control. Indeed, as we saw in the last chapter, he believed that an author should not aspire to such 'purposed domination'. It may seem strange that this belief did not prevent him from criticising severely various misreadings and distorted adaptations of his works. But there is no inconsistency in Tolkien's position. He hoped that people who had read and understood his work would freely apply it to their own experiences: he was not waiving the expectation that they would read it with understanding in the first place. Similarly, his youthful ambition that his cycle of stories would 'leave scope for other minds and hands, wielding paint and music and drama' did not envisage a free-for-all in which the distinctive 'tone and quality' of the original invention would be wholly lost.[1] Much of what has happened has disappointed – or is simply irrelevant to – Tolkien's hopes, but if we look for cultural phenomena which are both of value in themselves and intrinsically and necessarily related to Tolkien's invention, we will not by any means draw a complete blank.

Since the various forms taken by the cultural afterlives of major texts ought to be a theme of particular interest in cultural studies, it may be useful to approach the forms in an analytical rather than a chronological manner: *The Lord of the Rings* especially has attracted such a vast and diverse afterlife that it should be possible to evolve some kind of systematic account of what has transpired. The opening sections of the chapter will therefore examine some of the cultural processes whereby the distinctiveness of the original work is dissolved into wider cultural categories or practices; the longer closing section, on adaptations, will consider how successfully adapters have confronted the task of making a new work in their own medium that is yet essentially related to an existing original.

Relabelling

Let us start with the child-size packs of playing cards produced in 2002 by Character Games Ltd, under licence from New Line Cinema. These are standard playing cards, except that the 'court' or 'face' cards represent characters from the Peter Jackson movie version of *The Lord of the Rings*. Accompanying the pack is a leaflet of rules for card games such as 'Gollum's Gamble' and 'Elvish Whist'. These are easily recognised (though not necessarily by the children who are the intended market) as elementary variants of pre-existing games. Elvish Whist is just a very simple form of Whist, while Gollum's Gamble is a discard game in which the only significance of the title is that 'the last player left with cards is called "the Gollum", or whatever term of derision you wish'. Similarly, Winning Moves' card series *Top Trumps: The Lord of the Rings* largely reworks the devices of the Pokémon series.

This phenomenon can be called *relabelling*. An established type of cultural product, in this case the card game, is given a new lease of commercial life by association with a creative work to which it has no necessary connection: there is nothing, that is, in the activity of the player or the structure of the game to which the content of the creative work has made a difference. The *Lord of the Rings* Advent Calendar produced in 2002, under licence from New Line Cinema, also exemplifies relabelling, any connection between the Tolkien/Jackson narrative and the countdown to Christmas being purely arbitrary.[2]

A less clear-cut example is provided by the Playstation 2 games, EA's *The Lord of the Rings: The Two Towers* and Vivendi's *The Lord of the Rings:*

The Fellowship of the Ring.[3] With these games, in which the player manoeuvres on-screen figures through a series of environments, tasks and combats, one does gain an initial impression of tracking, and modifying, the narrative of the book or film itself, an impression aided by the superb graphics (in the case of *The Two Towers*, derived from and interwoven with footage from the first two Jackson films). However, the generic – in fact, abstract and logical – nature of the play itself ultimately undermines this impression. The player's actions consist of inputting electronic signals by finger pressure on the controller buttons; these generate output from the console according to the rules of a computer program, something that in itself, as Searle puts it, has a syntax but no semantics.[4] Though the on-screen graphics interpret the underlying algebra to present a surface semantics of running, jumping, axe-swinging, firing arrows, and so on, the narrative possibilities open to the player are, in the end, all too recognisably similar in structure to those in other computer games. To survive as he battles against giant spiders in the Vivendi game, for example, our Frodo figure must re-acquire 'Health' by eating a certain quantity of mushrooms which he picks up beside the path, just as other Playstation heroes are required to accumulate apples, butterflies or chocolate frogs[5] to restore their life chances: behind the screen, as it were, mushrooms and frogs are the same. In *The Two Towers*, one can choose to activate the figures of Aragorn, Gimli, Legolas or Isildur; graphically, they are differenti-ated, but their functional characteristics are expressed in numerical scores for arrows stored, spent and retrieved, 'health', 'experience', speed of movement, resilience and so forth, and it is these that determine the outcome of the combats in which they incessantly engage. The exceptional complexity of the play in *The Two Towers* reflects not so much the specific narrative resources provided by Tolkien's fiction as the success of children's brains and fingers in forcing ever greater logical ingenuity from the game designers.

Relabelling an existing formula to cash in on the exceptional popularity of a literary text is not, of course, a postmodern, or even a modern, phenomenon. Victorians dancing the 'Woman in White quadrille' or wearing a 'Woman in White' perfume presumably did not seriously believe that a dance tune or scent could, other than by arbitrary association, evoke the unique quality of Wilkie Collins's novel.[6] But arbitrary association can be a powerful thing: a trace of the glamour of the original text is transferred, however irrationally, to the new product. We can see this motive at work in the school playground, where children in mock fights assign themselves currently fashionable character-identities ('I'm Luke Skywalker'; 'I'm Legolas, you be Gimli'), just as a broken tree branch becomes a light saber one year, a wizard's staff the next. A related, but more complex phenomenon, not strictly relabelling, is the adoption of character names for one's children. This may be in part a way of publicly expressing one's admiration for the original work, but it is likely also to imply a degree of acceptance of whatever values or sentiments the work has succeeded in attaching to the character: Wendy (effectively invented in Barrie's *Peter Pan*) is a twentieth-century example, evoking an incipiently maternal bourgeois girlishness, irrespective of the actual attributes of its owners.[7] Thus to name a girl 'Arwen', as some readers of Tolkien have done, suggests a commendably adoring view of the new-born, if a slightly melancholy perspective on her future.[8] Yet the choice of this name is really as arbitrary in its relation to the thing named as the decision by Character Games Ltd to have Faramir rather than Robin Hood as the Jack of Diamonds.

Assimilation

In assimilation, the distinctive features of the original work, instead of forming the basis of an application to some new context, tend rather to be erased or eroded, in order to locate the work within some more familiar category. Assimilation, then, is the enemy of critical analysis or scholarly inquiry. At its crudest, it is the recourse of the lazy journalist who has not read *The Lord of the Rings*, but has seen the film *Conan the Barbarian*, and feels he must be on pretty safe ground talking about the *Lord of the Rings* as if it were *Conan the Barbarian*, since both of them appear to involve ancient sword-wielding heroes. In a common journalistic variant, assimilation is not even to other texts, merely to a supposedly generic taste among its readers. 'I never could do the Tolkien books, they were a bit too popular with the Dungeons-and-Dragons set',[9] is a typical apology along these lines, assimilation here taking the special form of guilt-by-association.

Assimilating the mysterious enthusiasm for Tolkien to various low-grade specialist tastes, or in the last resort to despised social or personality types, has in fact been a recurring strategy among hostile commentators. It might appear to be a doomed strategy, given the easily observable diversity in age, gender, nationality, occupation and lifestyles of Tolkien's vast readership, but it has nevertheless been persevered with to the point of absurdity, not to mention contradiction. An early view was that The Lord of the Rings, being after all the work of a pipe-smoking don, must appeal mainly to repressed middle-aged English males, public schoolboys who never grew up, the kind of readers who settle down with a ripping yarn every evening instead of getting a life. (Part of the point of this accusation may have been to explain away the enthusiastic reviews by W. H. Auden, Auden having admitted a few years earlier to an addiction to detective stories. But a look at Auden's writings will show that the claims he makes for Tolkien are at a very different level from his remarks on detective stories.)[10] There are hints of this view in the early attacks by Edmund Wilson, Edwin Muir and Philip Toynbee,[11] and it is still present in the 1983 collection edited by Robert Giddings, This Far Land. Giddings himself merely reiterates the public-school accusation (the characters 'are' prefects, fags, and so on), but Fred Inglis widens the line of fire, describing Tolkien's typical readers as 'honest worthies: English teachers, television producers ... interior designers ... clergymen ... Mrs Laura Ashley ...': the list seems to include pretty well any comfortably-off middle-aged person Inglis dislikes. Inglis imagines an archetypal Tolkien reader who was 'formerly head of art in a market town's shabby long-lived grammar school', and now runs a craft centre and has a 'battered Cortina'.[12] Yet from the 'Tolkien cult' period of the mid-1960s, people of a very different type, callow teenagers and dope-enraptured hippies (later, ex-hippies) gradually began to overtake 'honest worthies' in the role of despised or patronised fans. As late as 2001, many journalists seemed unable to get round to reporting or reviewing the film of The Fellowship of the Ring until the stock invocation of adolescence and 'flower power' was safely out of the way; while another critic revived the get-a-life slur with his claim to recall that, when he was a schoolboy, you either played sport or read The Lord of the Rings.[13] Regular guys, apparently, do not read Tolkien. As for regular girls, the presence of Naomi Mitchison, Iris Murdoch and the Queen of Denmark among Tolkien's earliest admirers has made it difficult to press the case that they are all male, but not to suggest that the female admirers are the wrong sort of females, like the 'full-grown women wearing puffed sleeves, clutching teddies and babbling excitedly about the doings of hobbits' in Germaine Greer's recollections of Cambridge.[14] The innuendo common to all these assimilations is that an admiration for The Lord of the Rings is not a unique literary judgement, picking out the distinctive qualities of the work: it is merely an epiphenom-enon of some deep psychological need, which might be satisfied by any one of a range of stimulants or sedatives.

Among reputable academic literary critics, confessing that you 'never could do' a book is less acceptable, as is dismissing it on the grounds that its readers wear puffed sleeves or drive battered Cortinas. The damaging assimilation has, in general, to be to other books, and to be based on some demonstrable resemblance, however fleeting. Fortunately (or unfortunately) the training provided by academic literary criticism is, in part, a training in making a great deal of fleeting details, inculcating as it does from high school onwards a routine in which large assertions are supported by small quotations. In practice this is hard to avoid. The examination candidate writes that Shakespeare in Othello makes extensive thematic use of animal images; and quotes – as she has been coached to do – a couple of lines from Act 3 to prove it. (This is called 'supporting your ideas with evidence'.) No one could possibly ask her to prove that these lines are in fact representative of a pattern visible across the play as a whole. The credibility of the proof by brief quotation depends on a prior consensus about the meaning of the play, to which the candidate is required to conform, as well as an essentially formalist poetics which views literary works as highly-wrought unities in which every detail may be assumed to subserve some thematic purpose of the whole. Once this routine has been inculcated, however, it can be exploited later in the student's career for a kind of glib dismissiveness. John Carey, for example, claims that The Lord of the Rings is 'a children's book', much of it in the style of Enid Blyton, and singles out as illustration a few sentences from an early chapter, including the phrase: 'and of course his special friends, Pippin Took and Merry Brandybuck' (FR, 76).[15] It is true that something like this passage could occur in Blyton, that Pippin and Merry are juvenile names, and that 'special friends' in many contexts could seem sentimental or arch. Colin Wilson says that The Lord of the Rings 'at its worst ... has touches of Enid Blyton', which is fair enough because it claims nothing beyond local resemblances.[16] I have myself noted some 'incongruous lapses' in the style of these early chapters. The problem with Carey's assimilation is the unfounded claim of typicality. There is, after all, nothing *exclusively* Blytonian about the phrase 'special friends' itself; what makes it reminiscent of her, especially if we pluck it out of its context and hold it up for inspection, is that Blyton rarely strays outside such cosy bourgeois-domestic intimacies as the phrase might capture. Readers turn to Blyton, as to other genre writers, because they know what they will get: lots and lots of the same. An attentive reading of the episode will show that Tolkien's style modulates into, and out of, the admittedly insipid passage to which Carey objects.[17]

Tolkien has suffered more than most writers from the '*this rather reminds me of ...*' critical mentality, both from admirers and neutrals overstating his indebtedness or affinity to other texts,[18] and from detractors. Long before Carey, Mark Roberts had provided a kind of template for the dismissive assimilators in his 1956 review of The Lord of the Rings in *Essays in Criticism*. Beginning 'Once upon a time' (a reductive assimilation in itself), and couched in tones of donnish ennui, Roberts' review shows us how, at the time of its publication, The Lord of the Rings might have struck an intelligent academic who has read so widely in modern English literature that he can make nothing of a unsettlingly new work except a collection of approximate resemblances. Even the multitudinous landscape descriptions (which he describes as 'lush' – surely hardly any of them are that) merely remind Roberts of Tennyson, except for being written in prose. At least Roberts, however, focused on the text. An assimilatory technique of a slightly later period – the politically indignant 'it is no coincidence ... ' manoeuvre, which does not require even fleeting resemblances among the actual texts – is exemplified by a remark by Giddings. 'It is interesting that the great success of Tolkien's epic has been coincidental with the cult of James Bond, the fashion for Len Deighton and John Le Carré, which collectively form such a revealing aspect of Cold War ideology.'[19] Under the protective vagueness of 'interesting ... coincidental with ...' (meaning 'non-coincidental, but I prefer not to offer any evidence') this contrives to smear Tolkien and his readers politically, while disallowing in advance the question of why a book which is not about the Cold War should be grouped with books which unquestionably are about it.

It is a relief to turn to a more innocent kind of assimilation, exemplified by the *Guardian* (London) of 30 November 2002. 'Take a leaf out of Tolkien's book and join the fellowship of the ring, with romantic chiffon and capes', begins a fashion feature. The sentence itself, starting with an allusion to a Tolkien title, removing the capitals from 'fellowship' and 'ring' to generalise their application, and finally justifying the chiffon and capes – neither especially redolent of Middle-earth – with the vaguely appropriate descriptor 'romantic', re-enacts the process whereby the specific content of Tolkien's invention has been dissolved into a wider, if not wholly alien, cultural landscape. The accompanying photographs set the model in woodland; one, showing her reclining rather awkwardly below tree roots on a steeply sloping bank, recalls not only an episode from the first Peter Jackson film, but also the widely used 1972 portrait of the elderly Tolkien by Snowdon. The garments themselves mostly emphasise earth and plant colours – brown, russet, cream, plum, lilac – and floral patterns; an impossibly long silver-grey dress ('£980, by Rafael Lopez') hints at the white and grey favoured by Galadriel and Arwen. They are indeed 'romantic', and so in a vaguely similar sense is Tolkien, but their style draws less on the (admittedly sketchy) indications of costume in the texts than on the Jackson films, themselves influenced by illustrators such as Alan Lee and John Howe, and more still on other 'romantic' traditions which have little to do with Tolkien: the pre-Raphaelite, and the 'gypsy'.

Both relabelling and assimilation are visible in the world of low-tech war games, in which the player uses lead or plastic figurines to enact battles governed by dice-throwing and by various abstruse rules of engagement. Games Workshop (again under licence from New Line Cinema) has recently produced a series featuring character types and devices from the Jackson films, but in essence very similar to other games from the same source. But thanks to the comparative antiquity of table-top war games, Tolkien's influence (whether direct or mediated through literary imitators like Terry Brooks, or through Gary Gygax's Dungeons and Dragons role-play games) has already had time to make its mark on the genre. Games Workshop's earlier Warhammer series, for example, has not only Orcs and Goblins, but High Elves (further proof of the general cultural success of Tolkien's dignifying transformation of the term 'Elf'); like the Eldar of Tolkien's legends, these Elves have experienced a historic 'sundering', are superior in power to the primitive races of men with whom they are coeval, have a language of their own (clearly indebted in style to Tolkien's Elvish tongues), and defend strongholds with names like 'Lothern'. However, in contrast to Tolkien's creatures their dignity lies solely in military strength: all the moral and religious, and most of the aesthetic, force of his invention is inevitably lost. The particular war games actually derived from the Jackson films have therefore relabelled, with elements direct from Tolkien, a pre-existing norm which is itself partly the outcome of the assimilation of his work into the older war game genre.

Imitation

If millions of readers of Tolkien have wished that there was more of Middle-earth to explore, thousands (at a guess) have attempted to create something to meet this need, or simply to satisfy their urge to imitate what one enjoys and admires. At the same time, the commercial success of Tolkien has lowered the threshold of quality at which publishers are willing to invest in work which can plausibly be thought to be reaching the same market. The combined result of these two factors has been a tidal wave of published fiction marketed either as, in effect, a continuation of Tolkien, or more subtly as post-Tolkienian or anti-Tolkienian fantasy, profiting by the liberation of respectable fiction from the tyranny of the here and now while renouncing the less generally fashionable elements in Tolkien's work, especially its religious orthodoxy and lack of irony. Writers as diverse as Stephen Donaldson, Philip Pullman and Terry Pratchett belong in this latter category.

The idea of 'fantasy fiction' as a niche market for which a kind of industrial production can be achieved (as with the detective story or the Western) was foreshadowed, in advance of Tolkien, by American fantasy magazines of the 1920s and '30s: notably Weird Tales, in which H. P. Lovecraft, among others, made his name. Its current flowering, however, is almost certainly the result of a process which began around the late 1960s, as Tolkien readers cast about for something to satisfy their quickened taste for imagined worlds, and writers, publishers and booksellers duly responded. Older authors like Lord Dunsany and E. R. Eddison, both of whom had died in the 1950s, were drafted on to the Tolkien shelf, as were slightly younger writers such as Mervyn Peake and T. H. White, who had already established reputations quite independently. More recently, a kind of marketing merger between fantasy and science fiction – genres already overlapping as far back as Weird Tales – has taken place.

Neither Peake's Gormenghast novels nor White's masterpiece The Once and Future King resemble Tolkien in emotional tone or moral temper, which is as it should be. As anyone who has tried it knows, the attempt to realise an invented world in fiction, and to make it distinctive and emotionally compelling, obliges the writer to search within himself or herself, to discover whether the resources of knowledge and imagination are there that can service the invention. If the pre-conscious mind co-operates, and the necessary compositional skills are also present, distinctive matter from deep regions of the personality and memory may be channelled into the finished work. For most people, however, it turns out that there is nothing very distinctive to be tapped, or the power to objectify it in art is lacking.

As I write, Waterstone's bookshops in the UK are displaying works by Tolkien in, or alongside, an alphabetical series which extends from Isaac Asimov to John Wyndham, both science-fiction writers, includes novelisations of the *Star Wars* films, but is dominated by the innumerable works of Terry Brooks, David Eddings, Robert Jordan, J. V. Jones ('As good as David Eddings or your money back!'), Anne McCaffrey, and other purveyors of Tolkien-derivative secondary worlds. Though entertaining enough if you can get past their mechanical prose, and do not reflect too much on the shortness of life, these are far closer in narrative content to Tolkien than are Peake or White, while at the same time lacking most of the qualities which, I have argued in earlier chapters, make Tolkien an important literary artist. Significantly, the qualities in which they tend to be most deficient are the 'modern', novelistic ones, the ones which are not exclusive to the fantasy fiction genre, but are required to give the inventions of fantasy the stamp of real human experience. The maps, the magic, the monsters, the races, the talismans, the names ending in -*ath* and -*eth* and -*or*, the Lords of this and the Masters of that are all there; what one misses are Tolkien's adequately motivated characters, diversity of dialogue styles, eye for three-dimensional landscape, leisurely but assured management of narrative, and combination of effectively realised character-perspectives with an underlying 'objective' vision.[20]

One is driven to the conclusion that just as Marx (he said) was not a marxist, Tolkien is not a writer of 'fantasy fiction' as now generally understood, and his ghost is entitled to disclaim paternity of Brooks, Jordan and the rest. His contribution has been the more general one of making departures from contemporary realism, especially in the direction of imaginary pasts rather than imaginary futures, more acceptable to an intelligent reading public. The genuinely creative minds who have seized this opportunity have moved away, not only from the surface features, but often from the fundamental aesthetic and metaphysical principles, of Tolkien's invention, such as the complete separation of the invented world from the real one. The recognition can be seen progressively dawning in the work of the children's writer Alan Garner, whose early books feature wizards, dwarfs and vaguely Tolkienian names (Gomrath, Elidor), but already depict, instead of an autonomous universe, the intrusion of other-worldly elements into the contemporary human world; by the time of his fourth and best-known work, *The Owl Service*, Garner had shed every trace of Tolkien's influence.[21] More recently, J. K. Rowling's 'Harry Potter' stories have triumphed by fusing elements reminiscent of Tolkien with a wholly different (and one would previously have thought almost defunct) genre, the public-school story. Tolkien would no doubt have deplored this hybrid quality, as he did in the case of Lewis's *Narnia* series, but he might have come to recognise that the unprecedented solidity of his own self-sufficient world, built up over a lifetime, could rarely be emulated, and that few would attempt it. (A partial exception which has proved successful, at least commercially, is George Lucas's *Star Wars* film series, a rare example of cinematic science fiction disengaged, at least in theory, from planet Earth.)[22] Terry Pratchett's *Discworld* novels combine world-invention with an ironic awareness of our own world, turning the resulting incongruities to comic effect. This kind of hybridity is a weakness, however, of Harvard Lampoon's Tolkien burlesque from 1969, *Bored of the Rings*.[23] Despite amusing moments at which it achieves genuine parody of Tolkien's tone and rhythm ('fishing their overnight bags out of the craft, [they] set out with Frito along the rising gorge that led to the next chapter'),[24] its essential strategy is the translation of Tolkien's epic narrative into the most bathetic terms of modern discourse, circa 1969. With its 'groovy' and 'stenographer', its 'Frito' and 'Spam', and its references to Chang Kai-Shek and Pandit Nehru, it has dated far more damagingly than its original.

Adaptation

'I think the book quite unsuitable for "dramatization"', Tolkien remarked within a year of the publication of *The Lord of the Rings*. In a 1956 letter to the radio producer Terence Tiller, he touched on some of the difficulties of adaptation: the sheer length of the book; the dependence of drama on dialogue to convey information; the impossibility of conveying adequately the physical setting (especially in a radio version).[25] In his essay 'On Fairy Stories', long before any prospect of adaptation had arisen, he had called drama 'an art fundamentally different from Literature', not least because of its resistance to fantasy: attempts to represent on stage fantastic elements (such as non-human creatures, or magical transformations), were more likely to achieve the 'buffoonery' of pantomime than enchantment. 'Fantasy is a thing best left to words', and their unmediated access to the human imagination.[26]

When, in 1958, Tolkien was shown the 'story-line' (by M. G. Zimmerman) for a proposed animated film of The Lord of the Rings, he wrote a long and mordant commentary.[27] I will return to this later when discussing the Peter Jackson films, but a number of Tolkien's observations have a general significance. He shows awareness that cinema, unlike stage drama, can be effective in suggesting 'scenery' and the change of the seasons. But most of his remarks are hostile. Some can be grouped as protests against various assimilations of his invention, to the dialogue style of science fiction (the Elvish waybread lembas as a 'food concentrate'), or to the visual style of French fairy-stories, especially as debased by Disney Studios. Others, however, touch upon narrative considerations which on the face of it are common to both film and fiction. An example is Tolkien's criticism of 'anticipation': the premature introduction of dramatic motifs or devices, with the result that the narrative is flattened out and the devices have lost their freshness when really needed. (Zimmerman had proposed to use Eagles to carry Frodo and his companions from the Shire, from Rivendell to the mountains, and so on. Tolkien argues against this on characteristic grounds of geographical realism – mountain Eagles do not alight in gently rolling countryside – but above all because it causes the 'staling' of the Eagles' appearances when they are really needed, to rescue Gandalf at Isengard and finally Frodo from the slopes of Mount Doom.) Further types of objection focus on the erosion of moral significance, such as the elimination of the temptation of Galadriel when Frodo offers her the Ring, or the reduction of Saruman's powers of persuasion, which the free reason can always reject, to an irresistible act of 'hypnosis'.

If we combine these insights of Tolkien with various points noted earlier in the present chapter, we may cautiously venture some criteria for the best possible adaptation of The Lord of the Rings. The best possible adaptation must not simply appropriate the characters and nomenclature of the original text in order to relabel an existing formula; it must not assimilate the original to generic styles or to other texts, thus losing its distinctiveness; it must resolve the problem of translation from narrative to dramatic form, while losing as little as possible of the original, and avoiding needless staling, repetition or loss of plausibility; and it must try to retain the special strengths of the original: its creation of an expansive and intensely perceived world whose survival is threatened, its steady momentum and coherence as a narrative, and its moral conviction and subtlety.

Notice that this is not an exercise in fan-club 'purism'. I am not suggesting that in a best possible adaptation nothing of the original needs to be changed or dropped. Nor do I want to imply for a moment that the best possible adaptation and the best possible drama, or film, are the same thing. On the contrary, we need to keep these assessments quite distinct. A wide divergence from a source text can sometimes produce a drama which is more effective than its source – or at least effective in a wholly different way, so that comparison is pointless. To take a well-known example, many people will agree that James Whale's *Frankenstein* (Universal Pictures, 1931) is a great film, even though it does not even attempt the dramatic adaptation of many powerful elements of Mary Shelley's novel,[28] and moreover assimilates the story shamelessly to other, post-Shelley traditions, including nineteenth-century melodrama and the Gothic aspects of 1920s German expressionism. Conversely, Kenneth Branagh's film *Mary Shelley's Frankenstein* (1994) may approach the status of best possible adaptation, but is not necessarily a better film than Whale's. At the same time, we should note that a significant divergence from an original source can often harm the adapted version, even in its own terms. It is hard to unravel just one thread of a plot – the whole thing can come apart in one's hands.[29]

Though these criteria for successful adaptation look daunting, an examination of the three main attempts now generally available – the BBC audio version, and the films by Ralph Bakshi and Peter Jackson – leaves one impressed by the attention and seriousness with which adapters have attempted the near-impossible. The first two are honourable failures, let down mainly by technical, and in Bakshi's case economic, constraints; the third a qualified success.

The 13-hour BBC radio production is, of course, fundamentally hampered by its inability to suggest the physical and cultural presence of Middle-earth, other than through inevitably rather generalised sound-effects such as the background roar and rumble of the Mordor scenes. The occasional passages of narrated text direct from the book give tantalising glimpses of a breadth of vision which fades painfully as the studio-bound dialogues resume. These are generally well delivered (there is a particularly fine Gollum by Peter Woodthorpe) and skilfully abridged. Its abridgements do, however, tend subtly to flatten the text in the direction of an adventure story. An example is the treatment of Pippin's oath of fealty to Denethor. In *The Return of the King*, Pippin swears to hold to his oath 'until my lord release me, or death take me, or the world end' (RK, 28). In the radio version the final phrase, with its reminder of the mythical framework of the story (and perhaps of the fact that Gondor is the survivor of Númenor, a world that *did* end) is eliminated, and Pippin's voice quavers histrionically at the words 'death take me'. The strength of the BBC version as an adaptation lies in its largely faithful, and nearly complete, realisation of the sequence of events (Tom Bombadil being the chief casualty, as in both film adaptations): in that sense, if no other, the criterion that as little as possible of the original should be lost is met more closely by this than by the movie versions.

At first glance, Bakshi's 1978 animated film is easy to dismiss, especially if one looks back at it with the computer-generated wonders of Jackson's version freshly in mind. Its Prologue on the history of the Ring combines crude silhouette figures with a portentously intoned narration; the voices are a mixed bag, to say the least; the character animation, aiming at a lifelike fluency, often creates curiously stilted movements, with the hobbits prone to facial tics and strange elbow-flapping gestures, while Gandalf is afflicted by an unexplained limp. If one looks forward to it from Zimmerman, on the other hand, one is struck by the close respect paid to the plot, and the appearance of many passages of dialogue from the original. Even the fact that Bakshi ran out of money at roughly the end of *The Two Towers* is a kind of compliment to his Jackson-like ambition. The moral and psychological implications of the Ring are recognised – there is a temptation of Galadriel, for example, and the Rivendell scene in which Bilbo shows an unhealthy interest in touching the Ring is present. The characters move through Middle-earth at a plausible pace, and in presenting the various settings some effort is made to mark out a distinctive visual style that will not recall earlier animated films. (The Elves, however, are Bambi-eyed, while Galadriel and Éowyn would not look out of place in Disney's *The Sleeping Beauty*.) The film is particularly good at evoking for the malign characters a frightening, *unheimlich* aspect which rightly goes beyond a merely physical threat. Gollum (ably voiced by Peter Woodthorpe again) is merely twitchy, but the Black Riders and the plug-ugly Orcs and Trolls of the battle scenes, seen as through a grey-green filter, and with eyes like points of red light, are genuinely ominous – they seem to come from a world of ghosts. Admittedly this goes beyond Tolkien's conception – his Orcs at any rate are physically quite solid – but it supports his general objective of evoking supernatural evil in the servants of Sauron. The score by Leonard Rosenman is also at its most effective in these disturbing episodes. It is only a pity that the 'rotoscoping' technique (where layers of animation, and even live action, are superimposed) has the effect that the Fellowship's antagonists rarely seem to be quite in the same visual plane as themselves.

Comparing Bakshi with Jackson yields a surprising number of resemblances, in addition to one admitted *hommage*, the placing of Odo Proudfoot's feet in the Party scene.[30] Most striking is the decision in both productions to begin with a Prologue: the sequence of events is quite similar, though narrated entirely differently, and certain images not necessitated by Tolkien's story – the bouncing Ring in Gollum's cave, for example – suggest that Bakshi's version may have lodged in Jackson's memory. Where the plot elements differ, as in the escape at the Ford of Bruinen, or the Mirror of Galadriel, it is generally Bakshi who stays closer to the original narrative. Nevertheless, Jackson's work – two of the three films have been released at the time of writing – represents such an advance in the adaptation of Tolkien's masterpiece that it is already difficult to imagine a movie version being attempted again for half a century. I will be arguing that it is less than the best possible adaptation, but it is adequate in scale and seriousness to its original. Many Tolkien readers who saw the Prologue for the first time in the cinema, knowing it to be the beginning of a nine-hour journey, will have been stunned not only by its amazing beauty – the panoramic battle scene, for example, bringing the grandeur and dignity of paintings by Altdorfer and Van Eyck to mind – but by the recognition that, almost beyond hope, exactly the right tone and pace were being set to allow the complexity of the work to unfold.

Why has this proved possible, at the turn of the millennium, when it was not possible before? I believe there are two main reasons. The first, of course, is the development of computer technology to the point at which a scene can be digitally assembled out of a multitude of images, some photographed live, others computer-generated, with little or no loss of visual credibility. In combination with more traditional techniques such as forced perspective and the use of body doubles, these resources put virtually any fictional scene, however fantastic, within the scope of literal cinematic representation. These devices are well known and extensively discussed by Jackson and his production team in interviews and commentaries. Because of them, it was in principle possible for someone who wanted to adapt the book seriously to do so.

The technology, however, cannot explain why the project largely escaped being devoured by any of the existing genre-clichés: why it was decided, rightly, that it would be more successful, even commercially, if it remained largely faithful to the book's conception; or why the attempt to be faithful did not, on the whole, founder at the level of detailed execution. The explanation, I believe, turns on the collective nature of film production: the fact that an aesthetically cohesive outcome can only be achieved in film-making if many people, from producers to designers and technicians of various kinds, are doing particular things as part of a collective activity which they all sufficiently comprehend.[31] With a routine genre production such as a Western, such collective comprehension can often, perhaps, be taken for granted. But the attempt to realise Tolkien's Middle-earth in its own terms, rather than to assimilate it to some pre-existing genre, requires a specially focused sensibility. In the 1950s, even if by some miracle a director of Jackson's gifts had grasped the aesthetic challenge of The Lord of The Rings and seen ways of meeting it, producers would not have understood the need to support him (and their scepticism would perhaps have been justified, since the core market among Tolkien enthusiasts would still have been quite small). And if they had backed him, it would have been necessary for the director to evangelise continually for his vision among a largely uncompre-hending cast and production team. But by the 1990s, there existed two or three generations of Tolkien readers, many in positions of influence, in sufficient numbers to provide the huge production company with a critical mass of sympathy and understanding of the book. This is not to say that everyone connected with the production was already a dedicated reader of Tolkien, but it is clear that many were, and that Jackson took care to recruit to the company specialists like the illustrator Alan Lee who had long reflected on how 'Middle-earth' might be realised. Nor is it to deny the ultimate accountability of the director as *auteur*. The finished product is conditioned finally by Jackson (and also initially, given the driving role played by his shot-by-shot 'storyboards'), but also partly by this diffused knowledge of the book within the company, so that to a certain extent contributors could be left to themselves, with Jackson merely signing off elements such as costume, artefacts, or computer-generated effects, or referring them back for revision. The time-scales for the production (for example, for the preparation of sets and the creation of artefacts) would in any case necessitate this degree of freedom.[32] No doubt much of this is true of any substantial film production. What *The Lord of the Rings* shows is that even a very challenging and immensely complex film adaptation of a work of fiction can survive the necessarily collective elements of production, if the original work has created a posterity capable of understanding it.

How successful is Jackson's adaptation, according to the criteria suggested above? In avoiding the worst excesses of relabelling and assimilation, it is exceptionally successful. Many had feared, if not *Conan the Barbarian* with hobbits, at any rate a degree of assimilation to other Hollywood or sub-Hollywood genres – the Indiana Jones, the James Bond, the Tomb Raider. Images of a wisecracking, eyebrow-raising Aragorn and a 'feisty', kick-boxing Arwen shoving Orcs over precipices in between their love scenes have happily been dispelled. A more insidious kind of assimilation, to the self-censoring conformities of the present, has also been avoided: Gandalf is allowed to smoke, for example, and the female characters are developed broadly within the terms of Tolkien's narrative, rather than those of political correctness. Some may cavil at Arwen's active role in the flight of Frodo to Rivendell, but while it does undermine the tender reclusiveness of Tolkien's character, it is not seriously against the spirit of his conception of the Elves, or of women: Lúthien in The Silmarillion, in many ways Arwen's prototype, is at least as adventurous. Crucially, the major female figures are allowed to be as different from one another as in the original: they are not flattened out into any generic female role.

There are moments at which the spell is broken. The absurd combat with wizards' staffs in The Fellowship of the Ring, an innovation of the film, is uncomfortably close to the light saber contests of Star Wars, though differentiated by a certain rawness in its violence. Merry and Pippin, at least in the first film, provide a kind of on-cue 'comic' relief more appropriate to the tongue-in-cheek style of the Indiana Jones series: they strike one as perpetual adolescents who would have been better left at home. (In contrast, the semi-comic treatment of the dwarf Gimli builds on elements traceable within Tolkien's text, and John Rhys Davies's boisterous performance carries it off.) Other episodes, enjoyable in themselves, suggest a different kind of exterior pull. In Tolkien's narrative, the fighting in the Chamber of Mazarbul is over in little more than a page: its focal point is the ominous fact that the orc-chieftain has selected Frodo for his spear-thrust (just as the Watcher in the Water has chosen Frodo to seize at the West Gate). In the film, the scene lasts over five minutes, and its theme seems to be: how very, very difficult it is to kill a cave-troll. It comes as no surprise that the Two Towers Playstation game features a version of just this scene, in which one is required to deplete the 'health' of the troll, as well as a version of the warg attack at the Gap of Rohan in The Two Towers, another dramatically unnecessary interpolation. I do not suggest that these scenes were expressly introduced to provide material for computer games, but the excitement they generate is the generic excitement of frenzied combat to which such games appeal.

A different, and more defensible, area of partial assimilation is the presentation of the Elves. Here Jackson and his team faced difficulties of adaptation which are perhaps insuperable. Little can be done with make-up or special effects to suggest how the Elves of Tolkien's narrative differ from Men: they are simply more beautiful, more serene, more wise: young and old, sad and blissful at once. The success of any attempt to suggest these qualities must turn largely on casting, and acting. The danger is that the female Elves will simper and look like beauty queens, while the male ones will sound arch (at best) and resemble ballet dancers or – given the need for tallness – well-groomed American football players. The performances of the principal actors, Cate Blanchett as Galadriel, Liv Tyler as Arwen and Orlando Bloom as Legolas, do much to transcend these dangers, but they are not entirely avoided. And there is a deeper problem. The environment the Elves fashion for themselves is only sketchily described in the text, but the dominant motif is of closeness to nature: in Lothlórien especially one has the sense that a perpetual summer allows its inhabitants to live in a continuous, tactile relation to tree, leaf, flower, sunlight, starlight and breeze – a breeze, moreover, which blows from the Elder Days, as much as from the river Anduin or the Bay of Belfalas. Such impressions are extremely difficult to convey dramatically. The film, drawing to some extent on the illustrations of Lee and Howe, tends instead to present both Elves and their culture in terms which can only be called sophisti-cated. Lothlórien, vernally green, silver and gold in the book, is phosphorescent blue and white in the film; when a light shimmers, or rather glows, around Arwen or Galadriel it seems to be the light, not so much of silver lanterns in the forest night, as of powerful floodlights. So far from being close to nature, Jackson's Elves often seem cut off from it by their lighting, their reverberant chorales, and their decorative apparatus. Yet their architecture and ornaments in the films are dominated by natural motifs, as if the intention is to suggest the Elves' integration with nature, but at one remove; and this works well in its own terms, especially in the Portmeirion-like idyll of Rivendell. Tolkien's own few illustrations of Elvish buildings, with their rounded, pencil-like towers and ochre-coloured sloping roofs, are very different in style: they suggest a simplified and more rustic version of the late-medieval world of the Limbourg Brothers.[33] But in view of his aversion to mechanical production, Tolkien would be likely to have endorsed Ruskin's approval of an architecture whose ornament follows the lines of nature,[34] and in many ways the film's designs evoke, appropriately, the post-Ruskinian taste of the period in which Tolkien grew up, in which pre-Raphaelite painting, the designs of William Morris, and Art Nouveau are dominant influences. The Elves of the original text could have been visualised by Tolkien in something like this way, even though they actually are not. We may regard these design features, then, as a case of assimilation in which the films, though they fail by the strict criteria of adaptation, achieve a coherence of their own which does not too seriously threaten the autonomy of the imagined world, or create gross stylistic anachronism.[35]

If we turn to the question of whether Jackson's version retains the special strengths of his original, we can give a positive answer on at least one point, indeed on the very point which might have been thought unachievable: the realisation of Middle-earth as a diverse and expansive world of lands and cultures under threat, a world we need to fall in love with in order to care sufficiently about the outcome of the plot. Here at least there is almost no disjunction between the film's success in its own terms and its success as an adaptation. The attentiveness to the original text's descriptions of locales is often quite remarkable: The West Wall of Moria, the Argonath and the lake of Nen Hithoel, Helm's Deep, Minas Tirith, all provide the Tolkien reader with a satisfying shock of recognition. (Again, the imagery is often mediated through earlier book illustrations, especially Alan Lee's.) Where elaboration is called for, as with the interior of Bag End, it is both consistent with the letter and spirit of the text and superbly executed. On repeated viewings, one perpetually looks over the characters' shoulders at some receding landscape or finely-crafted detail, and while with many films this would be an aesthetic indictment, here it is absolutely appropriate to the emotional sense of both book and film.

Quite apart from its consistent visual distinction, Jackson's work contains numerous particular images of exceptional beauty. Sometimes these are used in support of crucial narrative moments. One example is the sequence in *The Two Towers* which foreshadows Aragorn's death and Arwen's 'fading': here, the freedom of film narration to suggest time changes, and evoke a suitable emotional response, mainly through a rapid succession of images, makes possible the incorporation of an episode which Tolkien, obeying the more constrained narrative logic of fiction, had to relegate to an Appendix. Even more poetic are the scenes with Frodo and Sam at the close of *The Fellowship of the Ring*: the perilously self-conscious slow-motion scene of Sam's submersion is vindicated by its morally thematic reversal of Isildur's drowning in the Prologue, while the closing twilight shot, over the Emyn Muil to Mordor, hits just the right note of poignant sobriety. (The rejection of an alternative, action-driven ending, with an Orc suddenly rising from the water in the manner of *Fatal Attraction* – itself, at that point, a blend of *Carrie*, *Psycho*, and *High Noon* – must stand as one of Jackson's best decisions in defence of the film's autonomy.)[36] Other images – like the Shire sunset into which, after a moment, the Black Rider's horse ominously steps in *The Fellowship of the Ring* – are, if you like, individually more gratuitous, but cumulatively they sustain the sense of threatened joy and serenity. One's only reservation – strictly from the point of view of adaptation – is that these painterly images are, in a sense, too arrestingly beautiful, since they are composed in terms of the formal constraints exacted by the flat, rectangular canvas of the moving image: they are, in fact, too much like paintings, not least because of the digital colour grading which harmonises them. There is an aesthetic chasm here between prose narrative and film that cannot be crossed. As I argued in chapter 1, Tolkien's descriptions excel above all in three-dimensional views, in evoking the sensory experience of a moving spectator situated in the landscape. Though some mobility of perspective is given in the film by camera movement, the consequence is often that the audience becomes *aware* of camera movement, especially with the helicopter shots, where one cannot help thinking of the helicopter; this is not comparable to the sense of standing at one point or walking across the earth. (Oddly enough, the Vivendi Playstation game, which allows three-dimensional movement within richly visualised environments including a highly credible Hobbiton and Bywater, does give something of that exhilarating sense of being positioned within a world which one can explore at will – indeed, for clumsy-fingered adults this is perhaps the main attraction of such games.) Another proof of the gulf between fantasy and drama is that one is bound to be intermittently aware while watching the film that one is seeing New Zealand (more or less), whereas the book's Middle-earth, existing only in the imagination, is simply Middle-earth. However, granted the resources and limitations of the medium, it is difficult to conceive that the task could have been much better achieved.

In the other areas I have isolated as special excellences of Tolkien's work – its momentum and coherence as narrative, and its moral conviction and subtlety – the success of the film version, both in itself and as an adaptation, is a little more qualified, and we can discuss these areas together. Let us agree first that many of the modifications and excisions made for the film are necessitated by dramatic imperatives. The removal of Tom Bombadil and the Barrow-wights is justifiable because these episodes are largely self-contained: if the film has to be nine rather than ten hours long, they can go without significantly affecting its meaning. A more fundamental change is to the pace of the early sections. In the book, seventeen years elapse between Bilbo's departure and Frodo's, while Frodo, with Gandalf's approval, waits for some months between discovering the nature of the Ring and moving from Hobbiton. These intervals convey breadth of space as well as time, since they imply that the threat from Sauron is, at first, very far distant. The leisurely tempo established in this phase contributes much, I believe, to the comedic quality, the fundamental geniality and optimism, of Tolkien's story, as well as preparing for the contrasting effect created by the interwoven urgencies of the climactic chapters. But Jackson and his fellow writers have convincingly argued that for the purposes of the film, dramatic momentum requires that some of these leisurely intervals be elided.[37]

The characters of a literary fiction can be developed at various levels of complexity and inwardness, but on the stage or screen all have to begin by being physically represented by an actor (with or without digital metamorphosis). With those few characters who are developed in *The Lord of the Rings* to a more or less novelistic degree of psychological realism, their realisation in Jackson's film version is both intrinsically convincing and broadly faithful to the original conceptions. I would include in this category Bilbo, Frodo, Sam, Gandalf and Gollum – the last being the most psychologically complex and original; more grudgingly one might include Aragorn in this 'novelistic' group.[38] Gollum is one of the successes of the film version – as of the two other versions just discussed: he is evidently Tolkien's main gift to drama – in spite of a subtle softening of his role which makes pitying him seem a little easier than it should, given that (as Faramir says, in the book) he has done murder. The scene in The Two Towers in which he debates with himself is staged a little mechanically, with alternating half-profile shots representing the two sides of his riven mind, but a lesser director might have omitted it altogether. The relations among this group follow the original source quite closely, though with an important reservation: there is a move away from that (very English) understatement which is, again, inseparable from the geniality of the book, its emotional tact and spaciousness. In the film, Bilbo huddles whimpering into Gandalf's cloak after their disagreement over the Ring at Bag End. Sam's speech to Frodo in the boat at the end of The Fellowship of the Ring, and their tearful embrace, are more demonstrative, though not more moving, than the equivalent passage in the book. These scenes are certainly touching, and the latter is a finely judged moment of emotional release for the audience; but not all renunciations of understatement are so successful.

A second group of Tolkien's characters – Saruman and Denethor are the most interesting examples – might be seen as 'incipiently Shakespearean', in the sense that though they do not have novelistic inwardness, their heightened, formal utterance and their political importance give them the potential to rise to a kind of tragic dignity in a dramatic medium. Théoden also belongs to this group, as does Gandalf when in debate with them. Visually and vocally they achieve appropriate presence in their film incarnations, Christopher Lee's Saruman, for example, being a powerfully haunted and vindictive figure, if less self-deluding than Tolkien's. But the verbal confrontations among these characters seldom quite rise to the level one hopes for. Saruman, though he convincingly chides and sneers at Gandalf, makes no serious attempt to persuade him to form an alliance with him. Gandalf's 'cure' of Théoden, which in the book is as much an achievement of rhetoric and force of personality as of magic, is virtually reduced in the film of The Two Towers to a return match between the two staff-wielding wizards, coupled with a spectacular dissolution of Théoden's make-up. In general it is a weakness of the film version – and here the weakness seems intrinsic to its own value as drama – that it is too reluctant to dramatise rhetorical conflict when physical conflict can be substituted, or to allow a major character to influence events by dignity of presence or force of intellect. (In comparison to *Star Wars*, perhaps, it is sophisticated in its moments of verbal conflict, but Jackson's writers had Tolkien's dialogue as a starting point.) What makes this lack of rhetorical complexity particularly regrettable is that, in other respects, the film is exceptionally successful in conveying 'historical' authenticity, the importance of which Jackson has firmly grasped.[39] The court of Rohan, for example, is so thoroughly realised, not merely architecturally but in its social distinctions and its atmosphere of political intrigue, that one feels one could stage *King Lear* within it.

In certain other episodes, the aversion to understatement combines with the preference for external physical effects to create scenes that are at any rate very alien to Tolkien's invention. The temptation of Galadriel is an example. In the book, Galadriel as she imagines herself transformed by the Ring seems to Frodo 'terrible and beautiful' in the light of her own ring Nenya, which she holds aloft; the fact that Sam, who is present, does not even see this ('I wondered what you were talking about. I saw a star through your finger' (FR, 382)) confirms that Frodo's Ring-heightened perception is at work, and that Galadriel's terrible beauty is grounded in her actual charismatic presence. In the film, Sam is eliminated, and by means of uncharacteristically crude visual and auditory distortions (which make nonsense of her line 'All shall love me and despair!') Galadriel is literally transformed into a roaring seagreen hellhag: she staggers when the effect wears off. A case where the film works much better in its own terms is the shocking scene at Rivendell in which a suddenly demonic Bilbo snatches at the Ring. In the book the point of the episode is as much to indicate Frodo's developing possessiveness towards, or susceptibility of being deluded by, the Ring – there is a comparable scene with Sam in *The Return of the King* (RK, 188) – as to show Bilbo's residual desire for it: the image of Bilbo as a 'little wrinkled creature with a hungry face and bony hands' (FR, 244) is a matter of Frodo's perception, not an actual transformation. It is difficult to deny that the scene works well in the film, and it is consistent with the compelling, darker version of Bilbo's personality projected by Ian Holm's performance. But its approach is connected to another problematical aspect of the film version, its tendency to present the Ring almost exclusively as a brute magical force afflicting innocent victims, rather than as an insidious seducer of all-too-fallible wills. At one point in the text of *The Two Towers* it is expressly said that Frodo felt the external command to put on the Ring, but 'there was no longer any answer to that command in his own will ... only the beating on him of a great power from outside' (TT, 316): this stands in contrast to the earlier occasions on which Frodo's own will collaborates with the external pressure, not to mention the final occasion on which his will seizes the initiative. The ground for the film's conception of the Ring, however, is laid in its Prologue, where Sauron's wielding of the Ring looks like an exercise of overwhelming physical force. 'The power of the Ring could not be undone', declares Galadriel's voice-over, as Sauron's mace sweeps a line of Númenórian warriors hundreds of feet through the air. The scriptwriters defend this conception on the understandable grounds that the psychological aspect of the Ring is hard to realise in drama,[40] but I am not sure that more could not have been done by acting: Elijah Wood's eye-rolling facial expressions at moments when he yields to the Ring tend, especially in the first film, to suggest that he is swooning helplessly, rather than struggling with his own better judgement.

The danger of an overemphasis on the 'external' aspect of the Ring is that it will erode the moral realism of the story, its perception that everyone, however initially virtuous, is susceptible to corruption, not merely to misfortune. More generally, if the struggle between good and evil is reduced to a clash of competing magical powers, we are liable to lose any sense that the eventual overthrow of evil arises from the intrinsic myopia of evil, rather than from a fortunate superiority of strength or weaponry on the side of the virtuous.[41] The film version does not actually descend to this amoral level, but it does tend to replace the complex moral psychology of the original with a simpler message about the need not to lose hope, but to fight on because 'there is *some* good in the world' (to quote Sam's homily near the end of the film version of *The Two Towers*). The hobbits of the book would never have doubted for a moment that this was so. Both cultures and characters tend in Jackson's vision to be somewhat darkened, to sustain this theme. Bree, its inn and its people, for example, are far more 'Gothic' than the pleasant and hospitable society of the book. (Here what Jackson has done is to take Sam's inexperienced initial perception of the Inn as ominous and alien, and treat it as if it were the reality.)

On this view, the prime evil to be avoided among the virtuous becomes *defeatism*, and to keep this before the audience's mind, one after another of the characters is inexplicably afflicted by it. Elrond in his debate with Gandalf, Boromir at Lothlórien, Galadriel in her telepathic communications with Elrond, Théoden even after being 'cured', Legolas at Helm's Deep, Frodo on several occasions, all express despair, or at best deep pessimism. One consequence is to 'stale by anticipation' (to borrow Tolkien's terms from his critique of Zimmerman) the defeatism of Denethor, who genuinely *is* a defeatist character in the original work, and with adequate motivation for being so. The undue repetition of this defeatist note is an example of a more general weakness of the film version, a tendency to flatten out the plot by over-use of certain dramatic devices. Galadriel's repeated and calculatedly ambiguous musing about Frodo – 'the quest will claim his life' – exemplifies the trick whereby, by suppression of information, the audience is falsely induced to believe that something very bad has happened or will happen. Other examples are the implied death of Frodo after crossing the Ford of Bruinen; his implied death again when skewered by the cave-troll in Moria (followed by his, implausibly, seeming quite uninjured thereafter); the implication of a brief scene in The Two Towers that Arwen is going to relinquish Aragorn and go to the Grey Havens; and the implied death of Aragorn in the inter-polated scene where he falls over a cliff. One can only play this trick a couple of times before it, too, begins to 'stale'. Tolkien plays it only twice, with the 'fall' of Gandalf in Moria and the apparent death of Frodo in the pass of Cirith Ungol.[42] As a recurrent device, it belongs to the world of the serial adventure story; only when used very sparingly can it seem to foreshadow the special grace of Tolkien's 'eucatastrophe', just as tragedy ceases to be tragedy, and becomes merely gross misfortune, if the tragic fall is not a rare and special event.

Despite these reservations, the impressive achievement of Jackson and his team remains the only phenomenon in the cultural after-life of The Lord of the Rings that could conceivably threaten to occlude the work itself in our collective awareness. The further surge in sales of Tolkien's writings since the films began to appear may suggest otherwise. But it is conceivable that, as generations grow up who have had ready access to both versions from childhood, the film's representations of place, character, incident and theme may be the ones normalised in popular consciousness. Tolkien's original text would then recede to an unambiguously 'literary' status, rather like 'Mary Shelley's' *Frankenstein*. At worst, it might be read very much less, especially for as long as academic hostility excludes it even from the literary canon.

I do not myself believe that this will happen: partly because, for those who come to the film version first, its epic seriousness is likely to send them to the original text with some sense of what to expect, rather than with expectations which must be disappointed; and partly because I have a fair amount of confidence that, as Tolkien believed, the power of literature to quicken the imagination can survive any challenge from dramatic representation.

Further Reading (and Listening)

The Basic Kit

If I had to suggest a 'kit' for anyone wanting to understand Tolkien's literary work, it would contain the following five items – in addition, obviously, to the works of fiction and poetry themselves.

The Letters of J. R. R. Tolkien, edited by Humphrey Carpenter

The Monsters and the Critics: The Essays of J. R. R. Tolkien, edited by Christopher Tolkien

Humphrey Carpenter, J. R. R. Tolkien: A Biography

Tom Shippey, The Road to Middle-earth

J. R. R. T: A Film Portrait of J. R. R. Tolkien, written by Helen Dickinson, directed by Derek Bailey

The Letters and Essays are an indispensable resource of Tolkien's statements – sometimes emphatic, sometimes oblique – about his work, his ideas and his values. Carpenter's biography is straight-forwardly informative, and little or nothing has been added by subsequent biographers. It does not make much attempt to analyse Tolkien's creative intellect (and tends towards simplification when it does), but Carpenter's own later book The Inklings is valuable in filling out much of the context of thought and debate within which Tolkien pursued his lonely creative journey.

Shippey's earlier book remains the locus classicus of Tolkien criticism, written from a thorough knowledge and sympathetic understanding of Tolkien's mind and learning. The more recent J. R. R. Tolkien: Author of the Century contains much of the same material, is more transparently structured, and deals more fully with Tolkien's relevance to and standing in the present day. It would be worth having both, but Shippey's most distinctive insights are present, and sometimes more subtly developed, in *The Road to Middle-earth*.

All four of the books in the list are at present (2003) widely and cheaply available across the English-speaking world. At the time of writing it is much harder to get hold of the Dickinson/Bailey Film *Portrait*: it is to be hoped that it will soon be generally available, as it is – by a very long way – the best of the video or DVD commentaries. What makes it indispensable is the involvement of Christopher Tolkien, who here – and as far as I am aware, nowhere else – analyses his father's thought and vision with penetration, eloquence and cogency. It helps that he is relaxed with the cameras, unlike Tolkien himself who is seen in a few telling, but brief, clips from a BBC interview. The rest of the 110-minute production comprises effective analysis and comment from Tom Shippey, Verlyn Flieger, the publisher Rayner Unwin, Tolkien's friend Robert Murray, and other members of the Tolkien family, all interwoven into a sensible, not too hagiographical narrative of Tolkien's life and career. To hear more of Tolkien explaining himself, one has to turn to the BBC's *J. R. R. Tolkien: An Audio Portrait*, presented by Brian Sibley. Tolkien's remarks are fascinating, though this is very much an assembly of snippets, following a roughly biographical line but hopping to and fro among Tolkien, extracts from the BBC dramatisation of *The Lord of the Rings*, and controversy about Tolkien's merits, in which only John Carey is given space to develop a cogent argument.

Lines of Inquiry

The literature on Tolkien is vast, and extremely variable in quality. The volumes most visible in the bookshops include some of the best, but also some of the worst. Here I can do no more than suggest a few works, in addition to those by Pearce (HarperCollins, 1998), Garbowski (UMCS Press, Lublin, 2000), and Curry (HarperCollins, 1998) discussed in chapter 5, that I have found particularly thought-provoking even though I have not been able to engage with them in my main text. For dedicated students who wish to investigate more widely, Judith A. Johnson's bibliographical work *J. R. R. Tolkien:*

Six Decades of Criticism (Greenwood Press, 1986) is impressively comprehensive and informative for the earlier periods. Michael D. C.
Drout and Hilary Wynne's long article in Envoi 9.2 (Fall 2000),
awkwardly entitled 'Tom Shippey's J. R. R. Tolkien: Author of the Century
and a Look Back at Tolkien Criticism since 1982', contains an
excellent bibliography and surveys the field incisively.

Paul Kocher's Master of Middle-earth (Houghton Mifflin, 1972, but
available under several imprints) was once a lonely beacon of
competence: it remains a clear and painstaking introduction to the
whole range of the work published in Tolkien's lifetime, though
some of its findings have been superseded. Kocher's later work on
The Silmarillion, however, is little more than a running commentary.
The long, thoughtful but uneven chapter on Tolkien in Roger Sale's
Modern Heroism (University of California Press, 1973) does at least
attempt to set Tolkien in his time and among other writers. Verlyn
Flieger excels in placing Tolkien within a context of relevant ideas.
Her Splintered Light: Logos and Language in Tolkien's World (revised edition,
Kent State University Press, 2002) relates Tolkien's work to the
poetic/linguistic theory of Owen Barfield (an occasional Inkling
and friend of C. S. Lewis), and includes one of the most convincing
explanations of The Silmarillion. Her A Question of Time (Kent State
University Press, 1997) aims to locate Tolkien's use of dream and
time-transcendence within a more general early twentieth-century
preoccupation with the nature of time and consciousness. Jane
Chance's Tolkien's Art: A Mythology for England (revised edition, University
of Kentucky Press, 2001) skilfully juxtaposes Tolkien's work with
some of its probable or possible sources in pre-modern literature.
Robert E. Morse's short book Evocation of Virgil in Tolkien's Art (Bolchazy-
Carducci Publishers, 1986) suggests another source, with some
plausibility. Chance's The Lord of the Rings: The Mythology of Power (revised
edition, University of Kentucky Press, 2001) links Tolkien to
Foucault and to 1960s liberal values. William H. Green, The Hobbit:
A Journey Into Maturity (Twayne Publishers, 1995) is an ingenious psy-
chological interpretation of a work which tends to be marginalised
by critics, Shippey apart. Richard Purtill's readable J. R. R. Tolkien: Myth,
Morality and Religion (Harper & Row, 1984, but with a re-issue by
Ignatius Press announced for 2003) covers some of the same

ground as Pearce and Garbowski, without the doctrinal focus of the former or the exploratory quality of the latter.

There are numerous collections of essays about Tolkien, though few contain quite the density of distinguished work that one would wish. The standard is fairly high in George Clark and Daniel Timmons (eds.), *J. R. R. Tolkien and His Literary Resonances* (Greenwood Press, 2000): it includes one very good piece, George Clark's 'Tolkien and the True Hero' and one outstanding one, Geoffrey Russom's 'Tolkien's Versecraft'. The early (1970) collection by Neill D. Isaacs and Rose A. Zimbardo, *Tolkien and the Critics* (University of Notre Dame Press) is also generally good, having the freshness of early encounters with Tolkien's work: it includes W. H. Auden's important essay 'The Quest Hero'. (Auden's original *New York Times* reviews are also accessible at www.nytimes.com: they are full of insight.) Another early collection, Jared Lobdell (ed.) *A Tolkien Compass* (Open Court, 1975), contains not only a number of competent and sensible essays but a rare item by Tolkien himself, his 'Guide to the Names in *The Lord of the Rings*', written to assist translators. The best of the other collections are, in my view, Thomas Honegger (ed.) *Root and Branch: Approaches Towards Understanding Tolkien* (Walking Tree Publishers, Zurich and Berne, 1999), and Patricia Reynolds and Glen C. GoodKnight, *Proceedings of the J. R. R. Tolkien Centenary Conference* (Mythopoeic Press, 1995).

Notes

Introduction

1. For an analysis of the polls and the reaction to them, see Joseph Pearce, *Tolkien: Man and Myth* (London: HarperCollins, 1999), pp. 1–10, and Tom Shippey, *J. R. R. Tolkien: Author of the Century* (London: HarperCollins, 2000), pp. xx–xxiv.

2. Andrew Rissik, Review of Tom Shippey, *J. R. R. Tolkien: Author of the Century*, in the *Guardian* (London), 2 September 2000.

3. BBC's *Newsnight Review*, 14 December 2001. I discuss the political issues raised by Greer in chapter 5: see especially pages 160–7 and 178–86. See also chapter 1, pp. 35–47.

4. W. W. Robson remarks that the success of *The Lord of the Rings* 'has affinities with that of Ossian, and the more posthumous Tolkien material is published, the more it looks like Ossian' (*A Prologue to English Literature* (Batsford, 1986) p. 234). But (as this formulation implicitly concedes), *The Lord of the Rings* at any rate does not look much like Ossian: if it is set alongside the posthumously published but earlier written material, it is evident that an escape from what might be called 'Ossianic' style has taken place.

5. H. Bloom (ed.), *J. R. R. Tolkien* (Chelsea House, 2000), p. 2.

6. See, or rather hear, for example, John Carey's comments on the BBC audiotape *J. R. R. Tolkien; An Audio Portrait*, presented by Brian Sibley, BBC Worldwide Ltd 2001.

7. E. Wilson, 'Oo, those Awful Orcs!', *Nation* 182 (1956), pp. 312–13.

8. T. Shippey, *The Road to Middle-earth* (Allen & Unwin, 1982) p. 215.

9. I believe the best arguments in favour of interpretation as the recovery of a determinate and historically created meaning are those of E. D. Hirsch (see *Validity in Interpretation*, Yale University Press, 1967, and 'Past Intentions and Present Meanings', *Essays in Criticism*, Vol. XXXIII, No. 2, 1983) and Quentin Skinner (see 'Motives, Intentions and Interpretation' and 'Interpretation and the Understanding of Speech Acts' in his collection *Visions of Politics*, Cambridge University Press, 2002). I focus on Skinner's view in B. Rosebury, 'Irrecoverable Intentions and Literary Interpretation', *British Journal of Aesthetics*, Vol. 37, No. 1, January 1997, pp. 15–30.

10. Especially to anyone familiar with the title of John Livingston Lowes' book on the sources of Coleridge's inspiration, *The Road to Xanadu* (1927). Shippey acknowledges his borrowing of the formula with a delicate joke (p. 219).

11. Shippey, *The Road to Middle-earth*, p. 4.

12. HarperCollins, 2000.

13. Bryan Appleyard achieves a certain variation with 'tweedy academic whimsy', in *The Pleasures of Peace* (Faber, 1989) p. 13.

14. 'On Fairy Stories', *Tree and Leaf* (Unwin Hyman, 1988), pp. 21–3.

1   *The Lord of the Rings*: Imagining Middle-earth

1. Shippey, *The Road to Middle-earth*, p. 169.

2. D. S. Brewer, 'The Lord of the Rings as a Romance', M. Salu and R. T. Farrell (eds.), *J. R. R. Tolkien: Scholar and Storyteller: Essays in Memoriam* (Cornell University Press, 1979), p. 249.

3. *The Letters of J. R. R. Tolkien*, ed. H. Carpenter (Allen & Unwin, 1981), p. 239. Quotations from this volume reprinted by permission of HarperCollins Publishers Ltd © J. R. R. Tolkien, 1977.

4. 'On Fairy Stories', *Tree and Leaf*, p. 17.

5. H. Carpenter, *J. R. R. Tolkien: A Biography* (Allen & Unwin, 1977), p. 165.

6. D. Brewer, 'The Lord of the Rings as Romance', Salu & Farrell (eds.), *J. R. R. Tolkien: Scholar and Storyteller: Essays in Memoriam*, p. 255.

7. 'On Fairy Stories', *Tree and Leaf*, pp. 39–40.

8. C. Stimpson, *J. R. R. Tolkien* (Columbia University Press, 1969) p. 29.

9. 'On Translating Beowulf', *The Monsters and the Critics*, ed. C. Tolkien (Allen & Unwin, 1983) pp. 55–6. Quotations from this volume reprinted by permission of HarperCollins Publishers Ltd © J. R. R. Tolkien, 1983.

10. Shippey, *The Road to Middle-earth*, p. 120.

11. Shippey, *The Road to Middle-earth*, p. 121.

12. 'I have said the map was the most of the plot. I might almost say it was the whole … . It is my contention – my superstition, if you like – that who is faithful to his map, and consults it, and draws from it his inspiration, daily and hourly, gains positive support and not merely immunity from accident. The tale has a root there; it grows in that soil; it has a spine of its own behind the words' (R. L. Stevenson, 'My First Book', *Essays in the Art of Writing* (Chatto & Windus, 1920), pp. 135–6).

13. Shippey, *The Road to Middle-earth*, p. 121.

14. Shippey, *The Road to Middle-earth*, p. 79.

15. See p. 207 below.

16. The argument of this paragraph is developed much more extensively in my *Art and Desire: A Study in the Aesthetics of Fiction* (Macmillan Press – now Palgrave Macmillan, 1988).

17. It is the failure to recognise the aesthetic function of the expansiveness of Middle-earth that fatally weakens Christine Brooks-Rose's structuralist analysis of the work in *The Rhetoric of the Unreal* (Cambridge, 1983, pp. 233–55). Brooks-Rose recognises the highly developed realism of *The Lord of the Rings*, but finds the work littered with 'pointless' information (p. 245), 'irrelevant to the quest' (p. 244)

which her Todorovian scheme requires to be structurally definitive. She objects, for example, that Merry's oath of fealty to Théoden, and Pippin's to Denethor, are not 'functional' (p. 238), because Merry assists Théoden's niece not himself, and Pippin actually breaks his oath, disobeying Denethor's orders to save Faramir: but it is precisely these kinds of departure from a facile and predictable structuring of ethical action which exemplify the work's moral subtlety and openness to contingency. Brooks-Rose's essay is a *locus classicus* of the tendency of supposedly logical descriptive structures to turn into evaluative determinants, either explicitly (as the critic becomes increasingly irritated at the failure of the work to conform to the attributed structure), or covertly as terms like 'ambiguity' and 'reduplication' imperceptibly shade from a neutral into a pejorative meaning, and the features which the work happens to share with others are assumed to be its really important ones. (One is reminded of Hans Keller's remark that critics who analyse Mozart's symphonic movements in terms of the universal principles of sonata form are describing precisely what the music is not (*The Symphony*, ed. R. Simpson (Penguin, 1966) Vol. 1, p. 91).) A considerable number of minor, sometimes repeated, errors of spelling or accurate reading ('orks', 'Belin', 'Gamjee', 'Edora', 'Minas Mogul', 'Moria Mountain', Denethor as a 'king'), as well as certain exasperated turns of phrase jarring oddly with the general tone of dispassionate and concept-heavy structural analysis (e.g. the 'interminable' Council of Elrond, with 'each member adding his mite' (p. 242)) confirm one's impression that the distinctiveness of the work counts for less in this analysis than the deployment of the Todorovian scheme.

18. Tom Shippey suggests (*The Road to Middle-earth*, pp. 107–11) that there is in *The Lord of the Rings*, qualifying the Augustinian world-view, an element of Manicheanism, 'the heresy which says that Good and Evil are equal and opposite and that the universe is a battlefield' (p. 108). But the considerations Shippey cites – the formidable power of Sauron, and especially the power of Sauron's Ring to sway the wills of even the well-intentioned – do not take the book into Manicheanism. Nor do the barbarities of the twentieth century really provide, as Shippey suggests, an argument against the Augustinian view so persuasive that Tolkien is likely to have been swayed by them. To say with Augustine that evil is the absence or negation of good, and not a force co-equal and coeval with God and independently creative of life, is not to deny that evil persons may use the technology of their historical period with great effectiveness. The magical arts which have created the Ring and its power to disintegrate the personality of its bearers – compare, as Tolkien himself did (*Letters*, p. 252), twentieth-century 'brainwashing' – are in this sense merely technological: they do not amount to inherent powers co-equal with God's. Sauron is in fact consistently conceived as a master of scientific 'devices': hence his seduction, in the Second Age, of the Elven-Smiths of Eregion, in collaboration with whom the Rings of Power are made. Frodo would be helpless in direct contest with Sauron; but that is because Sauron is an immortal spirit and Frodo a mortal hobbit, not because Sauron derives strength from an independent powerhouse of Evil: he is, just the same as Frodo, the creation of an all-powerful, benevolent God who grants free will to his creatures.

19. 'On Fairy Stories', *Tree and Leaf*, p. 66.
20. W. H. Auden, 'The Quest Hero', N. D. Isaacs and R. A. Zimbardo (eds.), *Tolkien and the Critics* (University of Notre Dame Press, 1968) p. 51.
21. The issue only arises, of course, where a distillation of good and evil is projected. I have particularly in mind the example of Wilkie Collins's *The Woman in White*, where the problem (if there is one, granted the limited moral seriousness of the novel) is not so much that Count Fosco is genial, cultivated and amusing as that the ostensible hero and heroine (Walter Hartright and Laura Fairlie), with whom we ought warmly to sympathise, are humourless and vapid. In this respect the later novel *The Moonstone* marks an improvement, with its droll hero and spirited heroine. The God and Satan of *Paradise Lost* present a more serious problem, as is suggested by the critical debate that has raged inconclusively for two centuries over Blake's proposition that Milton was 'of the Devil's party without knowing it'.
22. Guy Davenport also notices the resemblance to Sherlock Holmes ('J. R. R. Tolkien, R.I.P.', *National Review*, September 28, 1973, pp. 1042–3).
23. V. Nabokov, 'On a Book Entitled Lolita', *Lolita* (Penguin, 1980) p. 313.
24. Nabokov, 'On a Book Entitled Lolita', *Lolita*, p. 313.
25. 'On Fairy Stories', *Tree and Leaf*, p. 61.
26. Thomas Traherne, 'Centuries of Meditation', in H. M. Margoliouth (ed.) *Centuries, Poems and Thanksgivings* (Clarendon Press, 1958), Vol. 1, p. 111.

2   *The Lord of the Rings*: Achieving the Narrative

1. A. Trollope, *Barchester Towers*, ed. J. Kincaid (Oxford University Press, 1980), chapter XV, p. 143.
2. *Letters*, p. 258.
3. 'On Fairy Stories', *Tree and Leaf*, p. 62.
4. Stimpson, *J. R. R. Tolkien*, p. 29.
5. 'On Translating Beowulf', *The Monsters and the Critics*, p. 55.
6. According to the *Oxford English Dictionary*.
7. There are also two occurrences in *The Two Towers* (TT, 156) where the meaning is again 'an islet in the middle of a stream'.
8. See, e.g., FR pp. 88, 185, 208, 227, 332, 402.
9. I do not mean to suggest that Tolkien was casual or perfunctory in his revision. On the contrary, the drafts of these chapters, edited by Christopher Tolkien and published as *The Return of the Shadow* (Unwin Hyman, 1988), reveal a many-layered revision, and a steady advance in breadth of conception and maturity of style. I mean that a few immature phrases or conceptions are left, as it were stranded, in the final text. The bath-scene at Crickhollow, for example, dates in essentials from the earliest phase of composition.
10. By E. A. Wyke-Smith (Ernest Benn, 1927).
11. The sentence was preserved unchanged from an early draft (cf. *The Return of the Shadow*, p. 258).

12. J. Carey, 'Hobbit-forming', The Listener, 12 May 1977, p. 631 (a review of Carpenter's biography of Tolkien).
13. E. Kirk, 'Language, Fiction and The Lord of the Rings', in M. Spilka (ed.), Towards a Poetics of Fiction (Indiana University Press, 1977), p. 300.
14. E. Kirk, Language, 'Fiction and The Lord of the Rings', Spilka (ed.), Towards a Poetics of Fiction, p. 300.
15. Francis Hope, 'Welcome to Middle-earth', New Statesman, 11 November 1966, pp. 701–2.
16. Carey, The Listener, 12 May 1977, p. 631. In a letter to Terence Tiller concerning a planned BBC dramatisation of The Lord of the Rings, Tolkien discountenances the use of 'accent-differentiation', in the sense of 'more or less consistent alterations of the vowels/consonants of received English'. He adds that 'it would probably be better to avoid certain, actual or conventional, features of modern "vulgar" English in representing Orcs, such as the dropping of aitches (these are, I think, not dropped in the text, and that is deliberate). But of course, for most people, "accent" as defined above is confused with impressions of different intonation, articulation and tempo. You will, I suppose, have to use such means to make Orcs sound nasty!' (Letters, pp. 253–4).
17. Hardy, The Return of the Native, chapter 1 (Macmillan, 1974), p. 35.
18. Roger Sale, Modern Heroism (University of California Press, 1973), p. 213.
19. Stimpson, J. R. R. Tolkien, p. 44.
20. E. Kirk, 'Language, Fiction and The Lord of the Rings', Spilka (ed.), Towards a Poetics of Fiction, p. 293.
21. 'On Fairy Stories', Tree and Leaf, pp. 52–5.
22. Wordsworth, Preface to Lyrical Ballads.

3 Fiction and Poetry 1914–73

1. LT1, p. 32. The poem is in Oxford Poetry 1915 (B. H. Blackwell, 1915), and is reprinted as an Appendix in J. S. Ryan (ed.), Tolkien: Cult or Culture? (University of New England Press, 1969), p. 209. Carpenter (J. R. R. Tolkien: A Biography, pp. 74–5) and Shippey (The Road to Middle-earth, p. 23) quote the first stanza only.
2. Carpenter, J. R. R. Tolkien, p. 70.
3. LT1, p. 29.
4. See Gryll Grange, chapter XV, for this touching poem.
5. See LT1, pp. 43–4.
6. Carpenter, J. R. R. Tolkien, pp. 183–4.
7. A. N. Wilson, C. S. Lewis: A Biography (Collins, 1990), p. 117.
8. Lays, p. 324.
9. Letters, p. 333
10. 'Leaf by Niggle', Tree and Leaf, p. 89.
11. 'On Fairy Stories', Tree and Leaf, p. 62.
12. See The Lost Road and Other Writings, Unwin Hyman, 1987, pp. 36–104, especially the two chapters dominated by somewhat intense, and learned, discourse between Oswin and Alboin Errol (pp. 36–53).

13. See LT1, pp. 45–63.

14. See pp. 178–92 below. For a different, but in its own terms lucid and persuasive, analysis of the creation symbolism of *The Silmarillion* as the key to much of Tolkien's work, see V. Flieger, *Splintered Light: Logos and Language in Tolkien's World* (Kent State University Press, 2002).

15. For a much more sympathetic analysis of this work and its predecessor 'The Lost Road', see V. Flieger, *A Question of Time: J. R. R. Tolkien's Road to Faärie* (Kent State University Press, 1997).

16. See chapter 5 below, pp. 178–92.

17. 'Intelligent children of good taste ... have always, I am glad to say, singled out the points in manner where the address is to children as blemishes' (draft letter to Walter Allen, *Letters*, p. 297).

18. Stimpson, *J. R. R. Tolkien*, p. 30.

19. 'On Fairy Stories', *Tree and Leaf*, p. 70.

20. Carpenter, *J. R. R. Tolkien*, p. 130.

21. G. Russom, 'Tolkien's Versecraft in *The Hobbit* and *The Lord of the Rings*, in G. Clark and D. Timmons (eds.), *J. R. R. Tolkien and His Literary Resonances* (Westport, CT: Greenwood Press, 2000), pp. 53–69.

22. It made an appearance, without citation, in a 'voice-over' anthology of verse and prose used by Sir John Betjeman for a 1970s television film about the English countryside.

23. *Poems and Songs of Middle-earth* (Caedmon Records TC 1231), 1967.

24. For Auden's praise, see the sleeve note of the Caedmon recording; for Tolkien's dispraise, see his letter to Pauline Baynes, 6 December 1961 (*Letters*, p. 312).

25. See LT2, pp. 267–77; and, for 'Imram', *Time and Tide*, 3 December 1955, p. 1561.

26. *Shenandoah: The Washington and Lee University Review*, XVIII, 2 (1967), pp. 96–7.

27. Tolkien, 'Sir Gawain and the Green Knight'; 'Pearl'; 'Sir Orfeo' (Unwin Paperbacks, 1979), p. 143.

28. It is, however, included in the most recent edition of *Tree and Leaf* (HarperCollins, 2001).

29. J. R. R. Tolkien, *The Father Christmas Letters*, ed. Baillie Tolkien (London: George Allen & Unwin, 1976).

30. J. R. R. Tolkien, *Roverandom*, ed. C. Scull and W. C. Hammond (London: HarperCollins, 1998). The Introduction and Notes by Scull and Hammond are excellent and I am indebted to them.

31. George Eliot, *Middlemarch*, 1871–72, chapter 15 (Penguin edition, ed. R. Ashton, 1994, p. 141).

32. John Fowles, *The French Lieutenant's Woman*, 1969 (Panther Books, 1977, pp. 15–16).

33. Carpenter, *J. R. R. Tolkien*, p. 196.

34. *Letters*, p. 389.

4 Tolkien and the Twentieth Century

1. The City of Birmingham has recently (and especially since the appearance of the movie version of *The Lord of the Rings*) woken up to the possibilities of Tolkien

tourism, but it must be admitted that the locations associated with Tolkien have often changed beyond recognition or are in any case quite undistinguished. The idea that Sarehole influenced Hobbiton/Bywater (which also had a prominent Mill) makes psychological sense, though Tolkien warned against naïve identification even in that case (see FR, 8). See http://www.virtualbrum.co.uk/tolkien.htm for a brief and sensible illustrated account of Tolkien's Birmingham childhood.

2. Richard C. West, *Tolkien Criticism: An Annotated Checklist* (Kent State University Press, 1974), p. 41, paraphrasing the claims of William Ready, *The Tolkien Relation* (Henry Regnery Company, 1968).

3. Proust, *Within a Budding Grove, Remembrance of Things Past*, tr. T. Kilmartin and C. K. Scott Moncrieff (Penguin, 1983), Vol. 1, pp. 589–91.

4. Wilson, *C. S. Lewis: A Biography*, p. 159.

5. 'English and Welsh', *The Monsters and the Critics*, p. 170.

6. *Letters*, p. 218.

7. Carpenter, *J. R. R. Tolkien*, p. 31.

8. Carpenter, *J. R. R. Tolkien*, p. 43.

9. Carpenter, *J. R. R. Tolkien*, p. 86.

10. Obituary of Tolkien, *The Times*, 3 September 1973.

11. H. Carpenter, *The Inklings* (Unwin paperbacks, 1981), *passim*.

12. Wilson, *C. S. Lewis: A Biography*, p. 294.

13. 'Dante doesn't attract me. He's full of spite and malice' (*Letters*, p. 377). Tolkien retracted any general disparagement of Dante ('a supreme poet') implied by this casual remark. Valentine Cunningham (*British Writers of the Thirties* (Oxford University Press, 1988, p. 151)) has no hesitation in finding that Tolkien 'openly neglected' his wife by attending these twice-weekly meetings with friends – or 'chums' as Cunningham prefers to call them. (I talk to my friends, you chat to your chums.) Or compare Carpenter's biography, and especially its balanced and sensitive account of the marriage, with the pharisaic fantasy John Carey weaves round its contents in his *Listener* review (12 May 1977). Carpenter tells us that Tolkien made frequent confession, while Edith hated doing so and in the end abandoned churchgoing. Carey glosses the point as follows. '[Tolkien] retained something of Father Francis's view of sex. Even marital relations had to be atoned for by frequent confession – a requirement Mrs Tolkien found distasteful, and hotly contested.' The implication (shielded by a theoretical ambiguity in Carey's sentence) is that what Mrs Tolkien contested, with understandable heat, was not confession *per se*, but confession of, or prompted by, 'marital relations'. Those readers of *The Listener* who had not already read Carpenter's book – i.e. virtually all of them – would naturally suppose that this bizarre insinuation is supported by the biography, which it is not. Carey's innuendo is that Tolkien – a father of four, and 'past master of bawdy in several languages' (Carpenter, *The Inklings*, p. 55) – was preoccupied by guilt about sex; but here it is Carey, not Tolkien, who takes it for granted that the mere practice of sexual intercourse may be a Catholic's

motive for confession. Carey goes on to find the women in Tolkien's fiction 'perfectly sexless'.

14. Carpenter, J. R. R. Tolkien, p. 231.

15. Carpenter, J. R. R. Tolkien, p. 231.

16. My former colleague Dr Wilf Gunther advises me that Tolkien's is a 'modified RP accent of a slightly old-fashioned type which is manifested in his pronunciation of mainly non-initial "r" as a so-called "flapped r", i.e. slightly rolled "r". "Jewil" and "curtinned" represent a common variant pronunciation that has only recently become "quaint". His accent also shows midlands influence in his pronunciation of, e.g., "ringing" as "ringging". Untypical either of RP or of the midlands is his "unaspirated p, t, k" (which means that "tide, pool, caves" sound almost like "dide, bool, gaves").' Dr Gunther speculates that this last feature may be a residue of South African speech patterns.

17. Interview with Denys Geroult, BBC Radio 4, 16 December 1970.

18. Letters, p. 353.

19. Letters, p. 116.

20. Letters, p. 390.

21. Letters, p. 53.

22. Carpenter, The Inklings, pp. 210–11.

23. Letters, p. 229.

24. Letters, p. 377n.

25. 'Tolkien in Oxford', BBC Television, 30 March 1968.

26. Letters, p. 376.

27. Carpenter, J. R. R. Tolkien, p. 223.

28. Letters, pp. 281, 376.

29. Carpenter, The Inklings, p. 157.

30. Carey, The Listener, 12 May 1977, p. 631.

31. Philip Larkin, 'Statement', Required Writing (Faber, 1983), p. 79.

32. 'Reflections on Some Aspects of the Experimental Novel', quoted in Malcolm Bradbury, The Social Context of Modern English Literature (Blackwell, 1971), p. 28.

33. See Carpenter, The Inklings, passim; J. Wain, Sprightly Running (Macmillan, 1962), pp. 179–85; K. Amis, Memoirs (Hutchinson, 1991), p. 102. Near the end of Tolkien's life, in 1973, Tolkien and Wain had a public disagreement in connection with Wain's candidacy for the Oxford Chair of Poetry. Tolkien declared to a newspaper that the Chair, which had previously been held by a sequence of practising poets, should now revert to a scholar interested in poetry, and voted for the critic John Jones (who in fact succeeded to the Chair in a later election). Wain replied in a radio interview to the effect that, if it was acceptable for a professor (such as Tolkien) to write a 'romance', it should be acceptable for a poet and novelist (such as himself) to become a professor.

34. Letters, pp. 236, 189.

35. Shippey, The Road to Middle-earth, p. 137.

36. See stanzas VIII–X. Shelley's horseman, also like Tolkien's (RK, 103), wears 'a kingly crown'.

37. R. Giddings and E. Holland, *The Shores of Middle-earth* (Junction Books, 1981), pp. 102–4, 106.

38. 'Tradition and the Individual Talent' (1919), *Selected Prose of T. S. Eliot*, ed. F. Kermode (Faber, 1975), p. 38.

39. J. W. Lambert, 'New Fiction', *Sunday Times*, August 8, 1954, p. 5.

40. FR, 6.

41. 'Leaf by Niggle', *Tree and Leaf*, p. 93.

42. Proust, *The Captive, Remembrance of Things Past*, tr. T. Kilmartin and C. K. Scott Moncrieff (Penguin, 1983), Vol. 3, p.186.

43. Nabokov, *Pale Fire* (Penguin, 1973), p. 58.

44. 'On Fairy Stories', *Tree and Leaf*, p. 53.

5 Tolkien in the History of Ideas

1. An example is John Carey, in his contribution to *J. R. R. Tolkien; An Audio Portrait*, presented by Brian Sibley, BBC Worldwide Ltd 2001.

2. 'Beowulf: The Monsters and the Critics', *The Monsters and the Critics*, p. 15.

3. C. Wilson, *The Strength to Dream* (Gollancz, 1962), p. 150n. Dodsworth claims that *The Lord of the Rings* is 'a shamefully self-glorifying account of how little England defeated the ogre Hitler' (in P. Rogers (ed.), *An Outline of English Literature* (Oxford University Press, 1998), p. 405.)

4. 'The Hobbit Man' (interview with Philip Norman), *Sunday Times Magazine*, January 15, 1967, p. 36.

5. *Letters*, p. 115.

6. 'Notes on W. H. Auden's review of *The Return of the King*', *Letters*, pp. 242–3.

7. J. R. Watson, 'The Hobbits and the Critics', *Critical Quarterly*, XIII, 3 (1971), p. 258.

8. See chapter 2, p. 82 above.

9. N. Otty, 'The Structuralist's Guide to Middle-earth', in R. Giddings (ed.), *This Far Land* (Vision Press, 1983), pp. 166, 172.

10. *J. R. R. Tolkien; An Audio Portrait*, presented by Brian Sibley, BBC Worldwide Ltd 2001.

11. BBC's *Newsnight Review*, 14 December 2001.

12. John Ruskin, 'Pre-Raphaelitism', *The Complete Works of John Ruskin* (Bryan, Taylor & Co., 1894), XV, p. 237.

13. Freud, *Civilization and its Discontents* (1930), tr. J. Strachey (W. W. Norton Co, 1962); Marx, 'Excerpts from James Mill's *Elements of Political Economy*' (1844 ms) in L. Colletti (ed.), *Karl Marx: Early Writings*, trans. by R. Livingstone and G. Benton (Penguin, 1975), pp. 277–8.

14. E. Fischer, *How to Read Karl Marx* (Monthly Review Press, 1996), p. 54.

15. Or so at least I interpret Marx's view. See David McLellan, *The Thought of Karl Marx* (Macmillan Press, 1971), pp. 138–50 for some relevant passages.

16. Or from elements which could not change without raising the question whether 'human' remained the appropriate name for the altered species.

17. 'Beowulf: The Monsters and the Critics', *The Monsters and the Critics*, pp. 25–6.

18. See Shippey, *J. R. R. Tolkien: Author of the Century*, pp. vii–viii, xxx–xxxi, 115–28, 157–9.

19. Shippey, *The Road to Middle-earth*, pp. 104–5.
20. Quoted in Carpenter, *J. R. R. Tolkien*, p. 128.
21. See FR, p. 168.
22. See FR, pp. 6–7.
23. See TT, p. 322.
24. J. Pearce, *Tolkien: Man and Myth* (HarperCollins, 1997).
25. p. 161.
26. Charles A. Coulombe, unpublished ms., quoted in Pearce, p. 160. Coulombe's essay subsequently appeared as 'The Lord of the Rings: A Catholic View', in J. Pearce (ed.), *Tolkien: A Celebration* (Ignatius Press, 2001),
27. Letters, p. 241.
28. See pp. 40–1 above.
29. 'On Fairy Stories', *Tree and Leaf*, p. 65.
30. *J. R. R. Tolkien; An Audio Portrait*, presented by Brian Sibley, BBC Worldwide Ltd 2001.
31. p. 112.
32. T. A. Olszański, translated by Agnieszka Sylwanowicz, 'Evil and the Evil One in Tolkien's Theology', in P. Reynolds and G. GoodKnight (eds.), *Proceedings of the J. R. R. Tolkien Centenary Conference* (Mythopoeic Press, 1995), pp. 298–300; C. Garbowski, 'Eucatastrophe and the Gift of Ilúvatar in Middle-earth', *Mallorn* XXXV (1997), pp. 21–7.
33. See 'On Fairy Stories', *Tree and Leaf*, pp. 52–4, 62.
34. C. Garbowski, *Recovery and Transcendence for the Contemporary Mythmaker* (Marie Curie-Skłodowska University Press, Lublin, 2000), pp. 180–1.
35. pp. 182–3.
36. P. Curry, 'Tolkien and His Critics; A Critique', in Thomas Honegger (ed.), *Root and Branch: Approaches Towards Understanding Tolkien* (Walking Tree Publishers, 1999), pp. 94–5. Aryk Nusbacher, whose contributions I have found the most valuable part of the Cromwell Productions/Eagle Vision videotape *J. R. R. Tolkien: Master of the Rings* (2001), argues persuasively that the tensions among the benign peoples reflect Tolkien's awareness of the frictions of 'coalition politics' in the 1930s and 1940s, and the need to overcome them.
37. P. Curry, *Defending Middle-earth: Tolkien, Myth and Modernity* (HarperCollins, 1997).
38. p. 54.
39. See Letters, p. 235, and note to letter 181, p. 446; and Carpenter, *J. R. R. Tolkien: A Biography*, p. 238
40. 'The Hobbits and the Critics', p. 258.
41. 'Hobbit-forming', *The Listener*, 12 May 1977, p. 631.
42. 'Leaf by Niggle', *Tree and Leaf*, pp. 87–8.
43. Curry, p. 73; Letters, p. 236; 'On Fairy Stories', *Tree and Leaf*, p. 49.
44. I am indebted here to Christopher Tolkien's exposition of his father's ideas in *J. R. R. T: A Film Portrait of J. R. R. Tolkien* (videotape), The Tolkien Partnership/Visual Corporation Ltd, 1992.
45. Curry, p. 142, quoting Brian Attebery, *Strategies of Fantasy* (University of Indiana Press, 1992).

46. Curry, pp. 80, 138, 154, 161.
47. *Letters*, pp. 63–4.
48. In *J. R. R. T: A Film Portrait of J. R. R. Tolkien*.
49. See L. Tolstoy, *The Kingdom of God is Within You*, trans. by Constance Garnett (University of Nebraska Press, 1983), *passim*. I am indebted here to T. Hopton, 'Tolstoy, God and Anarchism', *Anarchist Studies* 8 (2000), pp. 27–52.
50. Cf. *Letters*, p. 243.
51. *Letters*, p. 172.
52. Thomas Hobbes, *Leviathan*, Part II, chapter 31, 'Of the Kingdome of God by Nature', ed. R. Tuck (Cambridge University Press, 1996), pp. 246–8.
53. This sentence seems to me to undermine the less illiberal reading of the 'Job' passage offered by Alan Ryan, 'Hobbes and Individualism', in G. A. J. Rogers and A. Ryan (eds.) *Perspectives on Thomas Hobbes* (Clarendon Press, 1988), pp. 94–7. According to Ryan, Hobbes is concerned here to emphasise the *difference* between the right of God and that of the earthly sovereign, not the analogy between them: God, on this view, can do what he likes with us because he is 'the author of our being and therefore without further ado the author of our actions'; earthly sovereigns in contrast 'can only claim authorship of our actions when we have granted them that right over us' (96–7). But I think this interpretation is unconvincing. Hobbes writes not of the authorship of another's actions, but of the power and right to afflict another who is in fact capable of independent thought and action. (That some contemporary readers believed Hobbes to hold the heretical idea that God is the author of our sins should not, I think, constrain unduly our reading of the passage.) Moreover, Hobbes makes pointedly clear that the sovereign's right to afflict is not granted to him by others: like the others, he had it all along, but in his case, uniquely, it is 'not taken away' by the contract to obey.
54. Hobbes, *Leviathan*, ed. R. Tuck (Cambridge University Press, 1991), XV, p. 111. For an illuminating discussion of this point, see Q. Skinner, *Reason and Rhetoric in the Philosophy of Hobbes* (Cambridge University Press, 1996), pp. 316–26.
55. Hobbes, *Leviathan*, ed. R. Tuck (Cambridge University Press, 1991), XIV, p. 98.
56. See LT1, pp. 61–2.
57. *Tree and Leaf*, p. 99.
58. *Tree and Leaf*, pp. 44–5.

6 The Cultural Phenomenon

1. *Letters*, pp. 144–5.
2. Unless one makes something of the fact that the departure of the Fellowship from Rivendell takes place on 25 December (RK, 373); but the sequence of chocolate figures in the calendar did not allude to this connection.
3. Respectively Electronic Arts/New Line Cinema, 2002; and Vivendi Games/Tolkien Enterprises, 2002.
4. J. R. Searle, *Minds, Brains and Science* (Harmondsworth; Penguin Books, 1984), pp. 30–1.

5. Respectively: Crash Bandicoot, Spiro and Harry Potter.
6. See Julian Symons's introduction to The Woman in White (Harmondsworth: Penguin, 1974), p. 15.
7. And in spite of the failure of the OED to acknowledge the adjective 'Wendyish'. George Orwell uses it in 'The Art of Donald McGill', Collected Essays, Journalism and Letters, Vol. 2, p. 184.
8. I have taught one student named Arwen. In 1992 there were six Arwens on the admissions file (computerised student record) of a large English university.
9. Emily Perkins, 'My very own brush with movie glamour', Independent on Sunday (London), 12 January 2003.
10. W. H. Auden, review of The Return of the King (New York Times, 22 January, 1956); 'The Quest Hero', in N. D. Isaacs and R. A. Zimbardo (eds.), Tolkien and the Critics (University of Notre Dame Press, 1968); 'The Guilty Vicarage', in The Dyer's Hand (Faber and Faber, 1963), pp. 146–58.
11. E. Wilson, 'Oo, Those Awful Orcs!', Nation 182, 14 April 1956; P. Toynbee, Observer, 6 August 1961; E. Muir, 'A Boy's World', Observer, 27 November, 1955.
12. R. Giddings, Introduction, and Fred Inglis, 'Gentility and Powerlessness: Tolkien and the New Class', in R. Giddings (ed.), This Far Land (Vision Press, 1983), pp. 8, 29–31.
13. Mark Lawson on BBC's Newsnight Review, 14 December 2001.
14. W [Waterstones'] Magazine, Winter/Spring 1997.
15. In J. R. R. Tolkien; An Audio Portrait, presented by Brian Sibley, BBC Worldwide Ltd 2001.
16. Colin Wilson, The Strength to Dream: Literature and the Imagination (Gollancz, 1962), p. 141.
17. In fairness to Carey, his contribution to Sibley's audiotape can be construed as claiming merely that The Lord of the Rings is more like Enid Blyton, or like nineteenth-century historical romance (which he also mentions) than it is like Spenser's The Faerie Queene. On stylistic grounds, at least, this is plausible – it would be true of almost any novel of the last two hundred years or more. Moreover, Tolkien's dislike and avoidance of allegory sets his work far apart in conception from Spenser, whom he disliked (see Shippey, The Road to Middle-earth, pp. 42–3). Richard Hughes' offending comparison on the jacket-blurb of The Lord of the Rings simply says that 'nothing on this scale has been attempted since Spenser' (my italics) – which is hardly disputable.
18. Several of the essays in G. Clark and D. Timmons, J. R. R. Tolkien and His Literary Resonances, and in P. Reynolds and G. GoodKnight, Proceedings of the J. R. R. Tolkien Centenary Conference 1992 (Mythopoeic Press and the Tolkien Society, 1995) seem to me to drift into this overvaluing of approximate resemblances. I would except Tanya Caroline Wood's piece in Clark and Timmons, which convincingly argues that Tolkien's 'On Fairy Stories' resembles Sidney's 'Defense of Poesy' in its structure and rhetorical strategies.
19. This Far Land (Vision Press, 1983), p. 13.
20. For a somewhat more sympathetic view, see Shippey, J. R. R. Tolkien: Author of the Century, pp. xxiv–xxvi, 318–26.
21. Alan Garner, The Owl Service (Collins, 1967).

22. Though undermined by many a knowing glance back in its direction, from the intergalactic Wild West saloon of *Star Wars* itself to the Italian-Lakes vacation of *Attack of the Clones,*

23. Reprinted recently: London: Gollancz, 2002.

24. p. 130.

25. *Letters,* pp. 228, 254–5.

26. 'On Fairy Stories', *Tree and Leaf,* pp. 45–7.

27. *Letters,* pp. 270–7.

28. Overlooking even some of its most powerfully 'cinematic' elements, such as the framing episodes set in the Arctic.

29. A recent example is the good-looking but ineptly scripted 1997 BBC version of *The Woman in White,* directed by Tim Fywell. In Collins's novel, the young hero Walter Hartright leaves Limmeridge House because Laura Fairlie, with whom he is in love and who also fairly clearly loves him, is engaged to Sir Percival Glyde, fulfilling a promise to her late father. Laura's clever and spirited half-sister, Marian Halcombe, sympathises with Walter, but persuades him that to leave is the only honourable course. Evidently doubting the contemporary audience's ability to empathise with this characteristically mid-Victorian ethical dilemma, the adapters substituted a scene in which Walter is abruptly expelled from the house in disgrace by Marion, after being accused of sexual harassment – the anachronistic term is appropriate – by a servant. The problem with this amendment is the collateral damage it does to the consistency of Marion Halcombe's character and the social credibility of the drama: it shows us Marion, who is otherwise offered to our admiration as a highly perceptive and fair-minded young woman, condemning a gentleman from her own circle on the unsupported word of a servant woman, a leap to judgement indefensible in itself and inconceivable in the class-stratified culture of the drama.

30. Director's and Writers' commentary to the Special Extended DVD Edition of *The Fellowship of the Ring,* New Line Cinema, 2002.

31. This should not be confused with 'collective' production in the politically radical sense, i.e. a process in which, at least in theory, all production decisions are taken by the company as a whole. My point is that a film production, like a team game, is an example of 'collective intentionality', in which I do X as part of our doing Y. (See J. R. Searle, 'Collective Intentions and Actions', in *Consciousness and Language* (Cambridge University Press, 2002), pp. 90–105.) Christopher Garbowski points out [*personal communication*] that just this kind of collectivity is celebrated in Tolkien's myth of the Music of the Ainur, not least in its looking forward to the Music at the end of time, when 'each shall know the comprehension of each' (*Silmarillion,* p. 16).

32. Design team's commentary to the Special Extended DVD Edition of *The Fellowship of the Ring,* New Line Cinema, 2002.

33. See Christopher Tolkien (ed.), *Pictures by Tolkien* (London: HarperCollins, 1992), especially nos. 5–6 (Rivendell), 35 (Gondolin) and 36 (Tol Sirion).

34. See *The Stones of Venice*, ed. J. G. Links (New York: Da Capo Press, 1960), Book One, XI, pp. 100–11.
35. It is a fine judgement, however, and may depend on how alert individuals are to suggestions of 'exterior' cultural elements. For example, though generally admiring the Wagnerian aptness, cogency and diversity of Howard Shore's score, I am uncomfortable with the *Carmina Burana*-style choral incantations used for the appearances of the Nazgûl: this musical style has become such a cliché in horror films – compare, for example, Jerry Goldsmith's score for Richard Donner's *The Omen* (Twentieth Century Fox, 1976) – that it seems to me to place the terror of the Black Riders in inverted commas, as it were. But it may be that I am more sensitive to such resemblances in music than in visual design.
36. Director's and Writers' commentary.
37. Director's and Writers' commentary.
38. See Paul Kocher, *Master of Middle-earth* (Harmondsworth: Penguin, 1974), pp. 117–43 for a painstaking analysis of Aragorn's personality.
39. See his comments in 'Designing and Building Middle-earth', Special Extended DVD Edition of *The Fellowship of the Ring*, New Line Cinema, 2002. Jackson's determination to maintain historical credibility may have led him to change certain scenes which, though believable in narrative, would seem implausible if literally visually presented. For example, Arwen has to ride with the sick Frodo to the Ford of Bruinen because it is difficult if not impossible to suggest on screen – without some ostentatious display of 'fairy-tale' magic – that the Elf-trained horse would not let him fall. (I owe this point to Christopher Garbowski.)
40. Director's and Writers' commentary.
41. See W. H. Auden, 'The Quest Hero', and pp. 35–41 above.
42. Stephen Spielberg plays it only once in ET: *The Extra-Terrestrial*, and the emotional effect is proportionately greater.

Index

References to imaginary characters, places and objects in Tolkien's work are selective.